BETTER HOMES AND GARDENS®

Step·By·Step Successful Gardening

Trees & Shrubs

Catriona Tudor Erler

Better Homes and Gardens® Books
Des Moines

BETTER HOMES AND GARDENS® BOOKS
An Imprint of Meredith® Books

Step-By-Step Successful Gardening:
Trees & Shrubs
Senior Editor: Marsha Jahns
Production Manager: Douglas Johnston

Vice President and Editorial Director: Elizabeth P. Rice
Executive Editor: Kay Sanders
Art Director: Ernest Shelton
Managing Editor: Christopher Cavanaugh

President, Book Group: Joseph J. Ward
Vice President, Retail Marketing: Jamie L. Martin
Vice President, Direct Marketing: Timothy Jarrell

Meredith Corporation
Chairman of the Executive Committee: E. T. Meredith III
Chairman of the Board and Chief Executive Officer:
    Jack D. Rehm
President and Chief Operating Officer: William T. Kerr

Produced by ROUNDTABLE PRESS, INC.
Directors: Susan E. Meyer, Marsha Melnick
Executive Editor: Amy T. Jonak
Editorial Director: Anne Halpin
Senior Editor: Jane Mintzer Hoffman
Design: Brian Sisco, Susan Evans, Sisco & Evans, New York
Photo Editor: Marisa Bulzone
Assistant Photo Editor: Carol Sattler
Encyclopedia Editor: Henry W. Art and Storey Communi-
    cations, Inc., Pownal, Vermont
Horticultural Consultant: Christine M. Douglas
Copy Editor: Sue Heinemann
Proofreader: Cathy Peck
Assistant Editor: Alexis Wilson
Step-by-Step Photography: Derek Fell
Garden Plans: Elayne Sears and Storey Communications, Inc.

All of us at Meredith® Books are dedicated to providing you
with the information and ideas you need for successful gardening. We guarantee your satisfaction with this book for as long
as you own it. If you have any questions, comments, or sugges-
tions, please write to us at:

MEREDITH® BOOKS, *Garden Books*
Editorial Department, RW240
1716 Locust St.
Des Moines, IA 50309-3023

If you would like to order additional copies of any of our
books, call 1-800-678-2803 or check with your local
bookstore.

Trees & Shrubs

The World of Trees and Shrubs

*f*rom landscape design to planting methods, this book distills the vast store of knowledge about trees and shrubs into a concise and practical guide. • In the chapters that follow you're sure to discover new and beautiful plants as well as recognize old favorites, and you'll learn which trees and shrubs grow best in your particular climate. • When you're ready to put your landscaping plans into action, you'll find all the practical information you need to plant and maintain healthy trees and shrubs. This book illustrates various pruning techniques you can use to give them a graceful form, and gives you methods of propagating from seeds and cuttings to ensure a ready source of new plants. • By learning to make wise choices among the many species of trees and shrubs available, you'll add dramatic beauty, privacy, shade, shelter, as well as value to your property for years to come.

Literature and folklore are full of tales in which trees or forests have important meta-physical symbolism. Many European fairy tales take place in the woods, where characters make important discoveries about life and themselves.

The word tree *actually means "learning" in all the Celtic languages. As early as 1600 B.C., the ancient Celts used a 13-month calendar system in which each 28-day month was named for a tree that was believed to have seasonal magic and mytho-logical connotations.*

For example, the birch tree, which represents the time between Christmas Eve and January 20, was considered the tree of inception, and cradles were often made of birch because the wood was believed to repel evil spirits. Birch twigs, which make excellent brooms, were used to drive out the Spirit of the Old Year. Using the symbol-ic language of trees, a young woman in Pembrokeshire, Wales, would give a prospec-tive suitor a piece of birch wood to tell him he might begin courting.

*I*nstinctively you may know the difference between a tree and a shrub, but the distinction between the two is not always clear-cut. *Merriam-Webster's Collegiate Dictionary* defines a tree as "a woody perennial plant having a single usually elongate main stem generally with few or no branches on its lower part." Most trees are at least 10 feet tall at maturity, but there are exceptions. Although the flowering dogwood, *Cornus florida*, can reach a height of 20 feet in a garden, it rarely gets tall enough to be considered a tree in its native woodland habitat.

Shrubs are typically differentiated from trees by their shorter height and multistemmed form. Generally shrubs grow no higher than 20 feet, and some can be as short as knee height. Yet climate and growing conditions can contradict this rule. In warm southern regions and as far north as Washington, D.C., the sweet bay magnolia *(Magnolia virginiana)* is an evergreen tree that can grow more than 60 feet tall. Farther north to Massachusetts, it is deciduous and remains a multitrunked, spreading shrub reaching 30 feet at maturity.

To further confuse the issue, many trees, such as birch, grow multiple stems, and some shrubs can be trained as standards to grow on just one trunk.

For most home gardeners, however, the technical distinction between a tree and a shrub is immaterial. We are happy to leave it to the professionals to debate while we enjoy the benefits and beauty these plants bring to our homes.

Perhaps the most appreciated advantage of trees and shrubs is that they are generally very easy to maintain, requiring little or no watering once they are established and only occasional pruning. Many trees and shrubs produce fruit or flowers, yet they need vir-tually no care compared with flowers and vegetables.

Trees and shrubs also perform many valuable func-tions in landscapes and gardens, both environmentally and aesthetically. Their many leaves use the process of photosynthesis to absorb carbon dioxide from the air, combining it with water to form carbohydrates that nourish the plant and at the same time releasing oxy-gen into the air. Thus trees actually help to keep our air cleaner and to protect the planet's ozone layer.

Trees also provide climate control. If a deciduous tree is planted near the house, the leafy canopy helps keep the house cooler during the hot summer months, and the bare branches allow the maximum amount of sunlight to warm the house during cold, but sunny, winter days. Research has shown that this natural heating and cooling can save significantly on energy costs. In windy areas, a row or grove of trees can deflect the relentless air currents, again helping to cut heating bills.

A thick planting of trees or shrubs can also reduce noise. According to a United States Department of Agriculture (USDA) study, a dense wall of greenery will absorb as much as 50 percent of street noise.

Trees and shrubs provide habitats for the birds, beneficial insects, and other animals that reside in gar-dens. A bushy shrub makes an attractive, safe cover for birds that will eat unwanted insects. Butterflies and bees are lured by certain flowering shrubs, espe-cially *Buddleia* species, sweet pepperbush (*Clethra alnifolia*), and hackberry (*Celtis occidentalis*), and squirrels and chipmunks will nest in trees. Someone who truly wishes to encourage wildlife might even keep a fallen dead tree as part of the garden because it is host to such a wide spectrum of fauna.

With thousands of beautiful trees and shrubs avail-able to home gardeners, the aesthetic possibilities are limitless. Let an avenue of trees create a vista, or place

You can determine the color of hydrangea (H. macrophylla) *flowers by controlling the soil pH. The flowers will bloom blue or purple in acid soil up to about 5.5 pH. For pink or red flowers, add lime to raise the pH.*

Planted with deciduous trees and shrubs, evergreens add interesting contrasts in color, form, and texture, enhancing the overall landscape design.

Evergreen flowering shrubs, such as these rhododendrons and azaleas, are particularly stunning in spring, when they transform a woodland garden into a spectacular multicolored display.

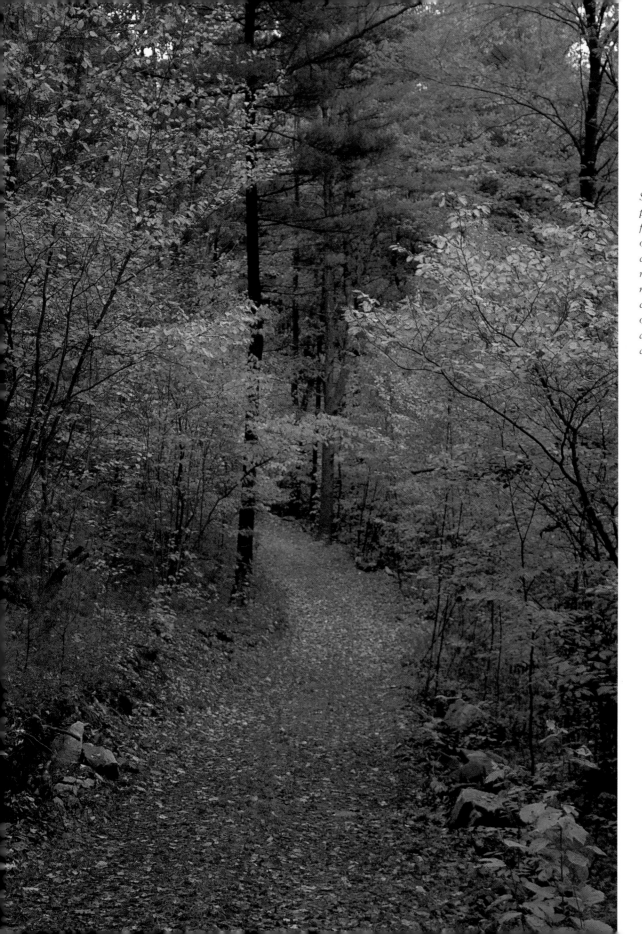

Shorter days in fall trigger a process that stops the flow of food and water to the leaves of deciduous trees. The green chlorophyll disappears, revealing a color that was masked by the green. This color—bright yellow, red, orange, deep red, or purple—depends on the leaf's main chemical.

a single outstanding tree on its own as a memorable specimen. Use a row of shrubs or trees to define your property line, build the walls of a private outdoor garden room, provide an evergreen background to a flower garden, or give structural form to your garden. By planting low-growing shrubs around a flower bed, you can create a frame, giving definition to the design. Try placing shrubs and small trees around your house as foundation plants, marrying your home to its environment. Or plant them on the periphery of a property to ensure privacy.

In addition to providing background and texture in a garden, flowering shrubs and trees can take center stage as important seasonal focal points. You may choose and value a tree or shrub for its flowers, fragrance, fruit, fall foliage, fascinating bark, winter interest, the shade it provides under its spreading canopy, or a combination of these reasons. Trees and shrubs can also serve as a play structure. A strong limb growing horizontal to the ground is perfect for a swing. Children—and even adults—enjoy climbing trees, and a tree house can be a cherished retreat, clubhouse, or fortress. In an essay on tree houses in her book *Green Thoughts: A Writer in the Garden*, Eleanor Perényi writes, "I can recall few keener pleasures, and climbed trees until well past the age when it was decent to do so. (One's own children with their embarrassed wails soon put an end to that sort of thing.) . . .When I spot a tree house on someone's property, I know civilized people live there."

If you don't have an appropriate tree to support a child's tree house, but want to give children a private outdoor retreat, consider creating a hideaway under arching branches of a large shrub.

Planting trees and shrubs, especially slow-growing varieties, is an investment in the future. In our mobile society, statistics show that the average person lives in a home for five years or less. As a result many people are loathe to put effort into planting a tree or shrub that won't come into its full beauty until they are long gone. That attitude, while understandable, is sad. Planting a tree or a shrub is a gift to the world.

In itself the growth of a tree or shrub can seem almost magical. It's easy to forget how small it was several seasons ago when it was first planted. Often it is only when you look at an old photograph that you realize how much it has changed. Observing change and growth is part of the joy of gardening—a pleasure missed by those who are unwilling to invest in planting slow-growing trees or shrubs. In his book *Creating Formal Gardens*, Roy Strong writes, "We are so obsessed with instant effect in this century that we have forgotten the joy of watching hedges grow to maturity, training and shaping them. Our ancestors lived far shorter lives. In the golden age of formal gardening, most would have been dead by forty but no one hesitated to devote ten to fifteen years of that span to making a garden."

Whether you choose to plant a rapid-growing tree such as the Leyland cypress, which grows as much as 3 to 5 feet a year, or opt for a slow grower such as a yew, which puts out only about 6 inches of growth a year, you're in for a treat. Trees and shrubs are important and exciting additions to any garden plan, providing both psychological and practical benefits.

America's Largest Trees

Trees continue to grow until they die, and those that survive to a venerable old age can be colossal. Concerned that these old trees would be destroyed, the American Forestry Association founded the National Register of Big Trees in 1940 to find and save the biggest trees of every native and naturalized species in the United States. The search for the champion trees continues as new finds supplant old winners. Among the winning living landmark trees as of January 1994 are a hackberry in Mason City, Illinois, that is 94 feet tall, with a spread of 88 feet and a circumference of 19½ feet, and a plains cottonwood in Hygiene, Colorado, that is 105 feet tall and 36 feet around, with a spread of 93 feet.

CHAPTER 1

Designing with Trees and Shrubs

*g*enerally long-lived, trees give a sense of time, history, and continuity to a garden and community. They also provide a sense of place, of geographic identity. Palm trees denote tropical climates, magnolias and bald cypresses mark the South, and fir trees suggest the cool forests of the North. In fact, it can be very jarring to the sensitive observer to see trees growing in a region to which they are not naturally suited. The joy—as well as the challenge—of designing with trees and shrubs is to specify the function the plant will have in the landscape and then to determine the best choice for the job. • You may want a tree to screen a view, provide shade, or give a splash of spring floral color or golden fall foliage. • Consider where the tree will be planted, and whether the environment there is shady, sunny, dry, windy, or wet. Is there a lot of space for the tree to spread, or do you need a compact variety that will fit in a tight corner? Once you have answered questions like these, you can begin to narrow down your selection to the best tree for your needs.

Trees and Shrubs in the Landscape

Shapes and Silhouettes

The illustrations below show five common tree shapes.

Conical or pyramidal trees include Colorado blue spruce (Picea pungens var. glauca), Lawson cypress (Chamaecyparis lawsoniana), and Nordmann fir (Abies nordmanniana).

For a weeping form, try Canada hemlock (Tsuga canadensis 'Pendula'), American arborvitae (Thuja occidentalis 'Pendula'), or weeping willows (Salix).

Some columnar trees are Italian cypress (Cupressus sempervirens), columnar maple (Acer platanoides 'Columnare'), and Lombardy poplar (Populus nigra 'Italica').

Spreading trees include silk tree (Albizia julibrissin), oaks (Quercus), and sycamore (Platanus occidentalis).

For a round or lollipop shape, consider maples (Acer), European hornbeam (Carpinus betulus), or common hackberry (Celtis occidentalis).

*T*here are several considerations to keep in mind when choosing trees and shrubs for your garden. First, the plant must be well suited to your climate and the specific soil, water, and light conditions on your property. Then make sure the tree or shrub is right for the particular site and function, keeping in mind the ultimate size of the plant and how fast it is likely to grow.

To have a healthy garden that needs minimal care and chemicals to keep it flourishing, choose plants that are well adapted to the environment. Make sure the climate zones for the trees and shrubs you want are suitable for where you live. Bear in mind, though, that the USDA climate zone ratings are only for cold temperatures. Some plants can survive the cold, but aren't adapted for long, hot, humid summers. In areas where summers are stressful, check with a local nursery or a county cooperative extension agent to be sure that the shrub or tree you have in mind can tolerate those conditions.

The type of soil you have also affects the success of a tree or shrub. Woodland plants such as azalea, rhododendron, mountain laurel, and holly all prefer acid soil with a low pH. You can try to grow these plants in soil with a pH above 7.5, but you will need to constantly add acidic fertilizer to lower the pH. On the other hand, juniper and mahonia prefer a more alkaline soil. Also bear in mind the plant's tolerance of extreme clay or sandy soil.

Moisture is another important factor to consider. Some plants thrive in damp surroundings, while others don't like to get wet. All newly planted trees and shrubs need to be watered, but once established they should be able to live off the natural rainfall. In dry climates, choose drought-tolerant specimens. If, on the other hand, you live in a rainy region and have spots where water accumulates, find trees that can take flooding. Other plants are suited to the salty air, strong winds, and sandy soil of the seashore.

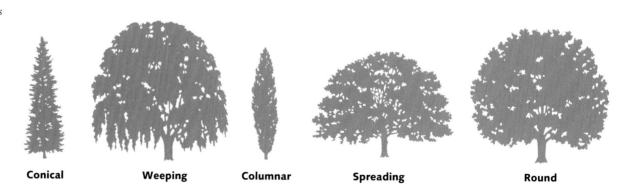

Conical   **Weeping**   **Columnar**   **Spreading**   **Round**

The trees and shrubs planted around the perimeter of this enclosed garden soften the hard lines of the brick wall, creating a wonderful sense of verdant privacy.

Rose-of-Sharon (Hibiscus syriacus) *is an excellent choice for a small garden. Actually a large shrub, it can be trained, as seen here, into a treelike form with a spreading, open canopy.*

The weeping cherry tree is a welcome break from the horizontal plane of this poolside garden, while the red-leaved Japanese maple in front droops gracefully over the edge of the pool.

Trees for Small Spaces

The following trees look good in small gardens: dwarf balsam fir (Abies balsamea 'Nana'), *Japanese maple* (Acer palmatum), *kousa dogwood* (Cornus kousa), *Asian serviceberry* (Amelanchier asiatica), *paperbark maple* (Acer griseum), *European hornbeam* (Carpinus betulus 'Fastigiata'), *showy crabapple* (Malus floribunda), *Korean mountain ash* (Sorbus alnifolia), *crape myrtle* (Lagerstroemia indica), *varnish tree* (Koelreuteria paniculata), *ornamental pear* (Pyrus calleryana), *dwarf white pine* (Pinus strobus 'Nana'), *and Hinoki false cypress* (Chamaecyparis obtusa).

Pay attention to the sun and light requirements of the plants you are choosing, and what's available in the site you have in mind. Even if a spot gets a few hours of direct sun, it may be very dark for the rest of the day—offering less overall available light for plants than a place that is continually in shade but is brightened by reflected light.

Once you have chosen plants adapted to your climate, think about how you plan to use them. If you want to plant along a driveway or patio or near the house, don't choose trees with invasive roots. Weeping willow roots, for example, are constantly seeking water and can even bore through drain pipes; ficus roots can lift the foundation of a house. Along a patio or deck, look for trees and shrubs that are attractive up close, perhaps with interesting bark and pretty flowers, fruit, or foliage. Avoid messy plants that drop sticky fruit or sap or constantly shed, as well as ones that hog water and nutrients from nearby lawns and plantings. If a tree or shrub is to be planted along a wall, it needs to have a contained root system and a narrow canopy.

Don't forget to consider the ultimate size of the specimen. It's unfortunate to see a tree with a potentially lovely form squashed up too close to a house. Clearly, when the tree was young it was planted at a logical distance, but no allowances were made for its inevitable growth. Don't plant trees that will ultimately be too large for a small lot. Instead, project the mature size of the plant and allow room for it to reach its limits. If the gaps bother you, consider mixing long-lived, slow-growing plants with quick-growing ones that have shorter lives. The rapid growers will soon fill in the gaps, and by the time they need to be removed to make room for the slow-and-steady plants, they will be past their prime anyway.

Deciduous Trees

Deciduous trees lose their leaves in the fall, generally remain bare through winter, and regenerate new growth again in the spring. There are deciduous trees for every garden need. Deciduous trees can be petite or towering, weeping or upright, spreading or narrow. Some are valued for their foliage, others for flowers or fruit, and still others for their fascinating skeletal structure. The variety of leaf shape, texture, and color is also immense.

The diversity and versatility of deciduous trees make them a mainstay in landscape design. Look for a specimen tree—one that is remarkable for its size, lovely form, or striking appearance—and place it where it will stand out as a special garden feature. One dramatic possibility is the red horse chestnut *(Aesculus × carnea)*, which can ultimately reach 45 feet tall and 30 feet wide. In mid-spring it blossoms with 8- to 10-inch-long upright flower spikes in red or pink, depending on the cultivar. Another beautiful choice is the silk tree *(Albizia julibrissin)*, which bears pink powder-puff flowers for several weeks in the summer. The sugar maple *(Acer saccharum)* makes an imposing specimen when planted in a large lawn, and offers spectacular fall foliage.

This staghorn sumac (Rhus typhina) *provides year-round interest in the garden. In spring the new growth clothes the small tree; in mid-summer tiny greenish flowers ripen into clusters of fuzzy red fruit; in fall the leaves turn a dazzling orange; and in winter the tree's fascinating form is revealed.*

Planted in neat rows, these flowering Yoshino cherry trees (Prunus yedoensis), *shown on the opposite page, add a sense of structure and drama to a garden design. They draw the eye down the avenue to a vista beyond. This planting would also be effective on a much smaller scale, such as lining a suburban driveway.*

Planted together to form a small grove of trees, the soft pastel flowers of the saucer magnolia (Magnolia × soulangiana) *and flowering cherries* (Prunus), *each a slightly different color, create a breathtaking scene.*

Deciduous trees that produce autumn fruit, such as this crabapple (Malus sargentii), *provide three-season interest. The bright red berries are a favorite of birds, adding to the pleasures the tree brings to the garden.*

Deciduous Trees CONTINUED

Other deciduous trees, such as paper birch *(Betula papyrifera)*, lend themselves to planting in small groves. The white peeling bark and bright green foliage of these trees make a beautiful landscape statement as an island bed in a lawn.

Many deciduous trees are treasured for their flowers. Perhaps best known are the spring-flowering possibilities such as dogwood *(Cornus* spp.*)*, redbud *(Cercis* spp.*)*, cherry and almond *(Prunus* spp.*)*, and Callery pear *(Pyrus calleryana)*, but don't overlook the pleasure of a summer floral display. Hawthorn *(Crataegus* spp.*)* and fringe tree *(Chionanthus virgini-*

Depending on your climate, you can find a tree that will bloom just about any month of the year. The ornamental flowers of this saucer magnolia (Magnolia × soulangiana) *bloom in spring. Deciduous shrubs, such as witch hazel* (Hamamelis)*, bloom as early as January and February, while others, such as the silk tree* (Albizia julibrissin)*, flower in late summer or early fall.*

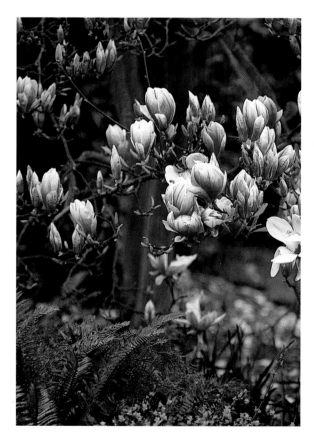

cus) bloom in late spring. For June blossoms, try the Japanese snowbell *(Styrax japonicus)*, which is covered in fragrant white fuchsialike flowers that stand out against the glossy, dark green foliage. The Japanese pagoda tree *(Sophora japonica)* produces creamy white pealike blossoms for six to eight weeks in summer. Crape myrtle *(Lagerstroemia indica)* blooms in August in colors ranging from white to reds, pinks, and lavenders.

A deciduous tree laden with berries or fruit in fall is a delightful sight, especially when it attracts birds to its feast. Crabapples *(Malus floribunda)* bear a profusion of fruit, ranging in color from bright red to pumpkin orange and golden yellow, depending on the cultivar. Harder to find, because the seed is difficult to germinate—but well worth the trouble—is the Korean mountain ash *(Sorbus alnifolia)*, which bears small white flowers in late spring that develop into orange-red berries. The late-spring flowers of hawthorn *(Crataegus crus-galli)* also ripen into bright crimson fruit.

Colorful autumn foliage is another reason to grow many deciduous trees. Maples aren't the only trees that turn into a blaze of color during the fall months. Sweet gum *(Liquidambar styraciflua)* will give a beautiful fall foliage display, even in warm climates. Purchase the trees in fall so that you can choose the coloration you like best. The maidenhair tree *(Ginkgo biloba)* has bright green fan-shaped leaves that transform into a golden yellow in the autumn months. Another tree that puts on spectacular yellow garb is golden-rain tree *(Koelreuteria bipinnata)*. The Chinese pistachio *(Pistacia chinensis)* is the only tree to produce scarlet leaves in the desert.

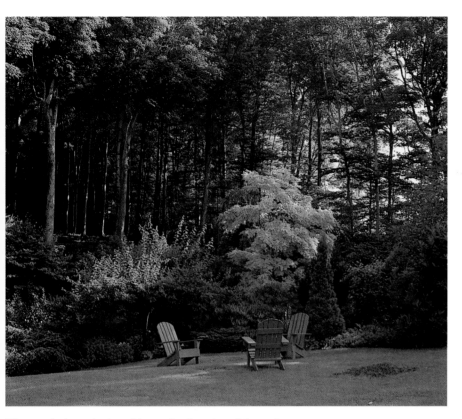

This stand of trees in the wild, woodland section of the garden provides a shady place to relax. The dense foliage creates a low-maintenance buffer that helps reduce noise from nearby traffic or other homes.

This copper beech (Fagus sylvatica ‘Atropunicea’) *is a spectacular landscape plant as well as a welcome shady retreat.*

For winter interest choose deciduous trees that have fascinating silhouettes once the leaves have fallen. Good possibilities include Japanese maple *(Acer palmatum)*, with its marvelous twisting branches, and Harry Lauder’s walking stick *(Corylus avellana* ‘Contorta’*)*, named for the Scottish comedian’s bent, gnarled walking stick. Large landscape trees, especially those growing out in the open with an even form, are lovely for the lacy pattern they make against the winter sky.

Many deciduous trees have multicolored or peeling bark that stands out dramatically, particularly in a winter landscape. Excellent choices for beautiful bark are birch trees, which offer a variety of colors. Try the red-brown peeling bark with tinges of pink of the Heritage river birch *(Betula nigra* ‘Heritage’*)*, or the classic white of the paper birches. Also consider crape myrtle and the paperbark maple *(Acer griseum)*.

Grouped together, deciduous trees can make a strong design statement. Long-lived forest trees such as beeches *(Fagus* spp.*)* or horse chestnuts *(Aesculus* spp.*)* are excellent for formal avenues or allées, although other, smaller-scale trees such as crape myrtle, dogwood, or flowering cherry can do the job as well in a restricted space such as lining a suburban driveway.

Deciduous Trees CONTINUED

When selecting deciduous trees, consider the site and the purpose of the tree. If you want a tree to soften the look of a bare wall, the tree needs to have a contained root system and a narrow canopy, so that it doesn't become too crowded. Consider trees from the maple family that are columnar in form, birches *(Betula* spp.*)*, European hornbeam *(Carpinus betulus* 'Fastigiata'*)*, Washington hawthorn *(Crataegus phaenopyrum)*, American holly *(Ilex opaca)*, crabapples *(Malus* spp.*)*, or pears *(Pyrus* spp.*)*.

When planting next to a patio, choose a tree that isn't too messy and that doesn't have roots that can push up paving. Good deciduous possibilities for patios include paperbark and Japanese maples *(Acer griseum* and *A. palmatum)*; birch trees; Persian silk tree or mimosa *(Albizia julibrissin)*, which is also beautiful when viewed from above, perhaps from an upstairs balcony; redbud *(Cercis canadensis)*; both the Chinese and white fringe trees *(Chionanthus retusus* and *C. virginicus)*; dogwoods *(Cornus × rutgersensis* and *C. kousa)*; and crabapples *(Malus* spp.*)*.

If you are looking for a shade tree, select one that will grow relatively quickly and has a broad crown. The sugar maple *(Acer saccharum)* grows rapidly to 100 feet with a wide spread, reaching as much as 60 feet in diameter. The Chinese pistachio is slower growing, but eventually reaches 35 feet with a wide, umbrellalike crown.

The sun shines through the leaves of the golden locust (Robinia pseudoacacia *'Frisia'). The color of the new-growth wood on this thorny tree is red.*

Variegated leaves can combine any number of colors, including yellow, cream, blue, silver, pink, and green. These variegated dogwood leaves belong to Cornus florida *'Welchii'.*

This European beech (Fagus sylvatica) *has tricolor variegated leaves of pink, green, and creamy white. It's a slow-growing tree, which may ultimately reach 25 to 60 feet in height.*

Sourwood (Oxydendrum arboreum) *has drooping clusters of fragrant flowers in spring and attractive fruits and brilliant red-orange foliage in fall. It needs soil that is acid.*

The silvery foliage of this weeping willow-leaved pear (Pyrus salicifolia *'Pendula') is a lovely soft accent in the garden.*

Evergreens

*E*vergreens are much loved in gardens and land-scapes because they stay green and alive in winter when everything else seems dead. They are divided into needle and broad-leaved types. In general, the needle evergreens are more cold hardy and heat sensitive, growing in the northern parts of North America, where the winters are cold and the summers don't get too hot. In contrast, the broad-leaved evergreens prefer the warmer climes of the southern region. Of course, there are exceptions. Mountain laurel species *(Kalmia latifolia)* are indigenous from Maine to Florida, and the Canary Island pine *(Pinus canariensis)*, a tender tree suited to zones 8 to 10, prefers hot, dry conditions.

We tend to think of coniferous evergreens in terms of Christmas trees, but that pyramidal shape is only one of several options. Some conifers, such as a

The glossy green leaves of the southern magnolia (Magnolia grandiflora) *are a delight in the landscape throughout the year. It is frost hardy through zone 7.*

A dark green evergreen hedge makes an ideal back-drop to a perennial border. Yew and small-leaved holly are often used to set off floral color and texture, although both grow slowly.

Evergreens CONTINUED

Dwarf Conifers

Dwarf conifers are a wonderfully diverse group of evergreens that are valuable in both large and small gardens. They come in all the colors, shapes, and textures of their larger counterparts, but the plants stay relatively small.

In confined spaces they make a definite visual statement. Set aside a spot in your garden to create a striking low-maintenance arrangement of dwarf conifers, combining several varieties to create a pleasing mix of texture, color, shape, and size. Include dwarf conifers in a rock garden to give background and a sense of scale to the smaller plants, and use them in mixed perennial borders to give structure to the design as well as winter interest.

mature deodar cedar *(Cedrus deodara)*, have irregular, open shapes. Other species, such as American arborvitae *(Thuja occidentalis* 'Pendula'*)* and Alaska cedar *(Chamaecyparis nootkatensis* 'Pendula'*)*, have pendulous branches that appear to weep. Still other evergreens shoot up tall and narrow like rockets; Italian cypress *(Cupressus sempervirens)*, common in classic Italian gardens, is a good example. Cold-climate options include Chinese juniper *(Juniperus chinensis)* and Rocky Mountain juniper *(J. scopulorum* 'Skyrocket'*)*. Some evergreens, including *Juniperus horizontalis*, make excellent ground covers.

The texture and color of conifers can vary widely. Some needles are long and soft, while others are short and sharp; they can be whorled, clumped, or growing individually along the branches. Or foliage may be scalelike. The foliage branches of needle evergreens

can be formed like fans or feathers, as on the Hinoki false cypress *(Chamaecyparis obtusa)*, or they can run along the main branches like raindrops down a window pane.

Colors range from distinct blues and grays through greens into bright yellows and golds, and there are even variegated combinations. The golden-tipped foliage of the Hinoki false cypress cultivar 'Crippsii' is particularly effective on cloudy days, when it appears to be perpetually bathed in sunlight.

Evergreens are an obvious choice for maintaining color and interest in the cold-season garden. Don't overlook boxwood and small-leaved holly shrubs pruned into clean-cut hedges. In summer they frame other plantings; in winter they become the substance of the garden.

A variety of evergreens is combined to create a stunning tapestry of color, form, and texture. This gorgeous backdrop of trees will be even more compelling in winter, when the golden-colored specimens give a spark of sunshine to even the cloudiest days.

Dwarf conifers are ideal for small gardens. Because they require little maintenance once established, they are perfect for a hillside or rock garden.

Evergreen shrubs such as these azaleas, rhododendrons, dwarf pines, and yews are excellent in a mixed border. In winter, when the annuals and perennials have died back, the shrubs are the focal point of the bed.

Conifers and deciduous trees make excellent garden companions. Here the pale green and distinct blue of the conifers contrast delightfully with the deep burgundy red of the Japanese maple in the center and the pale red-tipped foliage of the nandina in the foreground.

Evergreens CONTINUED

Evergreens with Unusual Foliage

For unusual foliage effects, consider the following.

Evergreens with golden foliage include Cupressus macrocarpa *'Goldcrest'*, Hinoki false cypress (Chamaecyparis obtusa *'Crippsii'*), *English yew* (Taxus baccata *'Aurea'*), *and Nordmann fir* (Abies nordmanniana *'Golden Spreader'*).

Blue Atlas cedar (Cedrus atlantica *'Glauca'*), *blue spruce* (Picea pungens *var.* glauca), *and Colorado spruce* (Picea pungens *'Koster'*) *have a distinctly blue color.*

Plants with drooping branches include Brewer's spruce (Picea brewerana), *American arborvitae* (Thuja occidentalis *'Pendula'*), *and Canada hemlock* (Tsuga canadensis *'Sargenti'*).

While excellent as dominant design features, evergreens also work well as unobtrusive backdrops in your garden. Mass-plant a dark green evergreen such as boxwood or holly as a tall hedge or screen to highlight brightly colored annuals and perennials planted in front. In summer the evergreens will be simply a foil to the rest of the garden, but in the winter, when the herbaceous plants are gone, the evergreens will become the central feature.

Evergreen trees are also excellent as screens and windbreaks. A screen of evergreens that protects your house from winter winds will reduce heating bills. On seaside properties evergreens can block strong ocean breezes and protect sensitive plants from the salty buffeting winds. Where you need salt-tolerant evergreens, good choices include Russian olive *(Elaeagnus angustifolia)*, eucalyptus, Colorado blue spruce *(Picea pungens var. glauca)*, and Austrian pine *(Pinus nigra)*.

Evergreens can also be planted as screens to block an unsightly view. Hemlocks planted close together make an excellent screen and can even be pruned to create a hedge. Leyland cypress *(× Cupressocyparis leylandii)* grows very quickly and is adaptable to both full sun and partial shade. It can be left to grow in its natural form or sheared as a hedge.

The dragon's-eye pine (Pinus densiflora *'Oculus draconis'*) *grows needles with alternating yellow and green bands.*

The Japanese umbrella pine has dark green needles in whorls at the end of each stem.

The pale, silvery foliage of the deodar cedar 'Silver Mist' is soft and almost feathery.

The Colorado blue spruce (Picea pungens *var.* glauca) *has stiff, sharp, bluish green needles.*

Shrubs

Shrubs, the "workhorses" of the garden, are too often taken for granted. Many are simply planted as a backdrop—missed if they are removed, but otherwise not particularly noticed. Yet a shrub can play a starring role in the garden, standing out as a specimen because of its beautiful flowers, decorative foliage, ornamental fruit, autumn color, attractiveness in winter, or arresting form, whether natural or pruned using topiary techniques.

Shrubs are the mainstay of most foundation plantings around the perimeter of the house. Generally low in maintenance, they help soften the architectural angles, hide the unsightly line between the walls and the ground, and visually connect the house to its surroundings. A well-designed foundation planting can be a marvelous combination of different-sized shrubs

A hedge of bridal-wreath spirea creates a spectacular spray of flowers every May. Other good possibilities for flowering hedges include camellias, azaleas, and box honeysuckle.

Include shrubs and even small trees in a perennial border to add structure to the design.

A beautiful shrub may warrant special placement as a specimen in your lawn. Here the smokebush (Cotinus coggyria) catches the eye with its soft, smoky display. The sterile hairs (pubescence) on the long panicles begin showing in June and continue, gradually changing colors through the season, until August or September.

Shrubs CONTINUED

Shrubs with Colorful Foliage

For colorful foliage, plant Japanese barberry: Berberis thunbergii *'Aurea' (yellow), 'Atropurpurea' (red), or 'Rose Glow' (variegated pink and white). Or try* Buddleia alternifolia *'Argentea' (silver),* Cornus alba *'Spaethii' (variegated golden),* Corylus avellana *'Aurea' (yellow),* Euonymus europaea *'Atropurpureus' (red),* Potentilla fruticosa *'Mandschurica' (silvery gray), or* Weigela florida *'Foliis Purpuriis' (red).*

with varying leaf textures and colors. Play the colors and textures of the different plants against each other. As a rule, avoid grouping only large-leaved plants together. While such a statement is assertive, no one shrub is displayed to full advantage. Instead, mix fine-leaved varieties with coarser-leaved ones, allowing them to enhance each other.

In a woodland garden, prune the lower branches of tall trees to create a glade, and then plant shade-loving shrubs such as holly, azalea, rhododendron, and kalmia underneath. Instead of dotting shrubs randomly about a lawn, making mowing more difficult, group them in an island bed. On a very large property, a series of well-placed island beds can form an informal walkway that encourages people to stroll through the garden.

Many shrubs, such as this cotoneaster, have lovely spring flowers and also set fruit that ripens in fall, creating a vivid display that lasts well into winter.

Small shrubs add structure and year-round interest to perennial borders and height to rock gardens. Since the warm summer months are generally the time you spend outdoors, design your border to peak in July and August, and choose shrubs that offer a floral display or pretty foliage during those months.

Like trees, large shrubs are superb for screens to block an unwanted view and secure privacy, as well as for windbreaks. Along the coast, check for varieties that can stand up to the constant buffeting from the wind and tolerate the salty soil and air.

Plant shrubs close together to form a hedge that defines your property line and adds privacy, divides one garden space from another, or encloses an outdoor garden room. A dark green hedge is also the ideal backdrop to a perennial border or flower bed.

Hedges can be pruned in a formal, clean-cut manner or they can be left to grow naturally, creating a soft, billowy barrier. In addition to the typical leafy hedges, you can plant a hedge of flowering shrubs such as camellias, large azaleas, box honeysuckle, or bottlebrush. Try alternating two different-colored flowering cultivars that bloom at the same time to create a checkerboard effect.

By planting a mixture of shrubs, vines, and small trees, you can form a hedgerow that evokes the old hedgerows lining the fields and roads in rural England. Your hedgerow will be an open invitation to a wide range of fascinating wildlife seeking food and lodging among the tangle of plants. Once established, a mixed hedgerow can be pruned or sheared to contain it and keep it looking tidy.

Within the same family, shrubs come in a wide variety of leaf colors. Here are two Japanese barberry plants. One, Berberis thunbergii *var.* atropurpurea 'Rose Glow', has deep reddish purple foliage. The other, 'Aurea', has vivid yellow foliage. Planted together, they form a dramatic contrast.

Pyracantha berries ripen in September and last well into the winter. As a rule, birds will eat the berries only as a last resort, so the display isn't decimated by their feeding.

TIMESAVING TIP

For an especially dramatic effect, combine same-type shrubs with different berry colors. For example, plant two gallon-size beautyberry plants in the same hole, one the purple variety (Callicarpa dichotoma) and the other a white form (var. albifructus). Both types are vigorous enough to survive in the same spot. If planted together when young, they look like one plant growing both white and purple berries.

The winged euonymus (Euonymus alata) *bursts into vibrant oranges and reds in autumn. It is one of the most consistent shrubs for fall foliage. The color is as vivid in the Midwest and South as in the Northeast. Here it rivals the red of the chrysan-themums in front.*

Shrubs CONTINUED

TROUBLESHOOTING TIP

Look for the new cold-hardy camellias that can tolerate temperatures as low as -12°F. These cultivars of Camellia japonica, classed as hardy in zones 6–10, are 'Snow Flurry', 'Winter's Interlude', 'Winter's Dream', 'Winter's Rose', and 'Winter's Charm'.

The row of boxwood (Buxus), *pruned into symmetrical ovals, gives an interesting formal pattern to this foundation planting.*

Whether deciduous or evergreen, shrubs enliven your garden throughout the year. Flowering shrubs attract bees, with their soothing, sonorous hum, and butterflies, the ballerinas of the garden. Many of the blooms, such as those of sweet pepperbush *(Clethra alnifolia)*, lilac *(Syringa vulgaris)*, and box honeysuckle *(Lonicera nitida)*, are deliciously fragrant.

Flowers generally last a month or so, but colorful foliage can be a visual treat throughout the season—it isn't limited to the autumn months. We think of leaves being green, but actually they can range from creamy white to golden yellow, silvery gray, blue, red, purple, and even variegated colors. For a striking shrub garden, combine plants with different leaf colors in an appealing tapestry of color, form, and texture. One caveat: don't overdo it. Too much variety in leaf color can look busy, contrived, and too clever.

Many shrubs produce spectacular fall foliage. One of the most brilliant is burning bush *(Euonymus alata)*. In fall, as its common name suggests, it

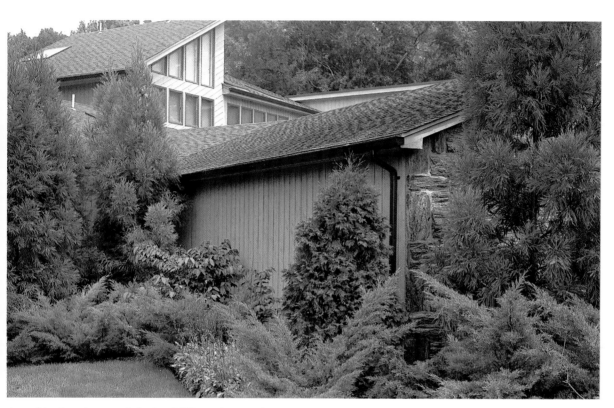

A combination of trees and shrubs of different forms, colors, textures, and growth habits makes an attractive planting along the edge of this house.

becomes a flaming mound of bright red foliage. This eye-catching display is followed by oval orange-red berries that cling through winter. *Fothergilla major* is another shrub that is remarkable for its incredible fall display of yellow, orange, and scarlet.

Even in winter shrubs can play an important role in the landscape. Many shrubs produce berries that last into the winter. Harry Lauder's walking stick *(Corylus avellana* 'Contorta') is a deciduous shrub whose marvelous twisted shape looks striking in the winter landscape, and the Siberian dogwood *(Cornus alba* 'Sibirica') is an upright, shrubby form with bright red stems that stand out dramatically once the leaves have dropped. Evergreen shrubs such as box-wood and the small-leaved holly bushes are also won-derful in winter, adding interest and structure when much of the rest of the garden is bare.

Home Foundation Planting

*T*his romantic garden, featuring spring-flowering shrubs and trees, is much more imaginative than the usual row of evergreen shrubs. In spring the garden is full of color, and the rest of the year the plants are an interesting composition of forms and textures.

Early in spring, the saucer magnolia is full of huge blossoms several inches wide, heralding the end of winter and the beginning of the gardening season. Saucer magnolia is a wonderful accent tree for the front yard.

The scarlet firethorn is an evergreen shrub that blossoms with clusters of white flowers, followed by bright red-orange berries that last from fall into winter. It can be trained to climb walls if you have an appropriate spot along your foundation.

The rockspray cotoneaster makes a lovely evergreen ground cover, spreading horizontally and staying low to the ground. Adding interest to the shiny leaves are white flowers in the spring and red berries by late summer.

Plant List

1 Saucer magnolia
(Magnolia × soulangiana)
2 Sweet box
(Sarcococca hookerana)
3 Common lilac
(Syringa vulgaris)
4 Scarlet firethorn
(Pyracantha coccinea)
5 Carolina rhododendron
(Rhododendron carolinianum)
6 St.-John's-wort
(Hypericum calycinum)
7 Rockspray cotoneaster
(Cotoneaster horizontalis)

The lilac has a wonderful rich scent that fills the air in late spring or early summer. Plant it near a window, so that the spring breezes can carry the scent indoors— a perfectly natural room freshener to air out your home after winter.

Rhododendrons are beautiful additions to foundation plantings. Their flowers tend to be long-lasting, adding color from mid-spring throughout midsummer.

Place rhododendrons in an area that is protected from winter winds, which can dry out the plants. Under the proper conditions, rhododendrons can be trouble-free for years, requiring very little pruning or extra attention.

Shady Woodland Garden

*I*f you have a wooded lot, use the existing trees to create the enchantment of a spring-flowering woodland walk. By pruning high, lopping off most of the lower branches of tall existing trees, you can admit enough light to grow smaller dogwoods and redbuds under the lacy canopy of trees.

After these spring shrubs finish blooming, the trees will be leafed out, creating more shade below. At this point the summer-flowering sweet pepperbush takes over, with its spires of yellow, white, or pink playing against the dark background of the foliage.

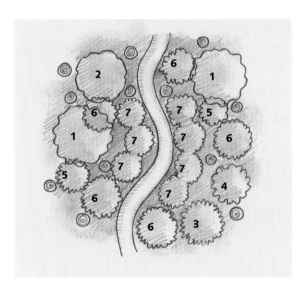

Plant List

1 Eastern redbud
(Cercis canadensis)

2 Flowering dogwood
(Cornus × rutgersensis)

3 Dexter hybrid rhododendron
(Rhododendron, white hybrids)

4 Dexter hybrid rhododendron
(Rhododendron, pink hybrids)

5 Sweet pepperbush
(Clethra alnifolia)

6 Japanese rose
(Kerria japonica)

7 Skimmia
(Skimmia japonica)

Creating a wood-chip path is not difficult and provides a quiet and soft cushion underfoot. Bark or wood-chip paths also allow access to an area that might otherwise tend to be soggy during the early spring.

Kerria frames the path with its attractive bright green leaves and clusters of yellow roselike flowers. This deciduous shrub grows well in hardiness zones 4 to 9, and is particularly well suited to shady sites with moist but well-drained soil.

Easy-Care Conifer Garden

The stone bench and stepping stones add a geometric element to complement the varied shapes of the evergreen shrubs, which range from low and prostrate to narrow and conical, and include weeping and rounded forms.

*I*n a hectic world, here's a respite with quiet serenity, inspired by traditional Japanese gardens. Time seems to stand still in this garden, where the slow-growing conifers give an impression of permanence, as if they would endure forever.

The stepping stones are set in sand, which can be raked into patterns in the Japanese custom. The ripples in the raked sand begin to look like water, the stepping stones like lily pads on the water's surface.

The rhododendron proclaims spring with clouds of delicate pink blossoms that appear before the leaves. At the same time the Mother Lode juniper provides a beautiful golden accent against the blues and greens of the other conifers.

Plant List

1 Chinese juniper
(Juniperus chinensus 'Kaizuka')
2 Creeping juniper
(Juniperus horizontalis)
3 Creeping juniper
(Juniperus horizontalis 'Mother Lode')
4 Rhododendron
(Rhododendron mucronulatum 'Cornell Pink')
5 Eastern hemlock
(Tsuga canadensis 'Gracilis')
6 Blue spruce
(Picea glauca 'Sanders Blue')
7 Japanese yew
(Taxus cuspidata)
8 Rocky mountain juniper
(Juniperus scopulorum 'Skyrocket')

Growing conifers in containers adds another architectural element to the garden. It also allows you to bring the plants indoors to enjoy during the winter. Before taking them outside in the spring, gradually harden them off by bringing the pots outdoors for an increasing amount of time each day. Hardening off prevents trauma to the conifers, which can be caused by changing their environment too suddenly.

Privacy Screen

When you turn an exposed area into a private corner, don't be surprised if the birds appreciate the shelter, too. Many species look for such a safe thicket, adding their songs and possibly a nest or

*H*ere's a terrific way to shield yourself from an unsightly view and cut down on noise, too. These densely growing shrubs turn an exposed area into a private corner.

Unlike a wooden fence erected for privacy, this natural hedge surrounds your patio with an ongoing show of color. Beginning with the white flowers of the cotoneaster in the spring and continuing with the abelia, vitex, and potentilla, there is a succession of new blossoms and colors. In the fall, the leaves of the cotoneaster turn yellow or red, and dark berries appear for the last of the changes before winter.

Plant List
1 Hedge cotoneaster
(Cotoneaster lucidus)
2 Abelia
(Abelia × grandiflora 'Edward Goucher')
3 Chaste tree
(Vitex agnus-castus)
4 Shrubby cinquefoil
(Potentilla fruticosa)

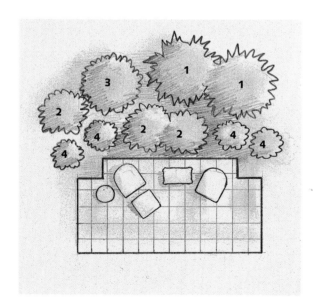

The shrubby cinquefoil is an especially noteworthy addition to this garden. The hedge is easy to maintain— seldom troubled by pests or diseases—and blooms for a long time, often continuing to flower well into fall.

two to your privacy screen.
Provide a birdbath and a
feeder to attract an even
greater variety of birds that
you can watch from indoors
or out.

CHAPTER 2

Growing Trees and Shrubs

*t*he ideal time to plant trees and shrubs is in the fall. At that time of year it's still warm enough for the roots to get a good start, but the weather is cooling, so the environment is less stressful for the plants. If you mulch the new plants well, the ground will stay warm, allowing the roots to continue to grow and develop even when the weather turns colder. Autumn rains water the soil deeply (if they don't, be sure to supplement with the hose), giving the plants a good store of moisture for the winter. • After their winter rest, most trees and shrubs planted in the fall should be ready for a spurt of growth in the spring. Spring is the second best time of year to plant trees and shrubs. • Again, the temperatures are moderate, not too hot or too cold, so the plant can begin settling in without too much stress and the roots can start growing. However, while some trees and shrubs will show growth their first summer after a spring planting, in most cases you'll have to wait a year to really see progress.

Soil

Create a compost heap with all your garden and kitchen waste, and use the broken-down compost as a topdressing around your trees and shrubs. Good ingredients for the compost include lawn clippings, prunings, dried leaves, potato peelings and other discarded vegetable parts, coffee grounds, and tea leaves. In addition to containing valuable nutrients that will leach into the soil, the compost will attract worms, which will help incorporate the rich, loamy material into the earth.

*I*t's a common practice to amend the backfill soil from a planting hole with organic matter such as peat moss, compost, or a commercially prepared planting mix. This enriched soil helps the newly planted tree make the transition to its new growing environment. But bear in mind that most trees have extensive root systems that will ultimately extend well beyond the area of the planting hole. In addition to bringing in nourishment, the far-reaching roots help hold the tree upright. The surrounding soil, therefore, must be adequate to sustain the tree.

In most cases the local soil is fine. However, soil around new homes or in areas with a lot of foot traffic can be so compacted that most roots cannot get through. Unless you break up the soil or dig the planting hole deep enough to get through the compacted area, you could end up with a root-bound or even a dead tree.

Shallow soils that have a layer of rock or hardpan (a compacted soil layer) just below the surface are also unhealthy for trees and shrubs. This condition is common in the southwestern United States. Depending on the depth of the hardpan layer, you can either bring in heavy equipment to plow the soil through the hard layer (generally effective to a depth of 1 foot) or use a soil auger or power posthole digger to drill through the hardpan to a layer of porous soil beneath. Or you can bypass the problem with a raised bed or planter. If the usable soil is deep enough to anchor a tree, but hardpan beneath will cut off drainage, use a tile drain that runs to a lower level of the garden to channel off excess water.

Some soils high in calcium carbonate (lime) have a high pH (between 7.5 and 8.5) and are considered alkaline. A soil is alkali if the pH is even higher. Acid soil has a low pH, ranging from 3.0 for extremely acidic to 6.0. A perfectly balanced or neutral soil is 7.0. Most plants are comfortable in a pH range of 6 to 8, although there are some trees and shrubs that prefer the more extreme ends of the pH spectrum. If you are unsure of the pH of your soil, have it tested by your local county cooperative extension office, and choose plants that do well in what you have.

Among the trees and shrubs that prefer alkaline soil, which is typical in western regions with low rainfall, are bottlebrush *(Callistemon* spp.*)*, cypress *(Cupressus* spp.*)*, and juniper *(Juniperus* spp.*)*. Those that thrive in acid soil include Douglas fir *(Pseudotsuga menziesii)*, fir *(Abies* spp.*)*, pine *(Pinus* spp.*)*, spruce *(Picea* spp.*)*, stewartia, western hemlock *(Tsuga heterophylla)*, azalea, rhododendron, camellia, pieris, styrax, and holly *(Ilex)*.

Soil also comes in different textures, ranging from the ideal crumbly, friable loam to the extremes of sand or heavy clay. Coarse, sandy soil provides excellent drainage and aeration, but nutrients tend to drain out along with the water. Heavy clay soil is high in nutrients, but the particles are so fine that water can take days or even weeks to move through. It's also hard work for roots to push through dense clay soil, and there isn't much oxygen for them.

To determine the type of soil you have, squeeze a damp handful. Clay soil will remain in a tight ball, sandy soil will crumble as you open your hand, and loam will hold its shape until gently prodded. Amend either heavy clay or loose sandy soil with organic matter, or choose trees and shrubs that thrive in that condition. The atlas cedar *(Cedrus atlantica)*, *Cotoneaster* species, *Pyracantha* species, Leyland cypress *(× Cupressocyparis leylandii)*, and oak *(Quercus* spp.*)* all tolerate clay soil. Barberry *(Berberis empetrifolia)* is a good choice for sandy soil.

Light

*E*very kind of tree and shrub needs some light to grow, but the amount varies depending on the species. Generally, shade lovers are the small trees and shrubs native to the eastern forests. Azalea, rhododendron, holly, dogwood, kalmia, and redbud all grow quite happily under the canopy of tall oaks, beeches, maples, and other forest trees. However, even plants that thrive in shade benefit from *some* light, especially if you want optimum bloom.

There are many degrees of shade. Shade can be a brightly lit environment where the sun makes dappled patterns on the ground, an area with no direct sun but some reflected light, or a shadowy place where the light is always dim. The brighter you can make a shady area, the better most plants will grow.

There are many ways to get extra light into a densely wooded area. Some of the trees can be removed, but if this isn't an option, consider pruning the lower branches of tall trees. An overhead canopy of foliage will still provide shade, but much more light will be available to the flora underneath—especially in the early morning and late afternoon, when the sun's rays are at an angle. Shrubs can also be pruned to create planting space for annuals and perennials beneath their skirts.

Another approach is to thin each tree, creating a loose, lacy pattern of branches. This "lacing" lets in more light and air, and enhances the form of the tree. It also makes large trees better able to withstand strong winds, because there are "portholes" for the wind to blow through. When thinning, avoid the temptation to head back the tree by cutting all the branches off at one level. You don't want a tangle of branches growing from each cut, creating an unattractive, hard-to-manage tree.

Some trees, such as tulip poplars or tulip trees (Liriodendron tulipifera), have very dense canopies that block most of the sunlight. Others, such as this weeping Higan cherry (Prunus subhirtella 'Pendula'), have a thinner leaf cover that allows light to shine through. The variation in light can make all the difference in what will grow under the tree.

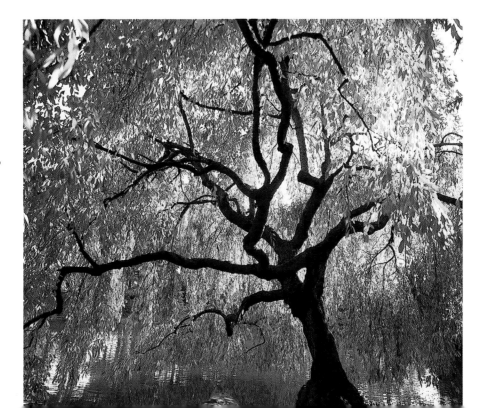

Choosing Healthy Trees and Shrubs

When choosing trees and shrubs, bear in mind that the biggest is often not the best. Resist the urge to buy the largest tree possible, even if you want to fill a space immediately. The larger, more mature trees and shrubs tend to have a harder time adjusting to being transplanted. Some large plants will spend several years reestablishing their root systems before they start growing again. Young trees planted at the same time as mature specimens of the same kind will catch up in size to the older tree in just a few years, and will often be healthier and better established.

The city of San Diego learned this lesson the hard way. Determined to have an instant grove of mature eucalyptus trees around the new stadium, the city invested thousands of dollars to bring in and plant full-grown trees. A few saplings were also planted for good measure. Many of the mature trees died from transplant shock. Within just a few years the eucalyptus saplings were as tall as the older trees, and much healthier because they were allowed to grow without being moved.

Be sure to start with a healthy plant. Buy only from reputable nurseries, and make sure they offer a guarantee. Most nurseries have a replacement policy for plants that die within three months to a year of purchase. The length of the guarantee may depend on whether the nursery staff plants the tree or shrub or whether you do it yourself.

When you buy plants in nursery containers, always check the roots. If plants have been left in containers too long or the potting practices were faulty, the roots will begin to circle and kink or, in extreme cases, grow into a tight knot. Do not buy trees or shrubs with such roots, unless you think you can amend the problem by uncurling or by pruning the roots. These defects will result in a weak, unstable trunk. Severe

1 *To "heel in" a bare-root plant until you can plant it in a permanent spot, soak the roots in a bucket of water while you dig a shallow trench.*

knotting will girdle the trunk, restricting the flow of water, nutrients, and food, ultimately slowing the tree's growth or even killing it. The problem will not be solved simply when the tree or shrub is planted in the ground.

When buying a tree, inspect the trunk for signs of injury to the bark caused by improper handling. Ideally the trunk should be able to stand up by itself, without a stake. Look for split, flattened, or dull-colored bark—an indication of sunburn damage. Sunburned bark heals slowly, leaving the tree vulnerable to borer infestation. Also check plants for signs of insects or disease. You don't want a plant that is already weakened by problems, and you certainly don't want to introduce pests into your garden.

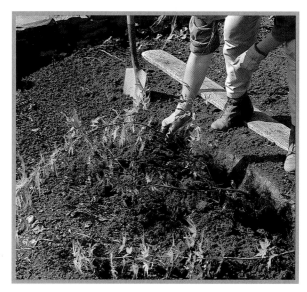

2 Slant one side of a trench or hole, and lay the bare-root plants on their sides in the hole. The position discourages the plant from rooting in the soil.

3 Bury the roots, and keep the soil moist. Ideally plants should be heeled in in a protected spot, away from the direct sun and wind.

If You Can't Plant Right Away

Ideally, you should plant newly purchased shrubs or trees right away, whether they are bare-root, in containers, or balled-and-burlapped. If a delay is necessary, take measures to protect the plants.

Put bare-root plants in a shady, weather-protected spot, and keep their roots moist. Cover them with damp sawdust, or "heel" them in, planting them temporarily in a shallow, angled hole with the tops resting along the ground.

Container plants are usually sold in black plastic pots. Left in direct sun, the dark pots absorb the heat, raising the soil temperature higher than is safe for the roots. Put unplanted containers in a cool, shady spot, and water frequently—soil dries out much faster in containers than in the ground.

Also keep balled-and-burlapped trees and shrubs shaded. Stand them in an upright position. On hot days, spray the foliage with water to help cool the plants.

1 To protect a dormant tree while bringing it home from the nursery, tie up the branches so that they are less likely to bend and break.

2 If the plant will be sticking out of a window or out the back of your vehicle while you transport it, wrap it in an old blanket to help prevent windburn.

Planting Bare-Root Stock

Deciduous trees and shrubs are generally available in early spring as bare-root stock. Because they are lighter and less bulky to ship, bare-root plants tend to be less expensive than those sold in containers, and often you'll have a better selection of varieties.

Examine the roots before you buy to make sure they are moist and plump. Don't buy plants with either moldy or dried, shriveled roots. Bare-root plants should be put in the ground as soon as possible. If a delay is unavoidable, protect the roots and keep them moist with a process called "heeling in." (See page 43.)

When you are ready to plant, soak the bare roots in a bucket of water for a few hours. Prune broken or damaged roots back to healthy tissue. Then dig a hole large enough to hold the spreading roots without cramping them. Mound the soil in the center of the hole so that roots can rest on top and fan out over the sides. Set the plant high enough so that its original soil line on the trunk (usually still visible) is level with the ground around the planting hole. Backfill the hole with the native soil (the roots will grow better if they don't have to adjust to different kinds of soils in the hole and surrounding area), tamping down firmly. When the hole is about half full, water thoroughly and allow the soil to settle. If the planting level drops, gently pull up the plant from its base to the correct level. Add more soil, and water again.

After the first thorough watering, bare-root plants need less water than other newly planted shrubs and trees because they are still dormant. Only irrigate if the soil is dry. Water as you would any new plant once active growth begins (see pages 52–53).

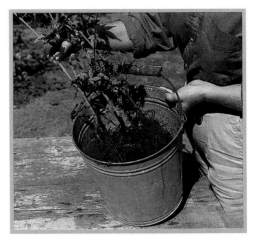

1 *Before planting a bare-root tree or shrub, soak the roots overnight in a bucket of water to make them plump and fresh.*

5 *Backfill the hole with the dug soil, until it is three-quarters full. Then water thoroughly, filling the hole and allowing the water to soak in.*

2 *Dig a hole wide and deep enough to accommodate the roots without cramping them. Mound some soil in the center of the hole.*

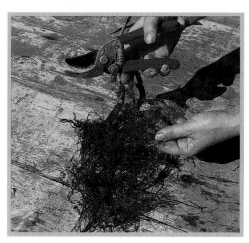

3 *Prune back any broken roots to healthy tissue. Also remove dead roots and ones that may be unduly twisted or kinked.*

4 *Set the plant in the hole, spreading the roots evenly over the soil cone. The original soil line should show just above ground level.*

6 *Fill the hole with the soil until it is even with the ground level. If the plant has settled in too deeply, pull it up gently to the correct level.*

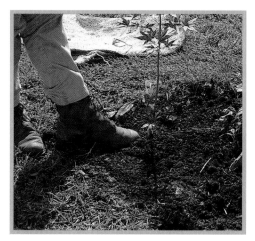

7 *Tamp down the soil with your foot to eliminate any air pockets left in the planting hole. Create a berm around the plant, and water again.*

8 *Prune off any unnecessary leaves and branches so that the roots can concentrate on growing, rather than on supporting excess foliage.*

Planting Balled-and-Burlapped Stock

*B*alled-and-burlapped (B-and-B) plants have been dug from their growing fields with a ball of soil around their roots. The soil ball is wrapped in burlap to hold it together. These plants can be put in holes together with their burlap wrapping, which will eventually rot away. Beware, however, of B-and-B plants wrapped in plastic fabric woven to look like burlap. Unless you remove this wrap, your plant will be root-bound and eventually die.

Dig a hole twice as wide as the root ball and about 6 inches deeper. Many B-and-B plants have been grown in heavy clay soil, and your garden soil may be lighter. The clay soil will absorb water more slowly than the lighter soil, so the roots may remain dry even though the surrounding soil feels moist. To help solve the problem, mix one shovelful of organic amendments (except manure) into three parts backfill soil. This mixture will retain water better and get it to the plant's roots.

Shovel a bit more than 6 inches of amended backfill into the hole, place the B-and-B plant on top, and water. The top of the root ball should be about 2 inches aboveground. When you water, the settling of the soil should lower the root ball to just above ground level. Refill the hole about half full, tamping down the soil as you go. Continue filling the hole to within 3 inches of the top. Untie the twine holding the burlap, and spread the burlap over the soil. Water thoroughly, allow the soil to settle, and then continue to fill the hole until the soil reaches ground level.

Create a watering basin around the new plant, a couple of inches from the trunk to keep the trunk from rotting. Watch the plant carefully for the first two years to make sure that the original root ball gets enough water. Once the roots have extended well into the surrounding soil, you don't need to worry.

1 *Dig a hole about twice the diameter of the root ball and 6 inches deeper. Backfill the hole with 6 inches of the original soil amended with organic matter.*

5 *Backfill the hole with amended soil, and press the soil with your foot to remove air pockets. Build a berm around the plant and water twice to settle the plant to ground level.*

2 *Place the plant centered in the hole. Check the position of the plant's branches, and rotate it if it looks better from a different side. Be sure the plant is properly upright.*

3 *Cut the ties around the burlap, but leave the burlap wrapping. Roots will grow through burlap, and the fabric will rot away in a few years. Synthetic burlap will not decompose.*

4 *Roll back the burlap wrapping so that none remains aboveground to draw moisture up from the roots like a wick. Remove any synthetic wrapping.*

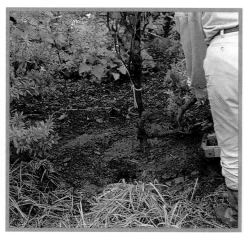

6 *Put a 4- to 6-inch layer of mulch around the plant to help conserve moisture around the roots and to deter weeds. The mulch will also keep the roots warm in cold temperatures.*

7 *Remove any ties that may have been wrapped around the plant to protect it during the transporting from the nursery to your property. Be careful not to damage any branches.*

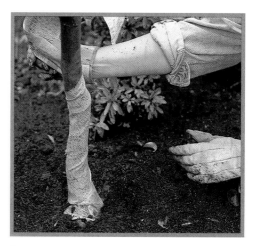

8 *The bark of young trees is particularly susceptible to sunburn. If your tree is planted in direct sun, wrap the trunk with burlap to protect it, or paint it with white latex paint or whitewash.*

Planting Container-Grown Stock

*B*efore you buy a container-grown plant, check that it isn't rootbound. If the roots are poking above the soil or growing out of the holes in the bottom, choose a different tree or shrub. Other signs of crowded roots are leggy plants, plants too big for their pots, and plants with dead twigs and branches.

There is no rush to plant container-grown stock; it can continue happily in its pot for months and even years as long as it isn't rootbound. Be sure, however, to water potted plants regularly, as often as twice a day during very hot, dry weather. Soil in pots dries out faster than soil in the garden.

Dig a generous planting hole. The native soil in your garden is probably much denser than the loose, quick-draining soil mixture generally preferred for container plants. If your soil is very heavy, loosen it in the planting area and over the area where roots will eventually grow. Amend the soil from the hole with organic matter to make it lighter and looser. Loosen the soil in the bottom of the hole, and return a few inches of the amended soil to the hole.

When you remove the plant from the container, check its roots. Straighten out any that are coiled, and if the root ball is tight, loosen it with your fingers, even removing the outer inch or so of roots. If the roots are too dense for your fingers, cut vertical slices up the sides of the root mass with a knife and pull it apart. This procedure improves the roots' contact with the fill soil and stimulates root growth.

Place the plant on top of the backfill so that the top of the root ball is just above the surrounding soil level. Replace the soil until the hole is about three-fourths full, then water and allow the soil to settle. The root ball should still be slightly above the ground. Continue filling the hole, create a basin for watering (see page 46), and then water again.

1 *Dig the hole twice the width of the container and several inches deeper. Remove the plant from the container by gently tugging on the stem and squeezing the sides of the container.*

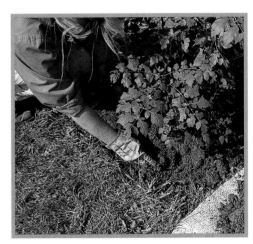

5 *When the depth is correct, backfill with the rest of the amended soil, pressing down firmly to remove air pockets. Water slowly so that the roots are thoroughly soaked.*

2 *Loosen the roots from the sides of the root ball so that they are pulled free from the soil. Don't worry: cut or broken roots will be stimulated to grow important new feeder roots.*

3 *Also loosen the roots around the bottom. Some people actually cut up into the root ball with an ax or sharp knife to butterfly it. Cut away any circled or kinked roots.*

4 *Backfill the planting hole with a few inches of amended soil. Place the plant in the hole, with the top of the soil ball slightly above ground level.*

6 *Spread mulch around the plant to retain soil moisture and deter weeds. Newspaper laid under the bark mulch is excellent for weed control and moisture retention.*

7 *Stake trees that are too tall to stand by themselves or those that have weak root systems. Place two stakes on opposite sides of the tree just outside the drip line.*

8 *Tie the tree to each stake, allowing enough slack for the trunk to bend a little in the breeze. Check the ties periodically to make sure they aren't constricting the trunk as the tree grows.*

Planting a Hedgerow

1 Mark the length of your hedge with string, and space the plants evenly along the line. The spacing will depend on the plants you choose.

2 Dig the holes where you had positioned each plant, following the appropriate directions for bare-root or container plants.

3 Place each plant in the hole, making sure it is upright and centered in the hole. Follow appropriate directions for planting on pages 44–49.

4 Firm the soil around each plant, pressing with your foot and using the full weight of your body. It is important to remove any air pockets.

5 Water generously, filling the basins around each plant at least twice to ensure that the entire root system is moistened.

6 Mulch the new plants with an organic material such as hay, shredded bark, or shredded leaves, making the layer 4 to 6 inches deep.

Care After Planting

TIMESAVING TIP

Determined grass and weeds can still emerge through the recommended 3- to 4-inch layer of mulch. To cut out all unwanted grass, put down a ¼-inch layer of newspaper before placing the mulch around newly planted trees and shrubs.

Young trees often have small branches growing lower on the trunk than you want. Unless these low branches are growing at the expense of the upper branches desired for the tree's ultimate framework, leave them on for the first three to five years. That way, the girth of the trunk will increase more rapidly.

Drying winds, hot sun, and winter freezes can damage young tree trunks. Protect the trunk with loosely tied burlap or tree tape. Check the wrap regularly and loosen it if it's too tight. Young trees grow quickly, and any constriction around the trunk can cause permanent damage. Young trees are also more vulnerable to chewing and clawing animals such as deer, mice, dogs, and cats. To keep these animals away, encircle young trees with wire mesh or hardware cloth.

Keep grass away from the trunk (as far as the outermost spread of branches, which is known as the drip line) for at least two to three years. Grass is a hearty feeder and will rob young trees of needed water and nutrients. Mulch is an excellent way to help keep back the turf and retain soil moisture. Permanent mulch protects the tree from possible lawn-mower damage (see page 55).

Ideally, new trees should not be staked. Waving in the wind actually helps the tree grow a strong, sturdy trunk. However, many young trees simply cannot stand on their own because of a small, undeveloped root system or top-heavy foliage. Sometimes pruning some branches is enough to allow the tree to stand on its own. If you must stake, do so in a manner that allows the tree some movement, and make sure that the trunk isn't constricted. (For more details, see the photographs on page 54.) As soon as the tree is strong enough to stand on its own, remove the stakes.

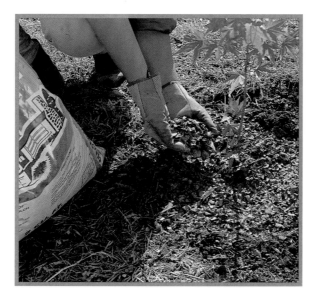

1 *Surround a newly planted tree or shrub with a layer of mulch 2 to 4 inches deep to conserve moisture and to keep the roots at an even, comfortable temperature. Mound the mulch away from the trunk of the tree.*

2 *To support small saplings, use a loop stake stuck into the ground close to the trunk. The space in the loop allows sufficient room for the tree to sway in the wind, so that the trunk builds up its strength.*

Watering

Drought-Tolerant Trees and Shrubs

Drought-tolerant trees and shrubs for a variety of climates include barberry (Berberis), broom (Cytisus), cotoneaster, firethorn (Pyracantha), ginkgo, hollies (Ilex), mahonia, varnish tree (Koelreuteria paniculata), mimosa or silk tree (Albizia julibrissin), oak (Quercus), privet (Ligustrum), sumacs (Rhus), and yews (Taxus). Some plants for dry gardens in warm climates are bottlebrush (Callistemon), California lilac (Ceanothus), crape myrtle (Lagerstroemia indica), and manzanita (Arctostaphylos).

Most plants die as a result of improper watering. New trees and shrubs need regular watering as they develop new roots. Immediately after planting, thoroughly irrigate the tree or shrub to settle the soil around the root system. Even if you choose a drought-tolerant specimen, continue to water the plant every seven to ten days during the growing season for the first year or two after it has been planted. After that the root system should be extensive enough to absorb adequate moisture from the surrounding soil. (Even well-established mature trees benefit from irrigation in times of extreme drought.) Otherwise they become more vulnerable to diseases and pests.

Signs of a thirsty tree or shrub include wilting, premature leaf fall, or a change in texture or color of the leaves—for example, from shiny to dull or from bright green to flat and yellowish.

Irrigate slowly, so that the water can penetrate deep into the soil without running off the surface. Frequent shallow watering is actually damaging to trees and shrubs. Most of the water evaporates quickly from the soil surface before reaching the roots, and the plant will stay shallow-rooted to remain near the water. Roots near the soil surface are extremely vulnerable to damage from hot sun and drought.

If you live in a dry region of the country or have many newly planted trees that need watering, it is probably worthwhile to install a drip-irrigation system. Drip systems are comprised of tiny hoses, called drip lines, that can be buried or laid on top of the ground. New lines can be added and old lines removed and the holes plugged, making it a versatile and flexible system. For trees, the lines should be run around each plant with one dripper or emitter for each 2 to 2½ feet of the canopy's diameter. For example, a tree that is 6 to 9 feet in diameter would require

Most drought-tolerant trees and shrubs grow happily without water once they are established, but even native desert plants need regular watering the first year. The tree growing in this cactus garden is a palo verde (Cercidium), native to the dry deserts of California.

three emitters. Small shrubs can make do with one feeder line and dripper to each plant.

Drip irrigation operates with low water pressure, delivering water at rates as slow as half a gallon per hour. Unlike sprinkling systems or hand-watering, there is no waste due to runoff or evaporation into the air.

This watering system has many benefits for plants. Water goes exactly where it is needed, and it soaks in more deeply because of the slow delivery. As a result, plants tend to grow faster and more evenly. Because the foliage never gets wet, there is less chance for disease organisms to take hold, thus reducing the need for chemical sprays. Liquid fertilizer can be added directly through the system, ensuring regular and accurately measured applications. When the system has an automatic timer, trees and shrubs get watered regularly, even when you're not at home to regulate the process.

If you do decide to water by hand, the basin around each plant should extend a few inches from the trunk to the edge of the branch spread, known as the tree's drip line. The ridge creating the basin should be about 6 inches tall for deep-rooted trees. Fill the basin slowly, so that the water pressure doesn't erode the soil and expose the plant's roots.

If the trees and shrubs don't have watering basins, run the water a long time on each plant. The flow should be gentle enough for the water to soak in without running off. Allow about half an hour for a small tree, three minutes for a knee-high shrub.

For newly planted specimens, check the soil for moisture every few days by digging down a few inches with your fingers. Water if it feels dry.

Trees and Shrubs for Wet Places

Some good trees and shrubs for wet soils in all but the coldest and very warmest climates include arborvitae (Thuja occidentalis), *ash* (Fraxinus), *bald cypress* (Taxodium distichum), *birch* (Betula), *black gum or tupelo* (Nyssa sylvatica), *dawn redwood* (Metasequoia glyptostroboides), *red maple* (Acer rubrum), *sweet bay magnolia* (Magnolia virginiana), *sweet pepperbush* (Clethra alnifolia), *and willow* (Salix).

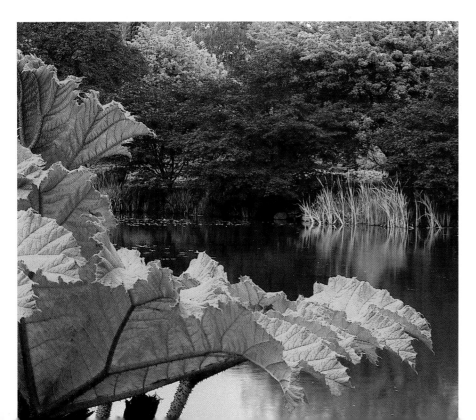

The deep burgundy red foliage of spectacular Japanese red maple trees contrasts beautifully with the bright green of the trees behind and with the paler green of the Siberian iris in the water.

Staking

1 *Stake kits come with webbed straps to wrap around the tree. This material won't dig into the tree's trunk and damage the bark.*

2 *The stakes, like tent pegs, allow you to adjust the tension of the guy wires so that the tree isn't pulled too much in one direction.*

3 *Like a tripod, three guy wires give ample support to the tree against wind blowing in any direction, while still allowing some flex.*

Mulching

*A*ll newly planted trees and shrubs should be mulched with a layer of loose material 4 to 6 inches deep. Arrange the mulch so that it rises away from the stem of the plant.

There are many benefits of mulch. In the winter it keeps roots warm. In spring, summer, and fall it blocks out weeds. As the summer sun grows hotter, mulch keeps plant roots cool, especially if the mulch is a light color that doesn't absorb heat as readily. Mulch also helps the soil to retain moisture by as much as 6 to 10 percent.

There is a wide variety of materials you can use as mulch. The organic choices are best because they will eventually decompose, adding valuable nutrients and humus to the soil and improving its condition. Even though the mulch layer will thin as it breaks down, needing to be replenished from time to time, you can rejoice in your enriched soil. Among the organic mulch possibilities are grass cuttings, straw, shredded leaves, cocoa bean hulls, sawdust, newspapers, and shredded bark.

A thick layer of newspaper is especially effective for keeping down weeds, and since it is 75 percent ground wood pulp and 25 percent purified fiber or cellulose (which contain nutrients and trace elements valuable to the garden), it will eventually break down into beneficial elements for the soil. Spread the newspaper several sheets deep around the base of the tree or shrub. Then cover the newspaper with a generous layer of shredded bark to keep the paper in place and to create a cosmetic cover. Newspaper will crackle underfoot at first, and the bark topping may slide around, but once the paper is well wetted, it will settle down and grip to both the ground and the bark.

1 *Organic mulches will break down, ultimately improving the soil. Spread mulch around a newly planted tree, keeping it away from the trunk, and replenish when it gets thin.*

2 *Inorganic materials such as gravel and stones also make excellent mulches. These stones are a striking decorative element in this shrub border.*

Fertilizing

EARTH·WISE TIP

Wait to feed newly planted trees and shrubs at least until you see new growth; some horticulturists now suggest waiting until the plant has been in place for a year. Fertilizer in the planting hole or backfill soil can actually harm the plant. However, a dose of vitamin B at planting helps the plant overcome the shock of being moved. Vitamin B for plants is available at garden centers. Follow the package directions for use.

Mature trees typically don't need fertilizing, but young trees and shrubs benefit greatly from feeding to increase their growth rate.

Ideally, maturing trees and shrubs should be fertilized in the spring and early fall, although a few shrubs, such as camellias, azaleas, and rhododendrons, benefit from three feedings, once at the end of their blooming season and twice more during the summer. Stop fertilizing by early August so the new growth stimulated by the fertilizer has time to harden before winter. Roses should be fed at the start of the first growth of the season and at the end of each bloom period. If you fertilize just once a year, do it in the fall, but not so late in the season that tender new growth will be vulnerable to freezes. Choose a slow-release all-purpose fertilizer so that the nitrogen is released into the soil gradually throughout the year. Follow the directions on the package for amounts and application procedures.

In alkaline soil, the leaves of some trees and shrubs may turn yellow with dark green veins, indicating chlorosis or iron deficiency (generally caused by too much lime in the soil, which makes the existing iron unavailable to the plants). Treat the soil with iron sulfate or, even better, chelated iron, which presents the iron in a form that is readily available to the plants.

1 *Sprinkle granular fertilizer that has a nutrient ratio such as 10-6-4 around the base of the plant, spreading it evenly. Read the directions on the package to learn the right dose for your plants.*

2 *Using a garden fork or a trowel, gently work the fertilizer into the soil, being careful not to disturb any shallow roots. Give the plant a good watering to let the fertilizer reach the roots.*

Controlling Pests and Diseases

A Safer Fungicide

Scientists at Cornell University developed a recipe for a nontoxic solution of baking soda and horticultural oil that is very effective in controlling powdery mildew and moderately effective in controlling black spot on roses when sprayed weekly. The proportions are 1 tablespoon of baking soda (sodium bicarbonate) and 2⅓ tablespoons of Sunspray Ultra-Fine Horticultural Spray Oil (available commercially and by mail order) per gallon of water. More concentrated sprays will damage the roses. Further studies have shown that the horticultural oil alone is as effective as the mix.

Probably the best technique is to spray the baking soda and oil mixture on a weekly basis from April through June, then switch to conventional fungicides during the warmer months of July and August when black spot is most likely to occur.

Healthy plants are usually able to cope on their own with pest and disease problems. But now and then a disease or pest overwhelms a plant and it needs extra help. If the tree or shrub is a manageable size, you can care for it yourself. Large trees are probably too tall to reach with home spraying equipment, and you should call in a professional.

When a plant needs help, first decide whether to use manual or physical methods of control, live controls, or packaged controls. Whatever control methods you choose, you will be most effective if you know the life cycle of the organism you are fighting, so that you can target it when it is most vulnerable. Check with a nursery or your county cooperative extension office for information on the best timing and techniques for combating the enemies plaguing your garden.

Manual measures include removing infected leaves and branches (see photographs on page 59), hand-picking caterpillars such as those of the gypsy moth, breaking up the nests of tent caterpillars and killing the inhabitants, and turning a hard spray of water onto shrubs to wash off unwanted aphids.

Many beneficial insects and birds feed on unwanted pests. With live controls, you simply introduce these creatures into your garden and allow them to go about their business. Cryptolaemus beetles, for example, prey on mealybugs; tiny encarsia wasps live off whiteflies; and lacewing larvae feed on aphids. Wrens will feed each of their fledglings as many as 500 insects in an afternoon; redstart young consume a minimum of 1,200 bugs daily; and a brown thrasher can eat up to 6,800 insects a day. Attract birds to your garden with birdbaths, feeders, and plantings that provide places for nesting as well as cover from predators.

Oil sprays are an effective, nontoxic means of controlling aphids, spider mites, scale insects, and other tree pests. Spray trees thoroughly with an oil that is specially formulated for horticultural use.

Packaged controls include nontoxic products as well as the traditional array of poisons. An excellent nontoxic solution to a caterpillar invasion is *Bacillus thuringiensis* (Bt). It destroys the digestive systems of caterpillars, so that they starve to death, but is harmless to other living creatures. Insecticidal soaps kill small soft-bodied pests such as aphids, psyllids, whiteflies, and mites, but you must spray the soap regularly and frequently. If you use toxic chemicals, choose a product that will target the pest or disease with the least effect to rest of the environment.

Controlling Pests and Diseases CONTINUED

EARTH·WISE TIP

Experienced staff at nurseries and your local county cooperative extension agents can help accurately diagnose both insect problems and diseases in plants. Before you spray an all-purpose poison, learn exactly what the trouble is, and then explore possible nontoxic solutions. Use poisons only with discretion and in moderation.

1 *Bands of burlap or cloth folded around your trees can help control gypsy moth infestations. Check under the burlap daily, collect the caterpillars, and destroy them.*

2 *For minor deer damage, try deterrents such as hanging bars of soap from string in trees. The soap can also be nailed to stakes around the edge of the garden.*

3 *If grazing deer are a serious problem in your garden, use special deer netting to cover vulnerable plants (they love azaleas, pictured here).*

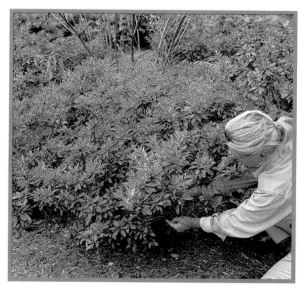

4 *Tie netting with twine or string, making sure that all the foliage is out of the deer's reach. Or encircle select plants with barriers made of galvanized hardware cloth.*

1 *Symptoms of the disease fire blight include sudden wilting followed by shriveling and blackening of blossoms, fruit, and young shoots.*

2 *Prune away infected wood. With trees, cut 6 to 12 inches below the blighted area. Cut several inches below the infection on small plants.*

3 *Sterilize the pruning shears between cuts with household bleach or another disinfectant. Avoid fertilizing and excessive watering.*

In addition to active control measures, you can create garden conditions that are less likely to encourage diseases and pests. A garden planted with a diversity of plants is less likely to suffer insect infestation or rampant disease than a specialty garden—but any messy garden that harbors unwanted insects, bacteria, and fungi can cause problems.

Anthracnose, a fungus that spreads by air or water, can plague trees and shrubs during long, wet springs. Rake away infected leaves from around the plant to keep rainwater from splashing off the leaves and back onto the plant. If this doesn't work, spray deciduous plants with copper or lime sulfur in the early spring while they are still dormant. This helps prevent anthracnose as well as other fungal diseases such as fire blight, leaf spot, scab, and shot hole. It also kills overwintering insects such as scale, mites, and certain caterpillars. The chemicals must be on the trees for at least 48 hours before a rain to be effective. Alternate copper and lime sulfur sprays from year to year to avoid building immunities to either fungicide.

When a particular disease or pest becomes unmanageable, the best measure is to avoid it altogether. Look for plant varieties and hybrids that have been bred to be resistant to specific diseases and problems.

Winter Protection and Care

TROUBLESHOOTING TIP

Prune the branches off your used Christmas tree, and lay the cuttings over tender ground-cover plants or low-growing shrubs. The cut branches will help insulate the plants from the cold and drying winter winds.

*E*ven trees and shrubs rated hardy for cold winter weather can benefit from some protection. Deep snowfalls weigh heavily on tree boughs and shrubs, often breaking brittle or weak branches. Snow sliding off a roof onto shrubs planted along a house foundation can severely damage plants. Fierce winter gales can topple shallow-rooted trees, as well as draw out all the life-giving moisture stored in the dormant branches and foliage. Even bright sunlight can damage or kill bark that in summer is shaded by leaves.

There are a variety of measures you can take to protect valued plants from these ravages of winter weather. Make a point of shaking or brushing heavy snow off trees and shrubs, especially trees with soft or brittle wood and specimen shrubs that you can see are becoming deformed or at risk of breaking because of the weight of the snow. Boxwood in particular turns

an ugly brown when damaged by snow, and gaps from broken branches take a long time to fill in. If you are ambitious, you may want to build a temporary wooden frame to shelter prized shrubs along the side of the house, so that they aren't broken or buried by an avalanche of snow sliding off the roof.

On the other hand, once trees or shrubs are encased in ice, it is best to leave them alone. Like a blanket of snow, the ice acts as insulation, protecting the plants from drying winds. Also, knocking ice off a branch can cause the branch to snap.

Scorch damage to trees and shrubs, caused by lack of water, is often mistaken for frost damage. This desiccation, caused by extremely low humidity or dry winds, is a common winter problem in the North, especially if there isn't a snow cover to insulate the plants. If fall rains are light, water trees and shrubs

1 *Protect tender young saplings from gnawing rodents by encircling the plants with wire-mesh cylinders that are buried 2 to 3 inches into the ground.*

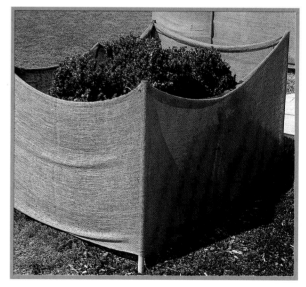

2 *Protect shrubs from icy, drying winds by encircling them with burlap. Drive four stakes into the ground, making sure they are deep enough not to topple or blow away.*

deeply before they go dormant for winter. Apply a thick layer of mulch to help retain the water. (If you want to keep the ground from freezing as long as possible, so that the roots can continue to draw up water, apply the mulch before the first freeze. If you want to keep the ground frozen to protect from the uprooting effects of ground heaving caused by alternating freezes and thaws, apply thick mulch after the ground has frozen to help keep it that way.) In early winter, spray an antidesiccant on the trunks, branches, and foliage of broad-leaved and needle evergreens if your garden happens to be subject to frequent drying winter winds.

To protect shrubs from the full force of drying, damaging winds, encircle them with burlap stapled to stakes, or place a screen of burlap attached to stakes on the windward side of the plant. Make sure the screen is well staked to the ground, so that it doesn't blow away.

Sunshine can damage trees in winter, when there are no leaves to protect the bark from strong sun. Sun scald, which can crack and kill the bark, tends to occur on the southwest side of the tree on bright, sunny days. Protect vulnerable trees by painting the trunk with whitewash or white latex paint, or wrap the trunk with burlap. As a last-minute measure, lay a board against the trunk on the sunny side to shade it.

Even subtropical areas sometimes get freezing temperatures. Orange growers in California and Florida have lost many a night's sleep keeping the smudge pots burning to heat the orchards, so that the trees won't freeze. In mild regions, where extreme cold snaps are rare, you may want to take special measures

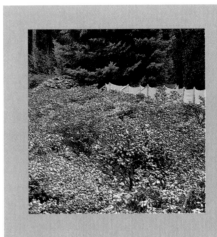

This group of azaleas is protected from winter wind damage by a "fence" of burlap and stakes on the side of the plants facing into the prevailing winds.

to protect a shrub that is frost-sensitive or of borderline hardiness from unusual cold. Move potted trees and shrubs to a sheltered spot out of the wind and near the house, where they can benefit from the warm walls during cold spells. If you hear predictions of freezing or colder-than-usual weather, throw a blanket, sheet, or even plastic sheeting over the tender plant (secure the plastic so that it doesn't blow away). That extra layer of protection and insulation will make an enormous difference to the plant if there are just a few degrees of frost. But be sure to remove the insulation as soon as the temperatures warm. The plastic sheet will act like a greenhouse once the sun hits it, and you could inadvertently bake your plant.

Regional Calendar of Tree and Shrub Care

 Spring

 Summer

COOL CLIMATES

Spring

- In early spring, plant bare-root trees and shrubs. Water well at planting, but wait for signs of growth to irrigate further. Container and balled-and-burlapped plants can go in the ground when the weather warms.

- Root softwood cuttings (new growth) of shrubs and ornamental cherries.

- Once you see signs of growth, fertilize newly planted and young trees and shrubs to give them a boost for summer.

- Mulch to conserve soil moisture and to keep the roots cool during the hot summer days.

- Remove any branches damaged by snow, wind, or ice. Remove new suckers, water sprouts, and branches that are growing in an unwanted direction. Train and prune new growth on espaliers.

- Wait to prune flowering trees and shrubs until after they have blossomed, or while they are in bloom if you want cut flowers for the house.

Summer

- In early summer prune azaleas, lilacs, and other spring-flowering shrubs to encourage new growth that will set buds for next spring's display.

- Prune flowering cherries now rather than in spring, when the vigorous new growth stimulated by the trimming is susceptible to leaf diseases.

- Keep an eye on the soil moisture, particularly around newly planted trees and shrubs, and water deeply if it is dry.

- Remove the dead or diseased branches of evergreens in late summer. Shear evergreens and hedges. Late summer is also the safest time to prune most shade trees; they are least likely to bleed then.

WARM CLIMATES

Spring

- After frost is past, feed avocado and citrus trees. Mature citrus trees use 1 pound of actual nitrogen per year; younger trees need proportionally less. Avocados require at least 2 pounds of actual nitrogen yearly; divide into four to six equal feedings given at regular intervals until June.

- Feed ornamental trees and shrubs with slow-release all-purpose fertilizer.

- Plant camellias and azaleas now, while they are in bloom. Apply fertilizer to camellias when bloom finishes, and then twice more at six-week intervals. Feed azaleas after they bloom and in September.

- Check junipers for juniper moths (tip damage, ¼-inch silver-white cocoons, silver-tan moths). If they are infested, spray with an appropriate pesticide.

- Control whiteflies on ash and fruit trees by washing off infested trees with insecticidal soap sprays every two to three weeks. Keep affected plants well watered and fertilized.

Summer

- Except in extremely hot inland areas, plant tropical and subtropical trees and shrubs such as hibiscus, gardenia, palms, floss silk tree *(Chorisia speciosa)*, and orchid tree *(Bauhinia* spp.*)*.

- Water established trees and shrubs deeply but infrequently to encourage a deep, more drought-tolerant root system. Mulch heavily to reduce water loss through evaporation.

- Layer camellias and azaleas to propagate new plants. See pages 91–93.

- Continue to prune and train espaliers.

- Prune branches of apples, pears, pyracantha, cotoneaster, plum, cherry, quince, and loquat that are infected with fire blight. Cut branches at least 8 inches below the visible damage, and disinfect shears in alcohol or bleach between each cut. Destroy infected prunings. See page 59.

Fall

🌲 *Winter*

- Take hardwood (mature wood) cuttings to root. Willows *(Salix spp.)* are among the easier trees to propagate from hardwood cuttings.

- If autumn rains are slight, give trees a deep watering to prepare them for winter.

- Except in the far North, plant container and balled-and-burlapped trees and shrubs. This is also the best time of year to move any trees or shrubs to a different spot.

- Fertilize young trees and shrubs to encourage faster growth next spring. Generally mature specimens do not need fertilizing.

- Mulch to retain moisture in the soil and insulate the roots. If you want to keep the roots warm as long as possible, mulch before the first freeze. If you want to prevent the soil from thawing and heaving, wait until after the ground is frozen.

- Protect young or tender plants from drying winter winds by making windbreaks with burlap stapled to stakes in the ground.

- Brush heavy snow off shrubs to protect them from breaking or becoming deformed.

- Apply white latex paint or wrap the bark of deciduous trees that get direct sunlight to protect them from scorching and other sun damage.

- Spray an antidesiccant on the trunks and branches of vulnerable trees and shrubs.

- Leave any ice that forms along branches of trees and shrubs alone, letting it melt naturally.

This table offers a basic outline of garden care by season. The tasks for each season differ for warm and cool climates: warm climates correspond to USDA plant hardiness zones 8 through 11, and cool climates to zones 2 through 7. Obviously, there are substantial climate differences within these broad regions. To understand the specific growing conditions in your area, consult the zone map on page 127. Also be sure to study local factors affecting the microclimate of your garden, such as elevation and proximity of water.

- Keep citrus and avocado trees well watered to prevent the fruit from splitting. Camellias also need regular watering to keep the buds from browning and dropping off.

- Disbud camellias, pinching off all but one bud from each cluster, leaving the one that is biggest or facing the direction you want. Disbudding gives you larger flowers. Mulch with pine needles.

- After September, tropical trees and shrubs begin to go dormant. Stop feeding these plants, so that they can begin to harden off for winter.

- Except for tropical trees, which adjust better when planted during the hotter months, fall is the best season for planting trees and shrubs.

- Encourage deciduous fruit trees into winter dormancy by withholding fertilizer. Also reduce water, but don't let the soil go completely dry.

- Apply dormant oil spray to roses, deciduous fruit trees, and sycamore trees to protect against fungus diseases. Spray fruit trees twice: once after leaves fall in November or December, and again in January before new buds swell. Prune fruit trees.

- Clean up fallen camellia blossoms to prevent petal blight, a fungus disease that causes brown, rotting blossoms. Spores are carried by the wind, so ask neighbors to pick up their camellia petals too.

- Protect tender shrubs from frost by covering them with a bedsheet, blanket, or plastic sheeting. If they are damaged by the cold, wait for signs of new growth before pruning off the frost-burned parts of the plant.

- Plant bare-root trees and shrubs. Transplant trees and shrubs that you want moved to new locations.

- Buy and plant sasanqua camellias now, while they are in bloom. Also look for early-flowering azaleas that bloom in winter.

CHAPTER 3

Pruning and Training

Some people may be uncomfortable pruning a tree or shrub, believing that the plant should grow unimpeded. Or they may be concerned that cutting will hurt the plant. • In fact, pruning is healthy for trees and shrubs, and nature has its own methods for removing growth. Branches, especially dead ones, break off trees in strong winds; animals such as deer, mice, rabbits, and beavers nibble on shoots; and forest fires (if they are not too hot and move through quickly) clean out deadwood while leaving healthy growth intact. • In a garden, however, we generally want more control over pruning than the somewhat random techniques that have evolved in the wild. People prune with specific goals in mind, such as guiding future growth, maintaining a desirable size or shape, encouraging more fruit or flower production, rejuvenating an old shrub, or removing diseased or injured limbs. The goal of pruning is to make your plant healthier and more attractive, and more useful in the landscape.

Pruning

*T*here are several ways to approach pruning, depending on what you want to accomplish. Some trees—especially fruit trees—are pruned when they are young to establish a network of major structural branches (known as scaffolds) that will support the tree's future growth. Pruning can enhance or refine a tree or shrub's natural growth habit, or you can use pruning to sculpt the plant into an idealized form and drastically change its shape. Topiary combines the latter type of pruning with other training techniques to force trees and shrubs into formal geometric or fanciful shapes.

Pruning to alter a plant's shape is not for beginners. Unless you're experienced, you can easily destroy a plant's shape by using improper pruning methods. Many a tree has been ruined by a well-intentioned gardener attempting to force it to grow against its natural inclination.

Pruning to change a plant's shape also takes time. Shoots growing in the wrong direction must be periodically removed throughout the life of the tree or shrub. If you fall behind, it will be obvious as the plant begins to lose its idealized form. Unless you are willing to make a long-term commitment of time and energy to maintaining the plant's shape, it's best to opt for a more natural form.

For good results, then, simply work with, rather than against, the plant's natural form. To reduce pruning needs and minimize the amount of time you must devote to pruning, choose trees and shrubs carefully before you plant them. Pick one whose ultimate size and shape will fit the available space. If you need a tree for a narrow space, for example, choose one with a naturally columnar or slender form rather than a wide tree that needs constant pruning.

Useful tools for pruning include various types of saws, long- and short-handled loppers, hedge shears, and anvil and scissor-type hand pruners.

1 *Pruning will improve the health and appearance of your plants. One approach to pruning is to shear evergreen shrubs to create neat formal shapes.*

2 *Cut back the new growth that extends beyond the outline of the shape you wish to maintain. Not all evergreens can tolerate this type of pruning (see page 72).*

▽ **Deciduous Trees**

The first time you may need to prune a tree is when you plant it. A large crown on a young plant, while attractive, also requires a lot of nourishment. Furthermore, when the root system is small it lacks the ability to grow and support the crown at the same time. To allow the roots to develop quickly, trim back all but a few leaves from the crown. Cut out any branches that cross each other and any thin or weak ones. Also cut back the side scaffold branches (the main structural limbs of the tree) if they are longer than the central leader (the tallest, strongest upright limb). On a tree that has a central leader, you want the leader to be the strongest and most dominant part. In windy areas, use an open branch form when

pruning, so that strong winds can blow through the tree without toppling it.

Once in a great while, it may be necessary to cut off the main leader on a young tree to about 6 to 12 inches from the ground or graft union, leaving just a bare stump of a trunk. But this drastic technique should be used only as a last-ditch effort to revitalize a weak sapling (first make sure the problem weakening the tree isn't poorly drained soil, insects, disease, or the like). If you do use this technique, when the lopped trunk begins to sprout, choose the most vigorous shoot to be the new leader, and remove all the others. Continue training as you would any other young tree.

Pruning CONTINUED

Beware of overpruning. Some trees and shrubs have remarkable regenerative powers (large eucalyptus trees will sprout even when cut to the ground, and old overgrown box, holly, and yew hedges can also be regenerated by cutting them back to bare stumps). Most plants, however, need some foliage in order to transform the light and air into life-sustaining nutrients.

Young trees benefit from early training to create the framework for them to grow into graceful, beautiful adults. Before you begin to prune, analyze the tree's natural shape and growth habits, and how this fits in with the function you want the tree to serve.

If you want the tree to screen a view, then you want it to grow in a tight form. Cut back the branches to an outward-facing bud to encourage bushier growth. For a wide, open tree, leave the terminal (end) branches, and instead cut off lateral (side) shoots. The branches will continue to grow long, but you will reduce the weight and density of the tree. You will need to continue pruning and training in this way for many years to correct and guide your tree.

As a tree matures, it may require maintenance pruning to keep a graceful form and a strong structure. Main scaffolding branches that grow from the trunk at a narrow angle have a much weaker crotch than those growing at a 45- to 90-degree angle from the trunk, and thus are more likely to break off. A branch is also at risk if it grows too thick, making it too heavy for the trunk to support. Remove any weak or heavy branches to encourage the development of other, stronger scaffold branches. Prune to keep the main radiating branches evenly spaced vertically and balanced around the trunk.

If children will be climbing the tree, you may want to leave the lower branches on to make it accessible. If it's along a street or walkway, however, remove the lower branches so that people and traffic can move comfortably underneath. Pruning lower branches also lets more light reach the ground, making it possible to plant a pretty ring of shallow-rooted annuals or perennials around the base of the tree. You can create a lovely glade in a woodland garden by removing tree branches as high as 40 feet (depending on how tall

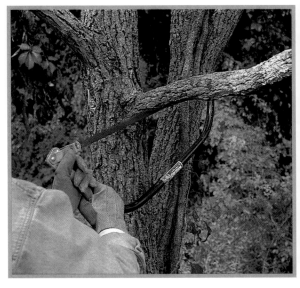

1 *To prevent the bark from tearing on large limbs, saw limbs off in three stages. Cut halfway through the limb from underneath, several inches away from the trunk.*

1 *Use long-handled loppers to remove small branches on the tree. Always cut close to the trunk with a clean, even cut of the loppers.*

2 Make your second cut from the top, slightly past the first undercut. The weight of the branch should cause it to fall without tearing the bark near the trunk.

3 Cut off the remaining stub close to the tree trunk. If the branch has grown from an enlarged collar, cut the stub flush with the collar to minimize the wound.

When to Hire a Professional

Many tree-pruning jobs can be done by the home gardener; however, it is wise to turn to a professional when the tree is very tall, the canopy is broad, or there are a lot of dangerous dead limbs. Professionals have special equipment for getting high into the tree safely, such as spiked shoes and safety belts. Professionals will also bring industrial equipment as needed, such as a cherry picker to prune the crown into a symmetrical, graceful form.

Find out what approach each professional takes, and choose someone who understands how to enhance the tree's natural form. The difference over the years to the tree's overall appearance is enormous.

2 Remove lower tree branches to let in the light, to make it easier to walk underneath, or to reveal the decorative bark of the trunk.

3 A grove of river birch (Betula nigra 'Heritage') is even more striking when the lower trunks are stripped to reveal the peeling bark.

Pruning CONTINUED

TROUBLESHOOTING TIP

In order to prevent temporary browning on the cut ends, shear narrow-leaved evergreens, such as balsam fir, yew, and hemlock, when they are wet. Choose a time after a rain or early in the morning, when the trees are still covered with dew.

the trees are) and planting shrubs underneath.

An important part of maintenance pruning is removing dead or diseased limbs. Dead branches are a hazard because they can drop, possibly hitting someone. They can also attract carpenter ants, which could then find their way to your house. Remove and destroy diseased branches or limbs as soon as you notice them. Often you can stop the progress of a disease if you get rid of infected areas. Sterilize your pruning equipment, including gloves, with rubbing alcohol or full-strength chlorine bleach after each cut so that you don't spread the bacteria. Pruning is especially effective for controlling canker, galls, and fire blight (see the photographs of pruning fire blight on page 59).

Older trees that have been neglected for many years generally require attention. If the crown has grown too heavy, it should be thinned. On the other hand, if the tree has grown too large for its space, the crown needs to be cut back.

Crown thinning, the process of removing inside lateral branches, lets light and air into the inside of the tree and allows wind to pass through the branches more easily. This increased light benefits not only the tree itself, but also any plants growing underneath it. If the tree is near a window, you'll be delighted with how much lighter the room is once the tree is thinned. Before you thin, study the tree and decide which branches most enhance its shape and structure, and which ones may be removed. Begin at the inside bottom, and work your way up and out.

This once-shaggy yew takes on a clean, formal look as it is sheared to emphasize its conical form.

Heading back, or cutting back, employs the same principle as pinching. When you cut back a growing stem, it activates latent buds farther down, which begin to grow shoots. You can cut back a tree canopy to make it smaller or bushier, or to stimulate flower or fruit production on the new growth. It is a good idea to combine some thinning with heading; simply heading produces a dense, unruly mass of foliage and lots of weak twiggy stems that exclude light and air.

Heading back is a technique that is often abused. The easiest way to cut back is to lop off major branches to the desired length. The tree responds by sending out a myriad of vigorous upright shoots that are weakly attached to the stem. Called "butchering" or "dehorning" by arborists, this approach is very damaging to the health and ultimate form of the tree, and it can take many years of careful pruning to undo the damage.

Pruning, especially heavy pruning, may stimulate water sprouts, quick-growing weak shoots that appear along a branch or trunk. Unless you need them to fill a gap in the tree, remove the sprouts, because they drain energy from the main branches.

1 *To train a new evergreen leader, select a flexible shoot located near the old leader. Bend it to an upright position, and stake securely until it holds the new position.*

▼ Pruning Instructions

Every time you prune back to a bud, you awaken it from dormancy and encourage new growth, but the direction of the growth depends on the location of the bud. As a general rule, make your cuts at an angle, ¼ inch above an outward-facing bud. The new shoot will grow away from the tree, thus promoting a graceful, open form that lets in more light and air. Branches cut at an inside bud will produce inward-growing shoots. Avoid cutting the entire tree that way, or the inside will eventually become a criss-crossed tangle. If you need to remove a limb com-pletely, make a clean cut, angled slightly away from the tree trunk, just outside the collar, the bulge where the branch joins the tree.

The correct time to prune depends on the type of tree and the results you want. Trees that flower in spring should be pruned while they are in bloom (take the flowers indoors to enjoy them) or immediately after the bloom has finished. Because spring-flowering trees form next year's buds during the summer months, any pruning done in midsummer will remove the following spring's display. Nonflowering trees can be pruned at any time, except during below-zero weather. If you want to increase vigor, prune in the winter. If you hope to slow the tree down, cut it back in the summer.

Pruning CONTINUED

▼ **Needle Evergreens**

The rules for pruning most types of conifers differ from those for deciduous trees because the trees' physiology is different. Deciduous trees will generate new growth at any latent bud along a branch, but the conifers whose branches radiate out from the trunk like spokes from an axis (pine, juniper, fir, and spruce, for example) will not. If you cut these trees back beyond the area of living foliage, the remaining section of branch will die. Therefore, it's important to begin shaping and sizing these conifers when they are young, and never remove more than one-third of the greenery per year. These conifers can be pruned at any time of year, but if you want to maintain a desired size, it is best to prune immediately after the new flush of growth in late spring or early summer.

In contrast, the random-branching conifers such as arborvitae, sequoia, hemlock, and yew can tolerate fairly drastic cutbacks. These plants all make admirable hedges, as they can be maintained far below the trees' natural height. They can also be grown as specimens, requiring little pruning other than to remove dead or diseased branches.

You can maintain compact growth on pine trees by cutting off part or all of the new growth "candles." (A look at a plant in active growth will show you why the new shoots are called candles.) This procedure has the same effect as pinching off leaf tips on broad-leaved plants.

1 *Shear conifers to encourage a tight, shapely form. Keep the top sheared to a point to make a natural-looking tree and to protect from any potential snow and ice damage.*

2 *Remove dead branches from evergreens. Hand clippers work well for small branches. Use loppers or a saw for the larger limbs.*

1 Shear broad-leaved evergreens, such as this holly, to encourage bushier growth and create an attractive form.

2 Use hand clippers to remove dead branches, cutting them back to living wood or to the main trunk.

3 With experience you will be able to clip a symmetrical shape freehand, although for complicated forms many professionals use special "jigs" as guides.

4 Clean up the debris left from pruning. If the clippings are not diseased or too woody, they are excellent material for the compost heap.

Pruning CONTINUED

1 *This mock orange (Philadelphus coronarius) blooms on the wood grown the previous season. For best flowering, don't allow the shrub to grow this dense.*

2 *To rejuvenate the overgrown shrub, remove the oldest canes after the plant flowers in the spring. Here the branches are being thinned first for better access.*

3 *Remove about one-third of the canes. Here the oldest, inner canes have been removed, allowing air to circulate and more light to reach the plant.*

4 *New wood will grow up from this thinned shrub, creating potential for bloom in future years. Plant shallow-rooted annuals around the newly exposed base.*

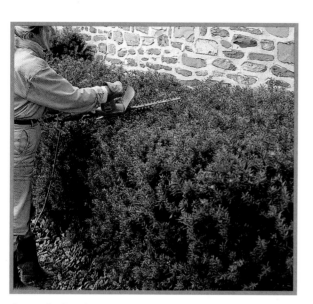

1 *Use hedge shears or electric-powered clippers to trim a hedge. If you aren't sure you can cut a straight, level line, run a horizontal string from two sticks as a guide.*

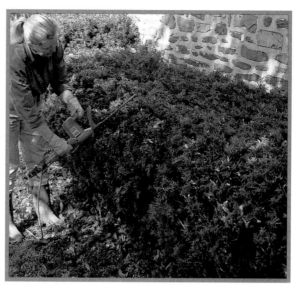

2 *Shear the sides of a hedge so that it flares out slightly at the bottom. Otherwise the light-starved foliage at the bottom will die back.*

TROUBLESHOOTING TIP

To ensure a straight cut along the length of a hedge, put a stake in the ground at each end, and run a length of line between the two at the desired height (make sure the line is level). Use the line as a cutting guide.

There is some controversy about whether it is possible to train a new central branch on a conifer if the original one is damaged. Success depends on how much of the leader is lost, the maturity of the tree, and the type of tree you're pruning. It is easiest to train a new leader on a young tree that hasn't suffered much loss. Simply choose a suitable side branch, then tie and stake it upward (see the photograph on page 71). The same procedure also works with older, badly damaged trees, but the result will look more spliced.

Most broad-leaved evergreens require very little pruning, other than to fine-tune their size and shape and to remove dead branches. If you want to encourage a dense, bushy form, pinch back the tips of the branches. If you prefer a more open, airy form, thin out unwanted branches, using the same principles you would for deciduous trees.

▼ Flowering Shrubs

By properly pruning flowering shrubs you can increase blossom production. However, if you prune at the wrong time of year, you can remove all the flower buds, costing yourself a season of beauty.

Azaleas and rhododendrons, for example, bloom in spring from buds developed the previous summer. If you trim them in early spring, you will remove that spring's flower buds. Instead, wait until the plants bloom and use the trimmings for cut flowers indoors. Or do not prune the plants until they finish blooming. Among the spring-blooming shrubs that should be pruned right after flowering are butterfly bush *(Buddleia alternifolia)*, daphne, deutzia, forsythia, honeysuckle *(Lonicera* spp.*)*, lilac *(Syringa* spp.*)*, mock orange *(Philadelphus* spp.*)*, pieris, and weigela. In contrast, summer-flowering shrubs such as glossy

Pruning CONTINUED

abelia, broom *(Cytisus* spp.*)*, butterfly bush (except *Buddleia alternifolia*), hibiscus *(Hibiscus syriacus)*, hydrangea *(Hydrangea paniculata)*, and potentilla blossom on new growth. You can stimulate more new growth—and more flowers—by pruning in late winter or early spring.

Knowing where the buds are formed helps you know the best place to cut. Azaleas form buds along their stems, so you can cut anywhere. In fact, shearing azaleas produces a bushier, more floriferous plant. Rhododendrons form their buds above the rosette of leaves. Always prune just above a leaf whorl or where a scar on the stem indicates a former whorl.

Another technique for pruning flowering shrubs is to cut selected older branches down to the ground. This method is recommended for rejuvenating old ole-ander, forsythia (which, by the way, should never be sheared since that spoils its arching, fountainlike form), mahonia, and nandina, to name a few.

Once a flowering shrub has finished blooming, it will channel all its energy into producing seeds. You can save that energy for future flower production by deadheading (removing all the spent blossoms). Although deadheading is impractical for plants that are covered with a multitude of tiny flowers, shrubs with large clusters of flowers, such as lilacs and hydrangeas, are relatively easy to deadhead. Cut them back to the next set of leaves. For azaleas, a light shearing will do the job. For rhododendrons, each dead flower needs to be snapped off where the brittle flower stem attaches to the main stem. They come off easily, but be careful not to damage the new buds.

▼ Hedges

Regular pruning is essential to maintain a dense but tidy hedge. How often the job needs to be done depends on the growth rate of your plants and the size you want your hedge to be. It is possible to keep a tall-growing evergreen, such as a white spruce that typically grows to 50 feet at maturity, as small as 3 feet tall with regular shearing. In these extreme cases, the shearing must be frequent (as often as every four months) and severe. In contrast, dwarf boxwood, popular for parterres because of its slow growth, needs clipping only once a year.

Small-leaved shrubs that have buds running close together along the entire length of the stem, such as boxwood, privet, and yew, should be sheared. Large-leaved hedges, such as English laurel *(Prunus lauro-cerasus)*, should be pruned with hand clippers branch by branch to avoid unsightly half-cut leaves.

All hedges should be tapered to be slightly wider at the base than the top so that sunlight can reach the entire surface of the plant. Otherwise, the lower, light-starved branches will begin to thin and die. You don't need to cut a dramatic pyramid; just slope the sides a little.

Espalier and Decorative Training

Espalier Tips

To save time when creating an espalier, choose a tree that already has branches in a way that fits your espalier design. If the ideal tree isn't available, begin with a year-old unbranched "whip." Use young, supple branches that can take the severe bending without damage. Tie them firmly, but not so tightly that the branch is constricted. Check periodically to make sure the branch has not outgrown its tie.

Once the final size and form are achieved, continue to prune espaliered trees several times in summer to keep the tight shape and encourage good fruit production.

Espalier, the art of training a tree or shrub to grow flat against a support such as a wall or trellis, is ideal for people who don't have enough room to grow trees and shrubs. If your garden is tiny, but you have a blank wall or a fence, you have enough space to grow a full-sized tree. Espalier is also a marvelous way to add beauty and interest to a stark, blank wall. In northern climates, the radiated warmth from the wall even helps the plant grow. Fruiting trees are popular for espalier because they are so attractive, but with a few exceptions, almost any tree or shrub can be trained to grow against a flat plane. It takes some effort and learning at the start to create an espalier, but once the shape is established, maintenance is easy.

There are many time-honored patterns used for espaliering plants. The least fussy is the cordon espalier, where the side branches are trained to grow in parallel horizontal rows, which can be either single or multiple. Another design is the palmette, where the parallel rows of branches are trained at a gentle upward angle so that the shape resembles a fan-leaved palm. You can also work with candelabra, diamond, V- or U-shaped, or triangular patterns.

Begin with a young plant that has soft, pliable wood—either a year-old whip (a young, unbranched tree) or one that's a few years old, but has branches approximately where you want them. With fruit trees, choose a dwarf variety since the very nature of espalier is to restrict growth. Full-sized trees must grow to a minimum size before they start producing fruit, and that may never happen if they are trained as espaliers.

To create a horizontal cordon style, begin in early summer by tying two side branches onto the support wire or trellis so that they are 45 degrees from the trunk. Many people tie them to dowels or stakes to

Espalier, where trees or shrubs are grown flat against a wall, fence, or trellis, can be a symmetrical or free-form pattern, such as this flowering quince (Chaenomeles speciosa).

hold them in place. Leave the central leader, but cut it off just below the second parallel wire, which should be about a foot above the first. That will activate another set of buds, which will produce branches for the next level. Allow three branches to grow: two for horizontal training and one for the leader. In late fall, lower the side branches that have been at 45 degrees to a horizontal 90 degrees. Continue the training each year until you have created as many rows as you want. At that point, keep the leader, or primary shoot, cut. Remove all extra growth from the trunk, and keep the lateral branches on your horizontal side limbs short. If you are espaliering fruit trees, you will need to prune in summer as well as spring to limit the growth of leaves that will take away from fruiting.

Branches that are in training need to be tied firmly, but not so tight as to restrict growth. Keep an eye on them, and loosen any ties that are constricting.

Espalier and Decorative Training CONTINUED

1 Begin a cordon with a young tree that has opposite lateral branches, or cut off the central leader of a young whip just below where you want the laterals.

2 In summer, tie the two cordon branches to support wires. All season, prune sublateral shoots, but don't remove spurs that will bear fruit.

3 In the case of an older tree that already has branches where you want them, cut away the unwanted side branches until you reach the next level for your cordon.

4 The branches on this apple tree aren't exactly symmetrical, but the result is still an attractive landscape feature that also provides fruit and takes up little space.

This trellis espalier, called a Belgian fence, is achieved by planting apple trees in a row and training two lateral branches on each to grow up at 45-degree angles. The tree at each end keeps its central leader along with just one lateral branch.

The palmette style of espalier resembles the leaf of the palmetto palm. To space the side branches correctly, cut the central leader to just below the spot where new branches should grow.

It is important to cut back the sublaterals (the little branches that grow from the main branches) to about 2 inches, so that energy goes into growing the lateral branches. This will ensure compact clusters of flowers as well as fruit in season.

Pyracantha is particularly effective as a multitiered cordon covering a fence or wall, providing striking year-round interest with dense clusters of flowers along each arm in spring, pretty green leaves all summer and winter, and berries in autumn that last well into winter.

Topiaries

Frequent hand clipping is essential in maintaining the precise shapes of topiary. If you have the time, patience, and skill, you can create standards, cones, spirals, or fanciful topiaries in the shape of animals, flying saucers, or abstract forms.

*T*he ancient art of topiary—pruning to create geometric shapes or recognizable forms—dates back at least to the first century B.C. The Roman writer Pliny the Elder (A.D. 23–79) described cypress trees trimmed to portray hunting scenes and fleets of ships. Topiary was revived in medieval times and flourished during the Italian Renaissance in response to the interest in ancient Rome. The English and Dutch reveled in creating fanciful forms from whimsical birds and mythological beasts to top hats, while the French preferred symmetrically clipped cones, globes, obelisks, and spirals.

There are many delightful ways to fit topiary into a modern garden, even a garden that isn't stylized or formal. Consider placing a matched set of junipers pruned into spirals (or any geometric shape you prefer) on each side of your front door. They can be placed in large ornamental pots or planted directly in the ground. A garden with a Japanese feel can be enhanced by pruning shrubs so that the branches are stripped of foliage except at the tips, which are trimmed to resemble layered, floating clouds. Hollies take well to being pruned into tidy cones, or you can

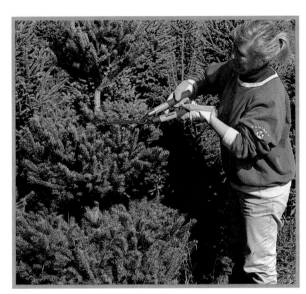

1 For a three-tiered "wedding-cake" topiary, cut away branches from the trunk to create the gaps between layers. Then shear the three sections to get the shape you want.

2 After the first shearing, allow the plant to grow for several months, and then shear it again to refine the layered wedding cake shape.

introduce some humor by shaping a large shrub to look like a bowling pin. Scallop the top of a hedge to echo the shape of a nearby fence, or create "posts" topped with finials.

Any shrub that takes shearing can be shaped into a topiary. Shapes such as cones, obelisks, and globes can be achieved almost immediately, simply by trimming the bush to that form. Fanciful animal shapes, layered wedding cakes, and other more intricate designs take more time. For the quickest results, work with the tree's natural shape. To create the wedding-cake form shown in the photos, prune so that each layer is slightly smaller in diameter than the one below it. The sides can be vertical or slightly rounded, but make each section slightly wider at the base than the top to allow light to reach the entire surface.

To grow an animal, for example, people generally purchase or make a wire frame in the desired shape and place it over a young plant. Yew and box, although slow growing, are particularly effective for topiaries that involve an intricate shape with a lot of detail. Once the plant starts to grow through the wire frame, trim it using the frame as a guide. Expect it to take from three to five years for a traditional topiary to achieve the desired finished look.

Once your topiary is established, the frequency of pruning will depend on the growth rate of the plant you chose. Plants such as holly or yew, which grow about 6 inches a year, need to be pruned only once or twice a year. Faster-growing shrubs, such as euonymus and box honeysuckle (*Lonicera nitida*) may require pruning as often as four times a year.

CHAPTER 4

Propagating Trees and Shrubs

*a*s you wait impatiently for a seed to sprout or a cutting to root, you may find it hard to believe that nature has a great urge to reproduce itself. But plants have many ways of proliferating. In addition to growing from seeds, a tree or shrub may produce roots from a dormant bare branch stuck in the ground. If a low branch is buried, it may sprout roots along its length, and each rooted section may become a new plant. • Many shrubs produce new plants from suckers that sprout from the roots or underground stems. By taking these natural propagation methods and improving on them, you can get faster results and higher success rates. • Through propagation, you can produce more specimens of a superior shrub or a difficult-to-find tree, or you can reproduce plants with valuable qualities such as unusual hardiness or disease resistance. It is wonderful to nurture a tiny sprout and watch it grow to a mature specimen. This chapter explains the basic techniques for making that happen.

Starting Seeds

Pretreatment for Seeds

Many seeds require special conditions to nudge them out of dormancy and induce germination.

One technique, called scarification, is simply breaking or softening the hard outer coating of the seed so that it will germinate more quickly. Large seeds can be nicked with a sharp knife or file, or rubbed with sandpaper. Shake small seeds in a sandpaper-lined jar.

Another technique, stratification, is used for plants from cold climates. Put the seeds between layers of moistened vermiculite or sand and peat either in a sealed jar or plastic bag. Store in the refrigerator. The time required to sprout varies with the tree. Conifers need about three weeks; some deciduous varieties take up to eight weeks. If you are uncertain, plant the seeds at intervals to ensure at least some germination.

Small seeds of trees and shrubs can be sown in flats, with the same techniques you would use for annuals or perennials. Always use a sterilized seed-starting mix. Large seeds, and those of trees with long taproots, need more space than smaller seeds. Plant them in single pots at least 4 inches deep.

Because seeds of trees and shrubs should be started outdoors or in cool greenhouses, you can also plant them in carefully prepared outside beds. The soil should be a well-tilled rich loam. Evergreen seeds are particularly susceptible to the fungus condition called damping-off. If damping-off is a frequent problem in your garden, treat the bed with a commercial product intended to destroy the fungi that cause damping-off before you plant evergreen seeds.

You can also germinate tree and shrub seeds in moist paper towels enclosed in polyethylene bags and placed in an unheated shed or garage over winter.

Space the seeds to allow enough room to grow, cover them with soil, and water well. Never let the soil dry out before the seeds have germinated—a process that can take a while. Some lilacs, for example, need as much as a year. Other seeds will sprout in a few weeks. If you are growing the seeds in containers or cold frames, keep the seeds covered with clear plastic to maintain the soil moisture.

If you have crowded many seeds into a small space, separate them once they have sprouted. Take each seedling out carefully, using a pencil, screwdriver, or other pointed tool to gently lift out the plant without

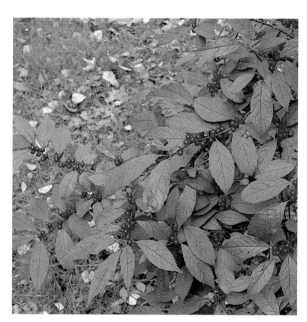

Some hollies grow easily from seed; others take a year or even longer to germinate. Although only female plants produce berries, you must have a male plant in the area for pollination.

You can grow viburnum cultivars from seed, planted immediately after harvest. The seed will germinate the following spring. However, take softwood cuttings to guarantee a plant that's true to its parent.

Propagate spirea from seed or by taking softwood cuttings in early summer.

In its natural, woodland environment, mountain laurel (Kalmia) will self-sow readily.

St.-John's-wort (Hypericum calycinum) roots easily from softwood cuttings taken in early summer; it can also be started from seed.

breaking the stem off the root. Make a hole for the plant in its new location, and press down the soil around the roots firmly but gently. Once the seedling has produced its first set of "true" leaves, begin fertilizing regularly with a weak dilution of fertilizer until mid-July. (True leaves have the same shape and characteristics of the plant's mature leaves, and are usually the second set of leaves to appear on the seedlings.) Then stop fertilizing, or new growth will still be tender when the winter cold comes.

When the seedling has a well-developed root system and top, it can be transplanted. Trees with long taproots should be transplanted before the root begins to grow too long, since cutting or even bending the taproot can inhibit the tree's growth or even kill it. If the young plants have been in a protected spot, such as a cold frame or cold greenhouse, harden them off before planting outdoors. Leave the top of the cold frame off for an increasing number of hours a day

and eventually overnight. Then transplant the seedlings. If the seedlings are in containers in a greenhouse, bring them outside, beginning in a sheltered, shady spot for an hour, gradually increasing the time and exposure to sun and other elements over a week or two.

Buy seeds from a company based in your region. Even if a tree is rated hardy to a much colder zone, it will be less cold hardy if the seed comes from a tree that is grown in a southern location rather than a northern-grown specimen of the same species. By the same token, seeds from northern-grown trees and shrubs may be less tolerant of heat and humidity than those produced by trees growing farther south.

Softwood Cuttings

Warm soil will accelerate the rooting process of softwood cuttings. Some people invest in soil-heating cables or horticultural heat mats for rooting cuttings and germinating seeds. If you don't want to buy one more gadget, look for ready-made warm spots in the house, such as the top of the refrigerator, dryer, or hot-water heater.

Softwood is the new growth produced on trees and shrubs in spring. As this new growth matures through the summer, it becomes harder and is known as semiripe or semihard wood.

Trees and shrubs to propagate from softwood cuttings in late spring include barberry, butterfly bush, flowering quince, deutzia, forsythia, bush honeysuckle, mock orange, Japanese pieris, shrubby cinquefoil, and viburnum. Some plants to propagate from semiripe cuttings taken in summer are glossy abelia, camellia, cotoneaster, daphne, hydrangea, mahonia, privet, pyracantha, spirea, and weigela.

Ideally, take softwood cuttings early in the morning after a rain or a thorough watering. Make each cutting 3 or 4 inches long. Although stems as long as 2 feet will root and produce a larger plant much sooner, you can't take as many from each parent bush. You can cut the stem about ¼ inch above or below a leaf joint—as long as you keep the cutting moist, it should

root either way. Cut at an angle to provide more surface for roots to develop.

If you can't pot up the cuttings immediately, keep them in water. Just before planting, strip off the lower foliage, leaving a few at the top (leave more for long cuttings). Also remove any flower buds. Dip the cut end in a rooting hormone powder, and plant it 1½ to 2 inches deep in a sterile, lightweight potting mixture such as a combination of vermiculite and perlite.

Keep the soil moist and warm. To maintain moisture, cover each pot or flat with plastic. The cuttings have rooted when you see signs of top growth, or when the stem resists a gentle tug. To acclimate cuttings grown indoors to the harsher outdoors, set them outside for half an hour the first day, gradually increasing the time over a week or so.

Follow the same procedure for semiripe cuttings. Since you are beginning later in the season, you may have to overwinter the cuttings indoors.

Barberry shrubs can be started from softwood cuttings in late spring or early summer.

The hard-to-find flowering chaste tree (Vitex agnus-castus) can be propagated by semiripe cuttings in summer or by seed in spring or fall.

The most reliable method for propagating broom is to take softwood cuttings in spring and treat it with a rooting hormone powder.

Camellias root easily from cuttings taken in midsummer and treated with rooting chemicals.

Crape myrtle will root from softwood cuttings, although the preferred propagation method is leaf cuttings kept misted.

1 Take softwood cuttings in late spring. If taken too early, the cuttings will be too soft, but if you wait until summer, the growth will begin to harden.

2 The softwood cuttings should be 3 to 4 inches long. Remove the lower leaves from each cutting to expose a length of bare stem.

3 For better rooting, dip the bottom of each cutting in rooting hormone powder. Pour out a small amount of the powder, and later dispose of the unused portion.

4 Plant the cuttings 1½ to 2 inches deep in a container of sterile rooting medium, and keep the soil evenly moist until rooting occurs.

Hardwood Cuttings

*H*ardwood cuttings are taken from dormant branches that have already had a full season of growth. In warm climates, you can begin to root these cuttings in fall. In regions where the ground freezes, take the cuttings during early winter and store until the ground is ready to work in spring.

Choose healthy, pencil-thick sections of branch, each 5 to 8 inches long and with three leaf buds. Remove all the leaves. Cut at an angle just below the lowest leaf bud to provide more surface area for rooting. Then cut straight across just above the top leaf bud, so that you can distinguish the two ends.

To overwinter the cuttings, tie like plants in labeled bundles and bury them in slightly damp sand, wood shavings, or vermiculite. Cover them to keep the storage medium moist, and keep them just above freezing, between 32° and 40°F.

As the temperature warms, each cutting will develop a callus on its cut end, which will help in producing roots. Wait until this callus has formed before planting. Cuttings can be planted directly into the ground, but it is best to put them first in pots or beds with prepared soil. Dip the bottom ends into rooting hormone powder, then plant each bare stick so that just the top bud pokes out of the ground. Tamp the soil down well around the cuttings; then water and cover with plastic sheeting to maintain an even moisture level.

You will know that roots have developed when you see signs of top growth. At that point apply a mild liquid fertilizer. Once the new plants are well established, you can transplant them to their permanent location.

Trees and shrubs to propagate from hardwood cuttings taken in fall include boxwood, false cypress, junipers, and yews. Take hardwood cuttings in winter for forsythia, gardenia, honey locust, aspen, cottonwood, spruce, and arborvitae.

Weigela (W. florida) is easily propagated from hard- or softwood cuttings.

Hardwood deutzia cuttings taken in the fall or winter can be planted directly in the ground in spring.

This summer-blooming hydrangea (H. Sargentiana) is propagated from hardwood cuttings.

Sweet mock orange (Philadelphus) is an easy plant to root from either hard- or softwood cuttings.

Rose-of-Sharon (Hibiscus syriacus) will root from either softwood or hardwood cuttings, although rooting chemicals are helpful.

1 Cuttings of broad-leaved evergreens are not exactly hardwood or softwood. Rhododendrons require special care. Take your cuttings in fall.

2 Dip the cut end of the stem in a rooting hormone powder. This is especially helpful for rhododendrons, which are difficult to root.

3 Plant the cutting in an acidic growing medium. In a nursery flat, such as the one shown here, you can root many plants in one place.

4 Trim off the tips of the leaves so that the cutting's energy can go into forming roots, rather than supporting the leaves.

5 Overwinter the cuttings indoors or in a warm greenhouse. If you see signs of disease, spray with a fungicide.

6 Once the roots have developed, transplant each cutting into an individual pot until it is large enough to plant outside.

Layering

TROUBLESHOOTING TIP

Some common household items can come in handy when propagating trees and shrubs. For example, cut a coat hanger into short lengths, bending them into U shapes like large hairpins. Use two, one at each side of the cut, to clamp the branch you want to layer to the ground.

*T*he easiest way to propagate new shrubs is by layering, a process that occurs when a stem or branch lies undisturbed on moist soil, eventually produces roots, and is then separated from the parent plant.

To propagate by layering, choose a flexible branch that will reach to the ground, and remove any foliage from the section you plan to root. Cut a slit halfway through the underside of the branch, and wedge it open with a small pebble or sliver of wood. (Or simply cut or scrape away a section of bark on the underside of the branch where it will touch the soil.) Dust the wound with a rooting hormone powder, and bury the treated section of branch, leaving about 6 inches of the tip end unburied. You may want to stake the end for it to grow upright, rather than at an angle. To make sure the buried portion of the stem remains buried, fasten it in place with U-shaped wire pins or wooden pegs, or weight it down with a stone.

If you want many new plants from the parent, you can mass-produce them by burying several sections of one long stem. This is called serpentine or compound layering. If the plant you want to layer doesn't have stems that can easily touch the ground, place a pot filled with damp soil underneath a suitable branch. Be sure you keep the potted soil moist.

It will take about a year for the branch to set roots and begin to grow. Watch for signs of new growth on the tip. When they appear, sever the new plant from the parent and replant it where you want it.

Some good shrubs to propagate by layering include forsythia, fothergilla, mountain laurels, shrubby cinquefoil *(Potentilla fruticosa)*, some rhododendrons, and spirea.

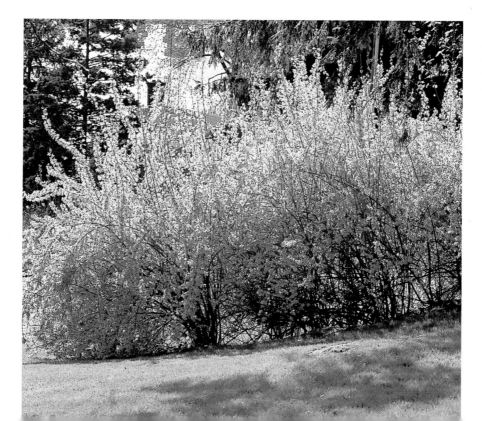

Forsythia is an easy plant to propagate. This can be done either by hardwood or softwood cuttings, dividing large shrubs, or layering.

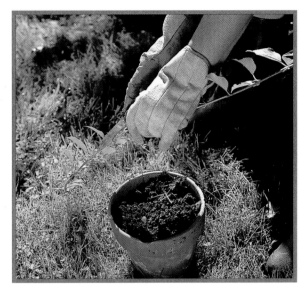

1 *To grow roots by layering, select a low-growing branch that can easily bend and lie on the ground or on the soil of a flower pot.*

2 *Speed up new root growth by wounding the stem. Gently scrape away the outside layer of bark on the side of the stem that will touch the ground.*

3 *Anchor the branch you want to root to the soil, making sure the scraped side is in contact with the ground. Hairpins make especially good pegs.*

4 *Depending on the plant, it can take up to a year for sufficient roots to develop. Once roots have grown, cut the new specimen away from the parent and plant.*

Air Layering

*I*f a tree or shrub branch won't reach to the ground for layering, use air layering to bring the "ground" to it. The best time for air layering is early spring, just as the leaves begin to appear. Choose a vigorous branch from the thickness of a pencil to an inch in diameter. Scrape away the outer bark, 1 to 1½ feet from the end, creating a wound about ½ inch wide that circles the branch. Dust the wound with rooting hormone powder recommended for hardwood cuttings, then wrap it with damp sphagnum moss (about as wet as a wrung-out sponge) or a moist mixture of equal parts perlite and peat. Wrap this rooting medium in black polyethylene (which keeps out the light) or clear plastic covered with foil. Seal it with furnace duct tape or electrical tape, so that air cannot get in and dry the material. You can air-layer many branches on one plant without hurting it.

Some trees and shrubs root fairly quickly using this method; others take a year or more. If you air-layer a plant in spring, check for roots in late summer or early fall by gently squeezing the plastic. If you unwrap the plastic to check and roots aren't properly formed yet, be sure to remoisten the rooting mixture and reseal the packet.

Once the wound has grown a good set of roots, cut off the branch below the new roots, being careful to keep the moss or perlite mixture around the roots. Plant it in a container filled with a good all-purpose potting medium. Immediately after planting, cut back the foliage by half to allow the roots to grow. Keep the potting medium moist and keep the new plant protected until it is clearly established and strong.

Fruit trees, citruses, many shade trees, magnolias, French lilacs, witch hazels, mountain laurels, azaleas, many tropical plants, and some rhododendrons can be air-layered.

The popular flowering dogwood (Cornus florida *var.* rubra) *can be propagated by air layering as well as softwood cuttings.*

Usually propagated by seed, new winter hazel plants can also be developed by air layering.

Smoke tree (Cotinus coggygria) *is best propagated by softwood cuttings taken in late spring or early summer, but it can also be air-layered.*

Most commercially grown evergreen holly is started from cuttings, but home gardeners may find air layering easier.

Flowering crabapple can be rooted with a modified air-layering technique in which the branch is cut off once a callus forms on the moss-covered wound and then is rooted in soil like a cutting.

1 To air-layer a tree or shrub, make a ½-inch-long wound all the way around a branch by scraping off the outer bark.

2 Cover the wound with a rooting hormone powder specifically recommended for hardwood cuttings.

3 Wrap the wound with damp (not dripping wet) sphagnum moss or a moist mixture of equal parts perlite and peat moss.

4 To maintain the moisture, wrap the ball of moss with plastic and seal the ends with twist ties or tape.

5 Once the roots have formed, cut the branch off the parent plant below the root ball, being careful to keep the moss around the roots.

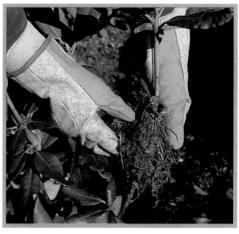

6 Plant the newly rooted shrub or tree where you want it in the garden. Cut back the foliage by half to allow the roots to grow.

Dividing Shrubs

*T*o multiply shrubs by division, simply take one plant and divide the upper portion and roots into two or more smaller plants. Be sure to get an adequate amount of root and a substantial branch with each piece of plant.

Among the shrubs that can be divided are deutzia, barberry, mock orange, potentilla, wild roses, service-berry, peony, and St.-John's-wort. Pick a healthy mid-sized plant, and cut away the outside edges where the shrub is less woody and there are more feeder roots. If you have a grafted shrub, such as French lilac or hawthorn, the divisions may not grow true to the original bush.

Early spring, when the plant is still dormant, is the best time to tackle division. You will need a sharp spade, clippers to separate smaller pieces, and a pruning saw or hatchet for tough roots. If the shrub is small, dig it up to see where you would like to cut. If the plant is large and this is impractical, choose the section you want to separate and dig straight through the roots with the sharp spade.

Replant the division immediately, before the roots dry out. Place it about an inch deeper in the soil than before. Trim back the top by about a third, so that the greenery doesn't drain energy from the roots. Keep the plant moist for the first few weeks.

Other shrubs—including box, heath, euonymus, kerria, some sumacs, and some Japanese spirea cultivars—produce suckers, which are shoots that grow from below the ground from the plant's roots or an underground stem. These new plants can be easily separated from the mother plant. Simply dig up the sucker, cut the main root that attaches to the parent plant, and replant it. If there is a lot of top foliage, cut it back by about a third.

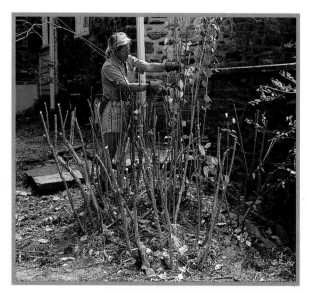

1 *It is best to divide shrubs in early spring, when they are still dormant. Using clippers, cut back the foliage by about a third.*

4 *For success in this method, each division should have at least one healthy branch and enough roots to sustain the new plant.*

2 *Examine the plant to make sure there will be sufficient roots to support each division. Mark where you plan to divide with string.*

3 *Work with a sharp spade to dig forcefully through the roots to cut them apart. Use a saw or ax to cut through very thick clumps of roots.*

E A R T H • W I S E
T I P

You can encourage a shrub to produce suckers for dividing. Dig around the parent plant in summer or fall to cut the roots. In the process of regenerating themselves, the damaged roots will probably produce suckers, which you can take the following summer.

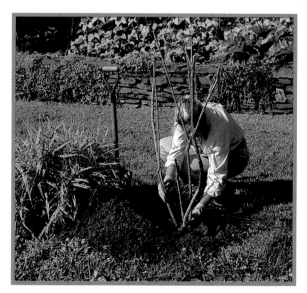

5 *Be prepared to replant the divisions immediately so that the roots don't become dry. Handle the root ball carefully to keep the soil in place.*

6 *Replant the divisions as you would any new plant. Use good-quality soil and make sure the planting hole is large enough to permit further growth.*

Trees and Shrubs for American Gardens

*T*his section provides concise information on more than 150 trees and shrubs recommended for American gardens. The plants have been selected on the basis of beauty, adaptability, and availability. If you're looking for plants for particular uses—of a certain height, for instance, or with flowers of a certain color—first check the Color Range, Height and Spread, and Ornamental Features columns. If you need plants for a shady spot, refer to the Growing Conditions column. Or you might prefer to look at the photos, read the descriptions, and then decide which trees and shrubs will grow well in your garden. Each photograph shows a species or variety described in the entry.

▼ About Plant Names

Plants appear in alphabetical order by the genus name, shown in bold type. On the next line is the most widely used common name. The third line contains the complete botanical name: genus, species, and where applicable, a variety or cultivar name.

Common names vary, but botanical names are the same everywhere. If you learn botanical names, you'll always get the plant you want from a mail-order nursery or local garden center. One gardener's sweet shrub may be another gardener's Carolina allspice, but both gardeners will recognize the plant if they know its scientific name: *Calycanthus floridus.*

When several species in a genus are similar in appearance and cultural needs, they are listed together in a single entry in the chart. In the case of a genus containing two or more vastly different species, each of the recommended species is given a separate entry in the chart. The second column of the chart provides a brief plant description. Look here to see if the plant is deciduous or evergreen, spreading or columnar. Check here also for flower, leaf, and bark descriptions.

▼ Color Range

The color dots following each description refer to the flower color of trees and shrubs noted for their bloom. Information on foliage color is included under Ornamental Features. Color dots indicate the color *family*; they are not a literal rendering of the flower color. A plant given a pink dot might be pale blush pink, clear pink, or bright rose pink.

▼ Height and Spread

This column indicates the eventual height of the mature tree or shrub, and the area over which it will spread. It is important when planting trees and shrubs to allow space for them to grow to their full size.

▼ Ornamental Features

In this column you will find the features that make the tree or shrub desirable for gardens. Check this column first if you are looking for a plant with fragrant flowers, colorful autumn foliage, or decorative bark; a conifer with a blue-green color; or a plant to use as a hedge, screen, or specimen.

▼ Hardiness Zones

Plant hardiness is generally an indication of the coldest temperatures a plant is likely to survive. But many plants also have limits to the amount of heat they can tolerate. In this chart hardiness is expressed as a range from the coolest to the warmest zones where the plant generally thrives. The zones are based on the newest version of the USDA Plant Hardiness Zone Map, shown on page 127.

▼ Growing Conditions

The last column of the chart summarizes the best growing conditions for the plant. Look here for information on the plant's light, moisture, and soil requirements.

			Flower Color	Height & Spread	Ornamental Features	Hardiness Zones	Growing Conditions
	ABELIA GLOSSY ABELIA *Abelia × grandiflora*	Semievergreen shrub used in shrub borders and in warmer zones as a hedge. Glossy leaves remain evergreen in warm climates but else-where turn deep bronze in autumn. Fragrant white or pink, trumpet-shaped flow-ers cluster at the branch tips.	○ ◐	Height: 3–6' Spread: 3–6'	Massing or hedge shrub. Fragrant white flowers in late spring to autumn. Glossy bronze leaves in autumn.	6 to 10	Full sun. Moist, well-drained soil that is rich in humus. Protect from winter winds in zone 7 and colder. Prune deadwood in late winter or early spring.
	ABELIO-PHYLLUM KOREAN ABELIALEAF, WHITE FORSYTHIA *Abeliophyllum distichum*	Deciduous shrub (not a true forsythia) that bears clusters of fragrant flowers early in spring before its leaves emerge. White, 4-petaled flowers are tinged with pink. White forsythia is best used in a shrub border or as a backdrop for spring bulbs.	○ ◐	Height: 3–5' Spread: 3–5'	Specimen or border shrub. Fragrant white flowers in early spring.	5 to 8	Full sun. Moist, well-drained soil that is rich in humus. This slow-growing shrub becomes bushier with age. Prune deadwood in late win-ter or early spring and again after flowering to encourage a more compact, bushy form.
	ABIES WHITE FIR ◄ *Abies concolor* NORDMANN FIR *A. nordmanniana*	Large, conical, evergreen trees with relatively soft, flat needles, grayish bark, and upright cones that shatter at maturity. A. concolor has 2-in. needles and is hardier than A. nordmanniana, whose notch-tipped needles are 1½-in. long.		A. conc. Height: 40–100' Spread: 15–25' A. nord. Height: 80–120' Spread: 15–25'	A. concolor has light blue-green needles. A. nordmanni-ana has dark green needles.	A. conc. 3 to 7 A. nord. 5 to 8	Full sun to very light shade. Evenly moist, well-drained, acid soil. Both species grow best in zones where sum-mers are cool.
	ACER AMUR MAPLE *Acer ginnala*	Large shrub or small tree that has purplish twigs, especially when young. Light yellow, fragrant flowers in spring produce reddish winged fruits in late sum-mer. Foliage turns reddish in autumn. Short cultivars make excellent hedges.	◐	Height: 3–15' Spread: 3–15'	Small speci-men tree or screen when planted in groups. Fra-grant yellow spring flowers. Red foliage in autumn.	3 to 8	Full sun to partial shade. Well-drained, humus-rich soil with ample moisture throughout the growing sea-son. Amur maple grows bet-ter in colder regions than in warm ones.
	ACER PAPERBARK MAPLE *Acer griseum*	Open-branching maple with unusual compound leaves of 3 small, glossy leaflets. Some cultivars turn brilliant colors in the autumn. Cinnamon brown bark peels freely with age. Trees are sometimes shrubby, growing as wide as tall.	◐	Height: 12–30' Spread: 15–30'	Colorful autumn foliage. All-season dis-play of peeling reddish brown bark.	5 to 8	Full sun to partial shade. Well-drained, humus-rich soil with ample moisture throughout the year.

◄ *Indicates species shown*

Trees and Shrubs for American Gardens

	Flower Color	Height & Spread	Ornamental Features	Hardiness Zones	Growing Conditions
ACER JAPANESE MAPLE *Acer palmatum* Small deciduous tree with a rounded crown that makes an ideal specimen tree where space is limited. Many cultivars of this species have red leaves with 5–11 deeply dissected lobes.	● ●	Height: 10–25' Spread: 10–28'	Specimen tree or screen when planted in groups. Purple, red, or variegated leaves. Small purple flowers in spring.	5 to 9	Full sun to partial shade. Well-drained, humus-rich soil with ample moisture throughout the year.
ACER RED MAPLE *Acer rubrum* Deciduous tree found from Canada to Florida but underutilized as an ornamental. Early spring's red flowers are followed by 3-in., light green leaves and red, 2-winged fruits. Trees usually bear brilliant scarlet autumn foliage.	●	Height: 50–100' Spread: 20–40'	Excellent shade tree. Bright red flowers and attractive red fruits in spring. Brilliant autumn foliage.	3 to 9	Full sun to light shade. Adaptable to a variety of soil conditions from well-drained, evenly moist to waterlogged situations. One of the most disease- and pest-resistant maples, this highly variable tree has many cultivars.
ACER HARD MAPLE, SUGAR MAPLE *Acer saccharum* A favorite northeastern native with a dense, oval crown that turns golden orange in autumn. Trees provide sweet sap in spring. The abundant 4- to 6-in., medium green leaves of this stately deciduous tree cast deep shade.	●	Height: 60–120' Spread: 40–60'	Excellent shade tree. Brilliant yellow-orange autumn foliage.	3 to 8	Full sun to shade. Well-drained, humus-rich soil with ample moisture throughout the year. Sugar maples grow better in colder regions than in warm ones.
AESCULUS RED HORSE CHESTNUT *A. × carnea* COMMON HORSE CHESTNUT *Aesculus hippocastanum* Deciduous trees with rounded crowns, large, palmate leaves, upright clusters of showy flowers, and spiny-husked fruits. Common horse chestnut has creamy white flowers flecked with pink; red hybrid has deep coral-pink flowers.	○ ●	A. × carn. Height: 30–45' Spread: 20–30' A. hippoc. Height: 50–75' Spread: 40–70'	Large specimen trees. Showy flower clusters in spring. Interesting fruits in autumn.	A. × carn. 5 to 8 A. hippoc. 4 to 7	Full sun to light shade. Moist, well-drained soil. To avoid leaf scorch and mildew problems, plant where trees will get good ventilation as they grow. Prune deadwood in early spring.
ALBIZIA MIMOSA, SILK TREE *Albizia julibrissin* Deciduous tree with much-branched, spreading crown. Clusters of striking pink pom-pom flowers festoon branches. Like other members of the pea family it has pod fruits. Doubly compound leaves have up to 60 leaflets.	●	Height: 20–35' Spread: 20–40'	Specimen or parkway tree. Silky, bright pink flowers in mid-spring to late summer. Flat fruit pods.	6 to 10	Full sun. Well-drained soil. Mimosas grow best in warm climates. They tolerate drought and wind but are susceptible to wilt disease, which has damaged many trees in the Southeast. Select resistant cultivars.

			Flower Color	Height & Spread	Ornamental Features	Hardiness Zones	Growing Conditions
	AMELANCHIER SERVICEBERRY SHADBUSH *Amelanchier canadensis*	Compact, small trees or large shrubs with smooth, gray-striped bark. White, 1-in., long-petaled flowers appear early in spring. Red-purple, 1/2-in., edible fruits mature in late spring. Foliage turns bronze to red in autumn.	○	Height: 10–25' Spread: 10–15'	Border shrub, specimen tree, or woodland edging. White spring flowers; purple summer fruits. Autumn foliage is bronze.	3 to 7	Full sun to partial shade. Moist soil rich in organic matter. Serviceberry is a bog plant that grows well in wet sandy soil.
	ARCTO-STAPHYLOS BEARBERRY, KINNIKINICK *Arctostaphylos uva-ursi*	Mat-forming, evergreen shrub that makes an ideal ground cover, especially for dry or sandy sites. Sprawling woody stems bear dense, 1/2- to 3/4-in., glossy leaves. Clusters of urn-shaped, pink-tinged white flowers produce bright 1/3-in. berries.	○ ◐	Height: 6–12" Spread: 10–50'	Dense, glossy evergreen ground cover. Small, attractive flowers in mid-spring. Red fruits summer to winter.	3 to 7	Full sun to light shade. Well-drained, sandy, slightly acid soil. Bearberry tolerates salt spray and winds. Set container-grown plants at 2-ft. intervals. Plants are sensitive to trampling.
	BERBERIS WINTERGREEN BARBERRY ◀ *Berberis julianae* KOREAN BARBERRY *B. koreana*	Popular spiny shrubs used for hedges. B. julianae has a mounded form and 2-in., spiny-toothed, evergreen leaves that are dark green above and light green below. Deciduous B. koreana has oval leaves that turn deep red in autumn.	◐	B. jul. Height: 6–8' Spread: 6–8' B. kor. Height: 4–6' Spread: 3–5'	B. julianae: yellow spring flowers, black fruits. B. koreana: yellow spring flowers, red autumn leaves, and red berries in winter.	B. jul. 6 to 9 B. kor. 3 to 8	Full sun. Moist, well-drained, slightly acidic soil. Prune in late winter to encourage dense growth form.
	BERBERIS JAPANESE BARBERRY *Berberis thunbergii*	Familiar deciduous hedge shrub whose prickles and dense leafy branches make an effective barrier. Plants bear attractive red berries in autumn. There are many cultivars, with leaf colors ranging from purple to yellow to variegated green.	◐	Height: 3–5' Spread: 2–4'	Barrier hedge. Red, orange, or purple foliage in autumn. Bright red berries into winter.	4 to 9	Full sun to partial shade. Ordinary garden soil. Plants tolerate dry, poor soil once established. Prune in late winter to encourage dense growth. Birds often spread the seeds far afield, causing it to be a pest in pastures.
	BETULA RIVER BIRCH *Betula nigra* 'Heritage'	Popular deciduous trees grown for their decorative bark. This cultivar has metallic red-brown bark when young; it peels with age to expose grayish or pinkish highlights. Toothed, 3-in., triangular leaves turn yellow in autumn.	◐	Height: 40–70' Spread: 30–60'	Specimen tree. Leathery, deep green leaves. All-season display of peeling gray to cinnamon brown bark.	4 to 9	Full sun to partial shade. Humus-rich, moist, acid soil. Do not plant in alkaline soil or top-dress with lime. Trees tolerate soggy or even dry soil once established. They grow better in warm regions and are less susceptible to borers than white birches.

◀ *Indicates species shown*

Trees and Shrubs for American Gardens

		Flower Color	Height & Spread	Ornamental Features	Hardiness Zones	Growing Conditions
BETULA CANOE BIRCH, PAPER BIRCH, WHITE BIRCH *Betula papyrifera*	Deciduous tree whose chalky white bark peels into paperlike strips with age. As a sapling it has brown bark. The rounded crown bears many toothed, oval leaves with sharply pointed tips. Leaves turn golden yellow in early autumn.	●	Height: 50–70' Spread: 25–35'	Specimen tree. Golden yellow autumn foliage. All-season display of peeling, chalky white bark.	2 to 7	Full sun. Moist, well-drained soil. Paper birch prefers cool climates. It grows rapidly but is not very long lived (60–90 years). Trees are susceptible to leaf miners and borers.
BETULA EUROPEAN WHITE BIRCH *Betula pendula*	A birch with a broadly conical crown. White bark develops black fissures and does not peel as much as on paper birch. Toothed, 2-in. leaves are generally triangular, but cultivars with deeply cut leaves are available. May be listed as B. alba.	●	Height: 40–50' Spread: 20–35'	Specimen tree. Silver-white bark. Graceful, pendulous branches.	3 to 8	Full sun. Moist, well-drained soil. European white birch grows best in cool climates. It grows rapidly but is not very long lived (60–90 years). Trees are susceptible to leaf miners and borers.
BUDDLEIA FOUNTAIN BUTTER- FLY BUSH *Buddleia alternifolia* BUTTERFLY BUSH, SUMMER LILAC ◀ *B. davidii*	Deciduous shrubs with spikes of fragrant flowers that attract butterflies. B. alternifolia has lavender flowers and narrow gray-green leaves. The more tender B. davidii has violet, lavender, pink, or white blooms. Good cut flowers.	○ ● ● ●	B. altern. Height: 8–12' Spread: 10–18' B. davidii Height: 5–10' Spread: 5–10'	Shrub or perennial border. Fragrant flowers in spring (B. alternifolia) or summer (B. davidii).	B. altern. 5 to 7 B. davidii 5 to 9	Full sun. Well-drained, evenly moist soil that is slightly acid. B. davidii dies back to the ground in zone 6 and colder; prune deadwood to ground level in spring. Prune B. alternifolia in early spring to remove old wood.
BUXUS LITTLELEAF BOX- WOOD *Buxus microphylla* COMMON BOXWOOD, ENGLISH BOXWOOD ◀ *B. sempervirens*	Shrubs with small, ever-green, aromatic leaves. Slender green branches can be pruned to form a dense hedge. B. microphylla has ½-in., medium green leaves, while B. sempervirens has ¾-in., deep green leaves.	●	B. micro. Height: 3–4' Spread: 3–4' B. semper. Height: 15–20' Spread: 15–20'	Excellent for formal hedges as a dark ever-green back-drop. Can be pruned into topiary.	B. micro. 5 to 8 B. semper. 5 to 8	Full sun to light shade. Moist, well-drained, slightly acid soil. Plant with protection from drying winds. Boxwood is shallow rooted; do not cultivate soil in immediate vicinity. Instead, mulch to suppress weeds and keep roots moist.
CALLISTEMON CRIMSON BOTTLE- BRUSH ◀ *Callistemon citrinus* LEMON BOTTLE- BRUSH *C. sieberi*	An Australian native shrub or tree with dense spikes of flowers clustered at the tips of twigs and lance-shaped, 3-in., evergreen leaves. Long, bright red stamens give flowers the appearance of bottlebrushes. The woody fruits look like beads.	●	Height: 6–20' Spread: 6–8'	Specimen tree or plant in groups as a screen. Bright red flowers in spring. Bead-like fruits good in dried arrangements.	9 to 10	Full sun. Well-drained, ordinary garden soil. Keep plants on the dry side to avoid root rot. Young plants need moisture to get established but are quite drought tolerant thereafter. To prevent rampant growth, keep soil fertility low.

			Flower Color	Height & Spread	Ornamental Features	Hardiness Zones	Growing Conditions
	CALLUNA HEATHER *Calluna vulgaris*	Small, evergreen shrub that covers hillsides in Scotland with soft lavender hues in late summer and early autumn. Heather is a superb ground cover or rock garden plant where winters and summers are not too severe. Flowers attract bees.	○ ◐ ◐ ●	Height: 6–24" Spread: 2–8'	Ground cover. Showy clusters of tiny rose, pink, or lavender urn-shaped flowers in late summer.	4 to 6	Full sun. Evenly moist, well-drained, humus-rich, acid (pH 6 or less) soil of low fertility. Do not fertilize or add lime. Prune in early spring. Japanese beetles can be a problem.
	CALYCANTHUS CAROLINA ALLSPICE, SWEET SHRUB *Calycanthus floridus*	Southeastern native deciduous shrub used as a specimen plant or in borders for its fragrant foliage and perfumed flowers. The 2- to 5-in., dark green leaves turn yellow in autumn. Dark, red-brown, 2-in. flowers are sweetly fragrant.	● ●	Height: 6–8' Spread: 5–8'	Specimen or border shrub. Clusters of fragrant, dark red flowers in late spring to early summer.	4 to 9	Full sun to light shade. Well-drained, moist soil that is rich in humus. This low-maintenance shrub may be pruned after flowering.
	CAMELLIA JAPANESE CAMELLIA ◄ *Camellia japonica* SASANQUA CAMELLIA *C. sasanqua*	Evergreen trees or shrubs with dark green leaves and showy white, pink, or red flowers that can be single or double. C. japonica is larger with bolder leaves and bigger (3- to 5-in.) flowers. C. sasanqua is denser and has 2- to 3-in. flowers.	○ ◐ ●	C. japon. Height: 10–15' Spread: 6–10' C. sasan. Height: 6–10' Spread: 5–8'	Specimen or borders. Lustrous foliage. Large flowers in winter (C. japonica) or autumn to winter (C. sasanqua).	7 to 10	Filtered sun to partial shade. Acid, humus-rich, moist, well-drained soil. These shallow-rooted shrubs benefit from mulching. Protect from drying winds during winter. Scale insects and mealybugs may be a problem.
	CARPINUS EUROPEAN HORNBEAM ◄ *Carpinus betulus* AMERICAN HORNBEAM, MUSCLEWOOD *C. caroliniana*	Small trees with smooth, sinuous, gray bark resembling flexed muscle, 3- to 5-in., toothed leaves, and drooping clusters of winged fruits. C. caroliniana, an eastern native, is smaller and has more autumn color than the European C. betulus.	◐	C. betul. Height: 40–60' Spread: 30–40' C. carol. Height: 20–30' Spread: 10–20'	Small specimen or screen hedge. Attractive smooth bark. Interesting fruit clusters.	C. betul. 4 to 7 C. carol. 2 to 9	Full sun to partial shade. Well-drained, fertile soil. C. caroliniana tolerates constantly moist conditions. C. betulus needs well-drained soil and grows best in full sun. Either can be pruned to form a hedge.
	CARYOPTERIS BLUEBEARD, BLUE MIST *Caryopteris × clandonensis*	Small, deciduous shrub grown as a specimen or border plant for its aromatic, gray-green leaves and fragrant flowers. Tubular, $1/4$- to $3/8$-in. violet-blue flowers are borne in dense, flat clusters.	● ●	Height: 2–4' Spread: 2–5'	Specimen, border plant, or informal hedge. Attractive blue flowers in summer.	7 to 9	Full sun in a sheltered location. Well-drained soil of low fertility. Caryopteris does not tolerate soggy conditions. Prune well after flowering to encourage vigorous growth during the next season. In zones 4 to 6, the top dies back in winter.

◄ *Indicates species shown*

101

Trees and Shrubs for American Gardens

			Flower Color	Height & Spread	Ornamental Features	Hardiness Zones	Growing Conditions
	CEDRUS BLUE ATLAS CEDAR *Cedrus atlantica* 'Glauca' DEODAR CEDAR *C. deodara*	Majestic conifers with dense clusters of evergreen needles covering their branches. They have pyramidal crowns when young but become increasingly broad with age. C. atlantica 'Glauca' has powder blue foliage.		C. atlan. Height: 60–90' Spread: 40–60' C. deo. Height: 70–100' Spread: 50–65'	Specimen trees. Gracefully drooping branches. C. atlantica 'Glauca' has light blue needles.	C. atlan. 6 to 9 C. deo. 7 to 9	Full sun. Well-drained, humus-rich, acid soil. Trees need deep, evenly moist soil but will not grow well in poorly drained soil. Protect from wind, especially as young saplings are becoming established.
	CELTIS HACKBERRY *Celtis occidentalis*	Handsome native tree with lopsided, lance-shaped, 4-in. leaves. Gray bark has corky ridges and thorny, warty bumps near the base of the trunk. Small flowers produce hard, dark, 1/3-in., pitted fruits that mature in autumn.	●	Height: 40–70' Spread: 40–50'	Sturdy shade tree. Yellow autumn leaves. Interesting bark.	2 to 9	Full sun to partial shade. Humus-rich, moist soil. This rugged tree withstands a wide range of environmental conditions, including dry and windy sites and heavy, sandy, or rocky soil.
	CERCIDI-PHYLLUM KATSURA TREE *Cercidiphyllum japonicum*	Deciduous tree with heart-shaped, 3-in. leaves that turn from light green to yellow orange in autumn. Gray bark becomes shaggy on mature trees. This often grows with multiple trunks and a bushy form. Several cultivars are available.	●	Height: 40–60' Spread: 20–50'	Specimen or shade tree with beautiful form. Attractive foliage with good autumn color.	4 to 8	Full sun to light shade. Well-drained, moist, fertile soil rich in humus. Trees are difficult to transplant. For best results, plant container-grown trees in early spring.
	CERCIDIUM BLUE PALO VERDE *Cercidium floridum*	Large shrub or small tree native to southwestern deserts. The name palo verde refers to its green bark. Yellow flowers appear in 2- to 4-in. clusters in early spring. A drought-deciduous species, it loses its leaves during dry spells.	●	Height: 10–30' Spread: 10–30'	Graceful form. Lacy leaves and green bark. Fragrant yellow flowers in early spring.	7 to 11	Full sun. Well-drained soil. Once established, it is quite drought resistant due to an exceedingly deep root system. Do not plant in the vicinity of septic tanks. Plants benefit from periodic fertilizer applications.
	CERCIS EASTERN REDBUD *Cercis canadensis*	A deciduous Southeastern native and one of the most attractive trees, not only for its dense clusters of rosy pink flowers, but for its lustrous, deep green, heart-shaped leaves. Cultivars with white flowers or purple leaves are available.	○ ◐ ●	Height: 20–30' Spread: 10–20'	Specimen tree suitable for small spaces. Profusion of pink, pealike flowers in spring. Attractive leaves.	4 to 9	Full sun to light shade. Moist, well-drained soil. Redbud tolerates a wide range of conditions except constant wetness.

		Flower Color	Height & Spread	Ornamental Features	Hardiness Zones	Growing Conditions
	CHAENOMELES JAPANESE FLOWERING QUINCE *Chaenomeles japonica* FLOWERING QUINCE ◀ *C. speciosa*	Spreading deciduous shrubs with spiny branches and clusters of showy, 1½-in. flowers in red, pink, orange, or white. *C.* japonica *is small and often used for foundation planting;* C. speciosa *is more erect and makes an excellent hedge.*	○ ● ● ● ●	C. jap. Height: 2–4' Spread: 3–6' C. spec. Height: 6–10' Spread: 6–12'	Flowering hedge, barrier, or border. *C. speciosa: late winter to early spring flowers. C. japonica: mid-spring flowers.*	4 to 9	Full sun to partial shade. Slightly acid, well-drained soil of average moisture and fertility.
	CHAMAE-CYPARIS ALASKA CEDAR ◀ *Chamaecyparis nootkatensis* 'Pendula' HINOKI FALSE CYPRESS *C. obtusa*	Evergreen trees with flattened sprays of small, awl-shaped needles, globular cones, and columnar crowns. *C. obtusa has deep green foliage; its branches droop less than those of blue-green* C. nootkatensis *'Pendula'. Brown bark shreds.*		C. noot. Height: 50–90' Spread: 15–40' C. obtusa Height: 50–75' Spread: 10–20'	Specimen trees. Elegant form. Attractive sprays of foliage.	C. noot. 4 to 7 C. obtusa 5 to 8	Full sun. Moist, well-drained, acid soil that is deep and rich in humus. *C. obtusa grows better where summers are warm;* C. nootkatensis *grows best where summers are cool and moist.*
	CHIONANTHUS CHINESE FRINGE TREE *Chionanthus retusus* WHITE FRINGE TREE, OLD-MAN'S-BEARD ◀ *C. virginicus*	Large shrubs or small trees with showy, 6- to 8-in. clusters of fragrant white flowers that hang below dark green, deciduous leaves. Dark blue fruits are produced by autumn. *C. retusus flowers later and usually is smaller than* C. virginicus.	○	C. ret. Height: 15–25' Spread: 10–20' C. virgin. Height: 20–30' Spread: 15–25'	Specimen tree or shrub. Clusters of long, white flowers in spring to summer. Yellow leaves in autumn.	C. ret. 5 to 8 C. virgin. 3 to 9	Full sun to partial shade with some afternoon shade in warm climates. Well-drained, fertile, slightly acid soil that never completely dries out. These trees grow slowly and may need 30 years to reach mature size.
	CHOISYA MEXICAN ORANGE *Choisya ternata*	Attractive evergreen hedge or screen shrub native to Mexico. Clusters of 1-in., 5-petaled, fragrant, white flowers are reminiscent of orange blossoms. Compound leaves have whorls of 3 thick leaflets with small transparent dots.	○	Height: 6–8' Spread: 6–8'	Specimen or border shrub. Attractive foliage. Fragrant white flowers useful for cutting.	8 to 10	Full sun to partial shade. Well-drained, acid soil. Choisya does not grow well where soil is alkaline, salty, or waterlogged. Prune at any time following bloom.
	CINNAMO-MUM CAMPHOR TREE *Cinnamomum camphora*	Evergreen tree with a broad crown and wood that is a commercial source of camphor. Aromatic, lance-shaped, 4- to 5-in. leathery leaves are dark green above and light blue green beneath. Small yellow flowers produce ¼-in. berries.	●	Height: 40–100' Spread: 30–40'	Specimen or shade tree. Attractive foliage. Dark brown bark.	8 to 10	Full sun. Well-drained, evenly moist, sandy-loam soil. Camphor tree does not grow well where soil is alkaline, salty, or waterlogged.

◀ *Indicates species shown*

Trees and Shrubs for American Gardens

		Flower Color	Height & Spread	Ornamental Features	Hardiness Zones	Growing Conditions
CLADRASTIS YELLOWWOOD *Cladrastis lutea*	Deciduous tree grown for its drooping clusters of fragrant white flowers and 12-in., pinnately compound leaves that are yellow in spring and autumn and green in summer. The light gray bark is smooth or slightly wrinkled.	○	Height: 30–50' Spread: 40–50'	Specimen tree. Clusters of white flowers in late spring to early summer. Beautiful foliage color changes.	3 to 8	Full sun. Well-drained soil. Yellowwood tolerates alkaline as well as acid soil. Prune young trees to prevent formation of weak limb crotches. Prune in summer to avoid excessive loss of sap.
CLETHRA SWEET PEPPERBUSH *Clethra alnifolia*	Deciduous native shrub found in eastern wetlands. Cylindrical clusters of fragrant white flowers festoon branch tips from mid- to late summer. The leathery, dark green leaves usually turn yellow or orange in autumn. Flowers attract bees.	○	Height: 3–8' Spread: 4–6'	Excellent for sunny or shady borders. Long season of fragrant flowers.	3 to 9	Full sun to full shade. Wet, acid soil that is rich in humus. Clethra does not grow well where soil is seasonally dry. It is good for seaside plantings in wet sites.
CORNUS FLOWERING DOGWOOD *Cornus florida* *C. × rutgersensis* KOUSA DOGWOOD ◄ *C. kousa*	Deciduous small trees or large shrubs used as specimen plants or massed. Trees bear white-bracted flower clusters, graceful branches, and attractive leaves that turn red or purple in autumn.	○ ◔	Height: 20–30' Spread: 20–30'	Small specimen trees. Beautiful spring flowers. Autumn foliage color. Red berries in autumn and winter.	5 to 9	Full sun to partial shade. Moist, well-drained, humus-rich soil. Dogwood grows poorly where soil is seasonally dry and hot. Both C. × rutgersensis and C. kousa resist anthracnose fungus, which has blighted native dogwoods (C. florida).
CORYLOPSIS BUTTERCUP WINTER HAZEL *Corylopsis pauciflora* SPIKE WINTER HAZEL ◄ *C. spicata*	Deciduous shrubs effective for woodland plantings. Slender, graceful branches bear drooping clusters of fragrant yellow flowers. The larger C. spicata has brighter, showier flowers and more crooked branches than the tidier C. pauciflora.	◔	C. pauci. Height: 4–6' Spread: 4–6' C. spic. Height: 4–6' Spread: 5–12'	Attractive screen or specimen shrubs. Fragrant yellow flowers in early spring. Blue-green foliage.	C. pauci. 6 to 9 C. spic. 5 to 9	Full sun to partial shade. Evenly moist, well-drained (even sandy), acid soil. Protect from drying winter winds and late spring frosts.
CORYLUS EUROPEAN FILBERT, HARRY LAUDER'S WALKING STICK *Corylus avellana* 'Contorta'	A cultivar of the shrub that produces hazelnuts. The branches are gnarled, giving the plant visual interest in the winter garden. Green, heart-shaped, 2- to 3-in. leaves with toothed edges turn yellow in autumn. The ³⁄₄-in. nuts are edible.	●	Height: 8–12' Spread: 8–10'	Specimen shrub. Interesting twisted twigs and branches and drooping male catkins in winter.	4 to 7	Full sun to light shade. Evenly moist, well-drained soil. 'Contorta' is a grafted shrub with European hazel as understock. Prune out all growth that arises from the understock.

		Flower Color	Height & Spread	Ornamental Features	Hardiness Zones	Growing Conditions
COTINUS SMOKEBUSH, SMOKE TREE *Cotinus coggygria*	Small, deciduous, multi-stemmed tree or large shrub grown for its wispy masses of plumed fruits that resemble pink smoke. Rounded, 2-in., blue-green leaves often turn red, purple, or orange in autumn. Smokebush is good for shrub borders.	○	Height: 10–15' Spread: 10–15'	Border or massing plants. Plumed masses of fruits in midsummer. Good autumn color in some cultivars.	5 to 8	Full sun. Well-drained soil on the dry side. Smokebush requires little maintenance. Be sure to buy a female plant. Male plants do not produce the smoke.
COTONEASTER BEARBERRY COTONEASTER *Cotoneaster dammeri* ROCKSPRAY COTONEASTER ◀ *C. horizontalis*	Low-growing, spreading shrubs with beautiful pink flowers that produce bright red, 1/4-in. berries by late summer. Tiny, shiny, evergreen leaves outline the horizontal branches of C. horizontalis. C. dammeri *has smaller branches.*	○ ●	*C. dam.* Height: 1–2' Spread: 3–6' *C. horiz.* Height: 2–3' Spread: 4–8'	Excellent semievergreen ground cover. Purple leaves in winter. Red berries in late summer.	*C. dam.* 5 to 8 *C. horiz.* 4 to 8	Full sun to partial shade. Well-drained, moist soil rich in organic matter. Once established, both species tolerate dry soil and even windy conditions. Plants spread horizontally with age.
COTONEASTER HEDGE COTONEASTER *Cotoneaster lucidus* WILLOWLEAF COTONEASTER ◀ *C. salicifolius*	Erect shrubs useful for hedges and screening. C. lucidus has 1- to 2-in., oval, pointed leaves that turn yellow or red in autumn and black berries. C. salicifolius has elongated semievergreen leaves, clusters of white flowers, and red berries.	○ ●	*C. lucid.* Height: 5–10' Spread: 3–5' *C. salic.* Height: 8–12' Spread: 8–12'	Useful for hedges or screens. Black or scarlet fruits.	*C. lucid.* 3 to 7 *C. salic.* 6 to 8	Full sun to partial shade. Well-drained, moist soil rich in organic matter. Once established, both species tolerate dry soil or windy conditions. Plants spread horizontally with age. C. salicifolius *is deciduous where winters are cold.*
CRATAEGUS COCKSPUR HAWTHORN *Crataegus crus-galli* WASHINGTON HAWTHORN ◀ *C. phaenopyrum*	Deciduous trees with white flowers, bright red 1/4- to 1/2-in. fruits, and 2- to 4-in. thorns on their twigs. The 2-in., oval, toothed leaves of C. crus-galli turn red in autumn. C. phaenopyrum has dark, sharp lobed leaves with pale green undersides.	○	*C. crus.* Height: 20–30' Spread: 20–35' *C. phaen.* Height: 20–25' Spread: 15–20'	Specimen or barrier trees, even hedges. White flowers in mid-spring. Red fruits in autumn and winter.	*C. crus.* 3 to 7 *C. phaen.* 3 to 8	Full sun to light shade. Ordinary well-drained garden soil. Prune deadwood in winter or early spring, but be careful of the stiff, sharp thorns. Trees get cedar-apple rust; do not plant near junipers (red cedar).
× CUPRESSO-CYPARIS LEYLAND CYPRESS × *Cupressocyparis leylandii*	Evergreen tree with an impressive columnar form. Awl-like, blue-green needles are arranged in flattened sprays. Globular, 1/2-in. cones mature in autumn.		Height: 75–100' Spread: 15–25'	Stately specimen tree; can be used in groups as screens. Attractive blue-green foliage.	6 to 10	Full sun to partial shade. Ordinary, well-drained soil. Leyland cypress thrives in a wide variety of soils and resists salt spray. Fast growing, up to 3 feet per year. Pruning is not necessary, but can increase bushiness when grown as a screen.

◀ *Indicates species shown*

Trees and Shrubs for American Gardens

		Flower Color	Height & Spread	Ornamental Features	Hardiness Zones	Growing Conditions
CYTISUS WARMINSTER BROOM ◀ *Cytisus × praecox* SCOTCH BROOM *C. scoparius*	Spreading, deciduous shrubs that quickly form mounds of pealike flowers and compound leaves with 3 leaflets. The larger C. × praecox has 1-in. flowers in white, yellow, pink, or red; C. scoparius comes in a bronze-flowering cultivar as well.	○ ● ●	C. × prae. Height: 8–10' Spread: 10–20' C. scopar. Height: 5–8' Spread: 5–15'	Rapidly growing border or screen. White, yellow, pink, or red flowers in mid-spring to late spring. Green twigs in winter.	C. × prae. 7 to 9 C. scopar. 6 to 8	Full sun. Sandy, very well-drained, acid soil of low fertility. Shrubs tend to spread by self-sowing and may become weedy with time. They tolerate poor soil and are also very resistant to salt spray.
DAPHNE GARLAND FLOWER ◀ *Daphne cneorum* WINTER DAPHNE *D. odora*	Low-growing shrubs with fragrant, colorful flowers and 1-in., dark, evergreen leaves. The shorter D. cneorum has pink, ½-in. flowers in spring. The more erect D. odora has purple-and-white or white flowers in late winter to early spring.	○ ◐ ● ●	D. cneor. Height: 6–12" Spread: 1–3' D. odora Height: 2–3' Spread: 2–3'	Low borders and ground covers. Fragrant pink, white, or purple-and-white flowers in late winter to mid-spring.	D. cneor. 4 to 9 D. odora 7 to 10	Full sun for D. cneorum; partial sun to light shade for D. odora. Moist, well-drained (even sandy) soil with a neutral pH for both species. Protect from drying winter winds. Prune annually after flowering.
DEUTZIA DEUTZIA ◀ *Deutzia gracilis* *D. × rosea*	Deciduous shrubs with dull green, lance-shaped leaves and 2- to 3-in., erect clusters of ½- to ¾-in. flowers. D. gracilis is larger, has white flowers, and forms larger mounds. The lower, more spreading D. × rosea produces light pink flowers.	○ ◐	D. gracilis Height: 4–6' Spread: 4–6' D. × rosea Height: 2–3' Spread: 4–6'	Useful border or hedge shrubs. Impressive display of white or pink flowers in late spring.	D. gracilis 4 to 9 D. × rosea 6 to 8	Full sun or very light shade. Moist, well-drained, slightly acid soil. Remove old stems and deadwood in summer to promote future flowering.
ELAEAGNUS OLEASTER, RUSSIAN OLIVE ◀ *Elaeagnus angustifolia* AUTUMN OLIVE *E. umbellata*	Deciduous large shrubs or small trees with thorny branches and 2- to 3-in., silver-flecked leaves. Small but fragrant yellow or white flowers in late spring. E. angustifolia is more tree-like, while E. umbellata is shrubbier.	○ ○	E. angust. Height: 15–25' Spread: 15–20' E. umbell. Height: 12–18' Spread: 15–20'	Rapidly growing hedge or windbreak. Fragrant spring flowers. Silvery branches and leaves. Colorful autumn berries.	E. angust. 3 to 7 E. umbell. 5 to 9	Full sun. Well-drained, sandy-loam soil. This wind-resistant, rapidly growing species tolerates any soil and can become weedy. Birds eat the attractive, sweet fruits, further spreading the species.
ENKIANTHUS ENKIANTHUS *Enkianthus campanulatus*	Deciduous shrub with clusters of elliptical, dark green leaves that turn intense yellow to orange in autumn. Clusters of light yellow-orange, red-tinged, bell-shaped flowers make a showy display in mid- to late spring.	○ ●	Height: 8–12' Spread: 6–8'	Specimen or border shrub. Dainty flowers in mid- to late spring. Brilliant autumn color.	4 to 8	Full sun to full shade. Moist, deep, acidic, well-drained, humus-rich soil. Adequate moisture and acidity are essential for this member of the heath family.

			Flower Color	Height & Spread	Ornamental Features	Hardiness Zones	Growing Conditions
	ERICA SNOW HEATHER, SPRING HEATH *Erica carnea*	Low evergreen shrub closely related to heather (Calluna) and requiring the same conditions. This species complements autumn-blooming heather by producing rosy, bell-shaped flowers in late winter to mid-spring.	● ●	Height: 4–8" Spread: 2–4'	Spreading evergreen ground cover. Abundant small red, pink, or white flowers in late winter to spring.	5 to 7	Full sun. Evenly moist, well-drained, humus-rich, acid (pH 6 or less) soil of low fertility. Acid soil is essential for its growth; do not fertilize or add lime.
	EUONYMUS WINTERCREEPER *Euonymus fortunei*	Highly variable species of woody evergreen. Both vine and small shrub forms are available. Its ¾- to 1-in., oblong leaves are typically dark green with yellow or white veins or variegations. Vine types are used as ground covers or climbers.	●	Vines Height: 4–8" Spread: 10–20' Shrubs Height: 3–6' Spread: 4–6'	Evergreen ground covers, climbers, and low hedges. Leathery, lustrous leaves. Purple leaves in winter for some cultivars.	5 to 9	Full sun to shade. Well-drained, ordinary garden soil. Euonymus is tolerant of almost any soil but will not survive in poor drainage. Plants are susceptible to euonymus scale insect attacks.
	FAGUS AMERICAN BEECH *Fagus grandifolia* EUROPEAN BEECH ◄ *F. sylvatica*	Deciduous trees with leathery, lustrous leaves, smooth gray bark, and triangular nuts enclosed in brown, spiny husks. F. sylvatica has many cultivars, including weeping and copper-colored forms. F. grandifolia often holds toothed leaves into winter.	● ●	F. grand. Height: 50–90' Spread: 40–75' F. sylvat. Height: 50–60' Spread: 35–45'	Superb, stately specimen and shade trees. Russet or golden bronze autumn foliage. Smooth, silvery gray bark.	F. grand. 3 to 9 F. sylvat. 4 to 7	Full sun to shade. Evenly moist, well-drained, slightly acid soil. Do not cultivate the soil around these shallow-rooted trees. Mature trees are quite large; plant only in open, unrestricted areas. F. sylvatica grows best in temperate climates.
	FORSYTHIA FORSYTHIA, BORDER FORSYTHIA *Forsythia × intermedia*	Very popular deciduous shrub with clusters of bright yellow, 1- to 2-in. flowers in spring, followed by medium green, toothed, lance-shaped leaves. Many cultivars of this hybrid vary in flower and leaf forms.	●	Height: 5–10' Spread: 6–12'	Border or massing shrub. Abundant bright yellow flowers in early to mid-spring.	4 to 8	Full sun to partial shade. Moist, well-drained, ordinary garden soil. Forsythia thrives in a wide range of conditions. Mulch during winter and protect from winter winds in colder climates. Prune in late spring after flowering.
	FOTHERGILLA FOTHERGILLA, WITCH-ALDER ◄ *Fothergilla major* *F. monticola*	Deciduous shrubs with 3-in., oval leaves, and showy, fragrant, 1- to 2-in. clusters of cream flowers borne in mid-spring. Flowers are composed of stamens only and resemble bottlebrushes. Some consider F. monticola the same species as F. major.	○	Height: 6–10' Spread: 4–8'	Specimen shrubs. Brilliant yellow to scarlet leaves in autumn. Clusters of cream flowers in mid-spring.	4 to 8	Full sun to light shade. Evenly moist, well-drained, moderately acid soil. Flower buds are formed in autumn. Prune only in spring after flowering.

◄ Indicates species shown

Trees and Shrubs for American Gardens

		Flower Color	Height & Spread	Ornamental Features	Hardiness Zones	Growing Conditions
FRANKLINIA FRANKLIN TREE *Franklinia alatamaha*	Magnificent deciduous tree native to the Southeast, but not found growing in the wild since 1790. The lustrous, dark green leaves of summer provide a beautiful backdrop for 3-in., white flowers with 5 petals and abundant yellow stamens.	○	Height: 15–30' Spread: 8–20'	Good specimen tree for small gardens. Large white flowers in summer and autumn. Red autumn foliage. Gray striped bark.	5 to 8	Full sun to light shade. Evenly moist, well-drained, humus-rich, acid soil. Full sun produces the most flowers and the best autumn foliage color. Trees are susceptible to vascular wilt disease.
FRAXINUS GREEN ASH, RED ASH *Fraxinus pennsylvanica*	Native deciduous tree with an upright, spreading form and deep green, compound leaves that turn yellow in early autumn. This fast-growing tree varies in shape and leaf color; named cultivars such as 'Honeyshade' or 'Summit' give best results.	●	Height: 50–60' Spread: 30–40'	Shade tree. Yellow or orange foliage in early autumn.	3 to 9	Full sun. Ordinary garden soil. Green ash is native to streamside sites in the East, but tolerates a wide variety of soil conditions. Once established it resists wind, drought, and salt spray. Separate male and female trees.
GINKGO GINKGO, MAIDENHAIR TREE *Ginkgo biloba*	A medium to tall tree with a strongly pyramidal crown. Light green, fan-shaped leaves turn golden yellow in autumn. Since female trees produce bad-smelling fruits, select male trees for planting.		Height: 50–80' Spread: 30–60'	Specimen or shade tree. Interesting branch patterns. Bright yellow foliage in autumn.	3 to 9	Full sun. Sandy, deep, moist soil. Ginkgo adapts to a wide variety of environmental conditions, including air pollution. It tolerates a wide variety of soil conditions and is a good choice for difficult sites.
GLEDITSIA HONEY LOCUST *Gleditsia triacanthos*	A large, bold tree whose 6- to 8-in., doubly compound leaves have about 100 leaflets. Pendant clusters of small, yellow-green flowers produce 8- to 18-in. flattened, brown pods. G. triacanthos var. inermis lacks the thorns of other varieties.	●	Height: 30–70' Spread: 20–30'	Dappled-shade tree useful for lawns. Long, leathery pod fruits.	3 to 9	Full sun. Moist, well-drained soil that is rich in organic matter and lime. Established trees are drought tolerant and adapt to a wide variety of conditions.
GYMNOCLADUS KENTUCKY COFFEE TREE *Gymnocladus dioica*	Deciduous tree native to the midwestern and central eastern states. The poisonous seeds, borne in 6-in. brown pods, were once roasted and used as a coffee substitute. The 2- to 3-ft., doubly compound leaves have dozens of 2-in., lance-shaped leaflets.	●	Height: 60–80' Spread: 40–50'	Shade or specimen tree. Dark bark with deep grooves. Attractive winter silhouette.	4 to 8	Full sun. Deep, rich, moist soil. This tree is native to moist bottomlands, but tolerates a wide range of soil conditions, especially when established. Plant male trees if you don't want to contend with dropping seedpods.

		Flower Color	Height & Spread	Ornamental Features	Hardiness Zones	Growing Conditions
HALESIA CAROLINA SILVER-BELL *Halesia carolina*	Small deciduous tree that makes a beautiful shade tree or addition to a woodland border. Clusters of white, drooping, ½- to ¾-in., bell-shaped flowers appear in spring. The dark green, 2- to 4-in. leaves turn yellow in autumn.	○	Height: 30–40' Spread: 20–35'	Shade or border tree. Beautiful, delicate white flowers in mid-spring. Yellow foliage in early autumn.	4 to 8	Full sun to partial shade. Deep, acid, well-drained, evenly moist soil that is rich in humus. When grown in its preferred conditions, it is a low-maintenance species.
HAMAMELIS WITCH HAZEL *Hamamelis × intermedia* CHINESE WITCH HAZEL ◀ *H. mollis*	Vigorous shrubs whose many cultivars provide a range of winter and early spring flower colors and autumn leaf colors from yellow to orange to red. H. × intermedia grows taller and flowers earlier than H. mollis, one of its parents.	○ ● ●	H. × inter. Height: 15–20' Spread: 12–18' H. mollis Height: 10–15' Spread: 6–12'	Specimen or border shrubs. Yellow to red autumn foliage. Yellow, red, or orange flowers in midwinter to early spring.	5 to 9	Full sun to partial shade. Moist, well-drained, slightly acid, humus-rich soil. These winter-flowering shrubs have no serious diseases or insect pests. They are a good substitute for the overused forsythias.
HIBISCUS TROPICAL HIBISCUS, ROSE-OF-CHINA *Hibiscus rosa-sinensis*	Tender, deciduous shrub that bears glossy, 3-in., pointed oval leaves and spectacular, 4- to 6-in., hollyhock-like flowers in a range of colors from white to pink to deep red or yellow. Stamens form a yellow column at flower center.	○ ○ ● ●	Height: 8–15' Spread: 3–5'	Specimen, hedge, or border shrub. Attractive summer flowers. Dark green, glossy foliage.	10 to 11	Full sun to light shade. Average, well-drained, evenly moist soil. This fast-growing shrub can be grown as a large container plant and brought indoors before frost.
HIBISCUS ROSE-OF-SHARON, SHRUB ALTHAEA *Hibiscus syriacus*	One of the few hardy deciduous shrubs in the genus Hibiscus. It looks much like H. rosa-sinensis but has 2- to 4-in. flowers in blue, purple, white, pink, red, or in various combinations. Light green leaves have 3 lobes.	○ ○ ○ ● ● ●	Height: 6–12' Spread: 8–10'	Excellent border shrub or screening hedge. Hollyhock-like flowers in various colors.	5 to 9	Full sun. Deep, moist, well-drained soil rich in humus. Prune in late winter or early spring to promote large, vigorous flowers. Plants typically leaf out late in spring. Leaf miners and Japanese beetles can be problems.
HYDRANGEA FRENCH HYDRANGEA, HORTENSIA *Hydrangea macrophylla*	Popular shrub grown for its showy clusters of pink, white, or blue flowers, whose colors depend on soil pH. Large (6- to 8-in.), thick, toothed, oval leaves are deciduous in zone 7 and colder but evergreen where winters are mild.	○ ○ ● ●	Height: 3–6' Spread: 3–6'	Border or specimen shrub. Showy clusters of pink, white, or blue flowers in summer.	5 to 9	Full sun to light shade. Moist, well-drained soil. Flowers are blue in acid soil, pink in slightly acid soil. Hydrangeas are often killed to the ground by severe winters. In colder zones plant in sheltered areas and cover with mulch before winter.

◀ *Indicates species shown*

Trees and Shrubs for American Gardens

		Flower Color	Height & Spread	Ornamental Features	Hardiness Zones	Growing Conditions
HYDRANGEA PEEGEE HYDRANGEA *Hydrangea paniculata* 'Grandiflora'	Large deciduous shrub or small tree that has large masses (typically 1 ft. or more long) of white flowers that turn pink in late summer and tan in autumn. Pointed, oval leaves are 3- to 6-in. long.	○ ● ●	Height: 15–20' Spread: 10–15'	Border shrub. Large, round-ed clusters of white flowers that turn pink in late summer.	3 to 8	Full sun to light shade. Moist, well-drained soil rich in humus. Prune in autumn after flowering, thinning stems to produce large flowers and a treelike form.
HYDRANGEA OAKLEAF HYDRANGEA *Hydrangea quercifolia*	Deciduous shrub native to the Southeast. Attractive, 6- to 8-in. leaves are shaped like those of red oak, and turn from medium green to orange, red, or purple in autumn. White flowers turn lavender in late summer and fade to tan in autumn.	○	Height: 4–6' Spread: 3–5'	Border shrub. White flowers turning laven-der in late summer. Orange, red, or purple foliage in autumn.	5 to 9	Full sun to light shade. Moist, well-drained soil rich in humus. Prune in autumn after flowering. Plants grow best if roots are kept cool and moist by covering with mulch.
HYPERICUM AARON'S BEARD, ST.-JOHN'S-WORT *Hypericum calycinum* *H. patulum*	Low shrubs with showy yel-low, 2- to 3-in. flowers that start to bloom in June. H. calycinum *spreads by under-ground stolons and is used as a ground cover. H. patu-lum is more erect and is used as a low shrub.*		H. caly. Height: 1–1½' Spread: 1½–2' H. pat. Height: 1–1½' Spread: 1–1½'	Low border or ground cover shrubs. Showy yellow flowers in early sum-mer to early autumn.	6 to 9	Full sun to partial shade. Well-drained, sandy, nutri-ent-poor soil. Prune in late winter to remove deadwood and stimulate vigorous growth and flowering.
ILEX JAPANESE HOLLY *Ilex crenata* AMERICAN HOLLY *I. opaca*	Stately evergreen plants used as specimen plants or in shrub borders. I. crenata *is a shrub with 1-in., oval leaves and ¼-in. black fruits. I. opaca is a conical tree with ⅓-in. red fruits and larger, spiny leaves. Many cultivars are available.*	○	I. crenata Height: 5–10' Spread: 5–15' I. opaca Height: 40–50' Spread: 20–40'	I. crenata: glossy dark leaves, excel-lent hedge. I. opaca: specimen tree, bright red fruits all winter.	I. crenata 5 to 7 I. opaca 6 to 9	Full sun to shade. Evenly moist, well-drained, acid soil that is rich in humus. To guarantee berries, plant at least one male for every couple of female plants. Both species resist salt spray. Hollies shed leaves in mid-spring.
JUNIPERUS CHINESE JUNIPER, PFITZER JUNIPER *Juniperus chinensis* var. chinensis 'Pfitzerana' SARGENT JUNIPER *J. chinensis* var. sargentii	Evergreen conifers widely used as foundation plant-ings, ground covers, or mass plantings, with sharp awl-shaped needles and gray-blue berrylike cones. 'Pfitzerana' is a large shrub. Sargentii is low-growing and a good ground cover.		'Pfitzerana' Height: 3–5' Spread: 5–10' var. sarg. Height: 1–2' Spread: 5–10'	Ground covers and low hedges. Green to blue-green or gray-green foliage. Light blue berrylike cones.	4 to 9	Full sun to partial shade. Light, sandy, moderately moist soil. These species do not tolerate soggy condi-tions. They may be troubled by slugs and snails and are susceptible to juniper blight.

			Flower Color	Height & Spread	Ornamental Features	Hardiness Zones	Growing Conditions
	JUNIPERUS COMMON JUNIPER *Juniperus communis*	*A spreading, clump-forming evergreen shrub or small tree. Plants bear dense, sharp, spiny olive green leaves and $1/4$-in., waxy, blue, berrylike cones. Many species are available, some erect and growing up to 30 ft. tall.*		Height: $1/2$–30' (varies with cultivar) Spread: 6–12'	*Ground cover, informal hedge, specimen shrub, or foundation plant. Evergreen, olive-colored foliage.*	2 to 6	*Full sun. Ordinary well-drained garden soil. Plants slowly spread with age to form sprawling mats or dense shrubs. Plants are susceptible to juniper blight and bagworms but quite tolerant of poor soil and windy exposed sites.*
	JUNIPERUS SHORE JUNIPER *Juniperus conferta*	*Evergreen, matlike, coniferous shrubs native to coastal dunes of Japan. Bright blue-green, $1/3$-in., awl-shaped needles are densely clustered in whorls of 3. Berrylike, $1/3$-in. cones are blue black and covered with a waxy bloom.*		Height: 1–$1 1/2$' Spread: 5–10'	*Excellent evergreen ground cover or prostrate rock garden plant. Blue-green foliage. Dark, waxy fruits.*	6 to 8	*Full sun. Ordinary well-drained garden soil. Shore juniper does not grow well if soil is poorly drained or clayey. It tolerates salt spray and sandy soil of low fertility.*
	JUNIPERUS CREEPING JUNIPER *Juniperus horizontalis*	*Low, creeping evergreen shrub that forms a mat. Dense, spiny or scaly, light blue-green leaves mostly cover the long, trailing branches. Plants produce $1/4$-in., waxy, blue, berrylike cones. Many cultivars are available.*		Height: $1/2$–2' (varies with cultivar) Spread: 2–15'	*Low ground cover, especially for rocky or heavy soil. Light blue-green foliage. Purplish foliage during winter.*	3 to 9	*Full sun. Ordinary well-drained garden soil. Creeping juniper tolerates hot, dry conditions and heavy or rocky soil. It is susceptible to juniper blight but is a useful ground cover for difficult or neglected sites.*
	JUNIPERUS ROCKY MOUNTAIN JUNIPER *Juniperus scopulorum*	*An evergreen, coniferous tree native to the foothills of the Rockies. The species grows in a narrow, columnar form, but cultivars are available with pyramidal or even globe-shaped forms. Trees bear dark, $1/3$-in., berrylike cones.*		Height: 4–40' (varies with cultivar) Spread: 3–12'	*Excellent screen or specimen tree. Blue-green foliage. Light blue berrylike cones.*	3 to 7	*Full sun. Ordinary well-drained garden soil. Rocky Mountain juniper tolerates hot, dry conditions and heavy or rocky soil. It is susceptible to juniper blight and bagworms.*
	JUNIPERUS EASTERN RED CEDAR *Juniperus virginiana*	*A coniferous evergreen tree (not a true cedar) native to the East. Young foliage is prickly and awl-shaped; mature foliage is flattened and scalelike. Trees bear light blue globular cones and reddish brown peeling bark. Many cultivars available.*		Height: 6–75' (varies with cultivar) Spread: 10–20'	*Specimen tree; also excellent for hedgerows and windbreaks. Deep green to light blue foliage. Light blue berrylike cones.*	2 to 9	*Full sun. Deep, well-drained, ordinary garden soil. Grows well in acidic or alkaline soils and withstands windy conditions. Do not plant near crabapples or hawthorns; it carries cedar-apple rust, a fungus affecting these plants.*

◀ *Indicates species shown*

111

ENCYCLOPEDIA OF PLANTS

Trees and Shrubs for American Gardens

		Flower Color	Height & Spread	Ornamental Features	Hardiness Zones	Growing Conditions
KALMIA MOUNTAIN LAUREL *Kalmia latifolia*	A handsome evergreen shrub native to the East. Plants bear lustrous, 2- to 4-in. leaves and showy clusters of white, pink, or rose, spotted, cuplike, 1-in. flowers in late spring. Laurels are ideal for naturalizing in woodland settings.	○ ◐ ●	Height: 4–10' Spread: 2–10'	Beautiful specimen or border shrub. Spectacular clusters of pink, white, or rose flowers in late spring.	5 to 9	Full sun to shade; partial shade where summers are hot. Acid soil that is cool, well drained, and evenly moist. Mountain laurels will not grow in alkaline soil. Protect from drying winter winds.
KERRIA JAPANESE ROSE, KERRIA *Kerria japonica*	Deciduous shrub with 1½-in., bright yellow, roselike flowers borne singly at the ends of pale green twigs. The 2- to 4-in., pointed, bright green leaves have toothed edges and persist into autumn.	◐	Height: 3–8' Spread: 5–10'	Group or specimen shrub. Beautiful yellow flowers in mid-spring. Attractive leaves and twigs.	4 to 9	Full sun to full shade. Evenly moist, well-drained soil of average fertility. Plant where it will be protected from drying winter winds. Overly fertile soil causes rampant growth and reduction of flowering.
KOELREU-TERIA GOLDEN-RAIN TREE *Koelreuteria bipinnata* VARNISH TREE ◀*K. paniculata*	Deciduous trees that have large, compound leaves and dense spikes of bright yellow flowers, which in turn produce seedpods. K. bipinnata has doubly compound leaves and pink pods, while K. paniculata has singly compound leaves and green pods.	◐	Height: 30–40' Spread: 30–45'	Specimen or shade tree. Lovely golden flowers in mid- to late summer.	K. bipinn. 8 to 10 K. panicu. 5 to 9	Full sun. Average soil conditions. K. paniculata withstands heat and drought and tolerates air pollution and alkaline soil. K. bipinnata is less winter hardy and more suited to warm climate zones.
KOLKWITZIA BEAUTYBUSH *Kolkwitzia amabilis*	Deciduous shrub covered in late spring by masses of ⅝-in., bell-shaped, light pink flowers dotted with yellow. Arching branches bear 2-in., lance-shaped leaves that sometimes turn red in autumn.	◐	Height: 6–10' Spread: 5–8'	Large, rapidly growing border shrub. Beautiful pink flowers in late spring.	4 to 8	Full sun to light shade with best flowers in full sun. Well-drained, evenly moist soil. Prune in early spring to remove deadwood. Periodically prune old shoots to the ground to promote new, vigorous growth and flowering.
LAGER-STROEMIA CRAPE MYRTLE *Lagerstroemia indica*	Deciduous shrub or small, multistemmed tree with smooth, gray bark that flakes off, revealing darker underbark. Plants bear showy 6-in. clusters of crepe-textured flowers and 1- to 2-in., elliptical leaves that turn bright red orange in autumn.	○ ◐ ◐	Height: 15–30' Spread: 10–35'	Specimen or grouping plant. White, pink, red, or purple flowers in summer. Bright foliage colors in autumn.	7 to 9	Full sun. Deep, moist, well-drained soil. Top may die back in severe winters. Prune back in early spring to remove deadwood and rejuvenate shrub.

112

		Flower Color	Height & Spread	Ornamental Features	Hardiness Zones	Growing Conditions
LEUCOTHOE DOG HOBBLE, FETTERBUSH *Leucothoe fontanesiana*	Evergreen shrub whose lustrous, dark green, 2- to 5-in., lance-shaped leaves darken in winter. In spring gracefully arching branches bear groups of drooping, fragrant, waxy, ¼-in. white flowers. Fetterbush spreads by underground stems.	○	Height: 3–6' Spread: 3–6'	Specimen for massing or naturalizing in an informal setting. Evergreen foliage. Fragrant, white flowers in mid-spring.	4 to 8	Partial to full shade. Moist, well-drained, acid soil. Prune after flowering, removing old wood to promote growth. Plants will tolerate full sun if given ample moisture. They will not tolerate drought or windy sites.
LIGUSTRUM JAPANESE PRIVET *Ligustrum japonicum* COMMON PRIVET, EUROPEAN PRIVET ◀ *L. vulgare*	Upright, dense shrubs useful for hedges and screens. Plants bear clusters of white, aromatic flowers, dense branches, and opposing pairs of oblong to lance-shaped leaves. L. japonicum is evergreen; L. vulgare is deciduous.	○	L. japon. Height: 6–12' Spread: 6–8' L. vulgare Height: 12–15' Spread: 12–15'	Hedge or screen shrubs. Creamy flowers in mid- to late spring.	L. japon. 7 to 10 L. vulgare 4 to 6	Full sun to light shade. Ordinary, well-drained garden soil. Privet adapts to all but waterlogged soils, withstands heavy pruning, and is easily shaped. Remove winter-killed branches in early spring.
LIQUIDAMBAR RED GUM, SWEET GUM *Liquidambar styraciflua*	Deciduous tree native to eastern and southeastern bottomlands bearing dark green, star-shaped, 5-lobed, 4- to 6-in. leaves that turn brilliant yellow, orange, and red in autumn. Female trees bear spiky, 1-in., russet, ball-shaped fruits.	●	Height: 50–75' Spread: 40–50'	Shade or specimen tree for large settings. Brilliant autumn foliage. Attractive fruits. Smooth gray bark.	5 to 9	Full sun. Deep, moist, slightly acid soil. Sweet gum adapts to all but dry soils. Some bud injury may occur in severe winters. Trees are susceptible to scale insects and leaf spot fungus.
LIRIODEN-DRON TULIP TREE, YELLOW POPLAR *Liriodendron tulipifera*	Stately deciduous tree native to the East. Interesting 4- to 7-in., squarish leaves and 2-in., green and orange, tulip-shaped flowers grace this relative of the magnolia. It develops a broad crown if grown in open.	● ●	Height: 60–90' Spread: 30–50'	Grand specimen tree for large spaces. Intriguing flowers in late spring. Attractive leaves.	4 to 9	Full sun. Deep, evenly moist, well-drained soil that is slightly acid. The wood is not particularly strong; protect from damaging winds.
LONICERA WINTER HONEY-SUCKLE ◀ *Lonicera fragrantissima* BOX HONEYSUCKLE *L. nitida*	Shrubs with pairs of evergreen or semievergreen, elliptical leaves and fragrant flowers that produce ¼-in. berries. L. fragrantissima has ½- to 3-in. leaves, very fragrant flowers, and red fruits. L. nitida has ¼- to ½-in. leaves and purple berries.	○	L. fragran. Height: 6–10' Spread: 6–10' L. nitida Height: 2–3' Spread: 3–4'	Hedge or border shrubs. Fragrant, creamy white flowers in late winter or early spring for L. fragrantissima and spring for L. nitida.	L. fragran. 4 to 9 L. nitida 7 to 9	Full sun to light shade. Moist, well-drained, humus-rich soil. Plants will not tolerate very dry or water-logged soils. Prune severely after flowering. Leaf blight and powdery mildew can be problems.

◀ *Indicates species shown*

Trees and Shrubs for American Gardens

			Flower Color	Height & Spread	Ornamental Features	Hardiness Zones	Growing Conditions
	MAGNOLIA SOUTHERN MAGNOLIA *Magnolia grandiflora*	Ornamental evergreen tree grown for its large, fragrant flowers. These pyramidal trees bear leathery, evergreen leaves, creamy white, 6- to 9-in. flowers with thick petals, and conelike fruit with vermilion seeds.	○	Height: 60–80' Spread: 30–50'	Specimen tree. Magnificent flowers in late spring to early summer. Lustrous, evergreen foliage.	6 to 9	Full sun to partial shade. Evenly moist, well-drained, acid soil that is rich in humus. In northern zones plant in sheltered areas away from dry winter winds and direct sun.
	MAGNOLIA SAUCER MAGNOLIA *Magnolia × soulangiana*	Small flowering deciduous tree or large shrub with 3- to 6-in., pointed oval leaves. The 5- to 6-in., chalice-shaped flowers are creamy white and tinged with purple or lavender on the outside. Bark is smooth, silvery gray.	○	Height: 20–30' Spread: 15–30'	Small specimen tree. Beautiful white-and-purple flowers in early spring.	5 to 9	Full sun to partial shade. Evenly moist, well-drained, acid soil rich in humus. Protect from drying winter winds. Trees are sensitive to ice damage, and late spring frosts may kill emerging flower buds.
	MAGNOLIA STAR MAGNOLIA *Magnolia stellata*	Flowering deciduous shrub to small tree with elliptical, 2- to 4-in. leaves and a dense crown. Abundant, 3-in., fragrant, white flowers have narrow, daisylike petals.	○	Height: 15–20' Spread: 10–15'	Small specimen tree. Beautiful, fragrant white flowers from early to mid-spring.	3 to 8	Full sun to partial shade. Evenly moist, well-drained, acid soil that is rich in humus. In northern zones plant in sheltered areas away from dry winter winds and direct sun. Late frosts may kill emerging flowers.
	MAGNOLIA SWAMP LAUREL, SWEET BAY MAGNOLIA *Magnolia virginiana*	A deciduous flowering tree in cold climates but evergreen where winters are mild. The 3- to 5-in., lance-shaped leaves are dark above and light green below. Fragrant, creamy white, 2- to 3-in. flowers bloom all summer long.	○	Height: 10–40' Spread: 10–30'	Specimen tree. Fragrant white flowers from late spring to early autumn.	5 to 9	Full sun to partial shade. Evenly moist, well-drained, acid soil rich in humus. This species tolerates deeper shade and wetter soils than other magnolias. In northern zones protect from drying winter winds and direct sun.
	MAHONIA OREGON GRAPE, HOLLY GRAPE *Mahonia aquifolium* ◀ *M. bealei*	Evergreen shrubs bearing showy clusters of small, yellow flowers and glossy, compound, spiny leaves that resemble American holly. Both plants bear prominent clusters of dark, blue-green, grapelike berries from mid-summer to fall.		*M. aquifol.* Height: 3–6' Spread: 3–5' *M. bealei* Height: 10–12' Spread: 8–10'	Massing shrubs. Clusters of yellow flowers from late winter to mid-spring. Masses of grapelike berries.	*M. aquifol.* 5 to 9 *M. bealei* 7 to 9	Light shade to full shade. Moist, well-drained, acid, humus-rich soil. Plants prefer a moist woodland setting. Protect from drying winter winds and sun. Use M. bealei in southern zones only.

			Flower Color	Height & Spread	Ornamental Features	Hardiness Zones	Growing Conditions

MALUS
JAPANESE CRAB-APPLE,
SHOWY CRABAPPLE
Malus floribunda
SARGENT CRABAPPLE
◀ *M. sargentii*

Small deciduous tree or large shrub with a profusion of fragrant flowers having 5 rounded petals. Flowers typically open deep pink, or even red, and fade to paler colors. M. floribunda *is more treelike than the shrubby* M. sargentii.

Flower Color: ● ●

Height & Spread: M. flor. Height: 20–30' Spread: 25–35' M. sarg. Height: 8–12' Spread: 15–20'

Ornamental Features: Single specimen or group plantings. Flowers in mid-spring. Fruits yellow and red in M. floribunda, and red in M. sargentii.

Hardiness Zones: 4 to 8

Growing Conditions: Full sun. Well-drained, evenly moist, slightly acid soil. Trees grow well in heavy loam soil. Prune after flowering in late spring. Trees host cedar-apple rust; don't plant near Eastern red cedar (Juniperus virginiana).

METASE-QUOIA
DAWN REDWOOD
Metasequoia glyptostroboides

Deciduous, coniferous tree known only from fossils until 1944, when it was discovered growing in China. A relative of bald cypress (Taxodium distichum), *it has a conical form, shreddy bark, and soft, needlelike leaves arranged in rows.*

Height & Spread: Height: 70–100' Spread: 20–25'

Ornamental Features: Single specimen or group plantings. A good seasonal screen for large areas. Attractive red-brown bark.

Hardiness Zones: 5 to 9

Growing Conditions: Full sun. Well-drained, moist, acid soil that is rich in organic matter. Avoid alkaline soil. Allow plenty of room for growth.

NYSSA
BLACK GUM,
TUPELO
Nyssa sylvatica

A native deciduous tree with architectural, horizontal branches. Elongated, 3- to 4-in., glossy green leaves turn bright red in early autumn. The unobtrusive spring flowers produce pairs of round, 1/4-in., blue-black fruits usually hidden by foliage.

Flower Color: ○

Height & Spread: Height: 30–90' Spread: 20–30'

Ornamental Features: Specimen or shade tree. Brilliant red or purple autumn foliage. Interesting horizontal branches.

Hardiness Zones: 4 to 9

Growing Conditions: Full sun to light shade. Moist, humus-rich, acid soil. Black gum is native to eastern swamps, but grows in well-drained sites as long as soil is evenly moist. Shelter from winter winds.

OXYDENDRUM
SOURWOOD
Oxydendrum arboreum

Medium-sized deciduous tree native to the East with branches that droop toward the tips and a narrowly pyramidal crown. Trees bear clusters of fragrant, white, bell-shaped flowers. Leaves turn yellow, red, and purple in autumn.

Flower Color: ○

Height & Spread: Height: 25–30' Spread: 15–25'

Ornamental Features: Specimen or shade tree. Fragrant white flowers in mid- to late summer. Multicolored leaves in autumn.

Hardiness Zones: 5 to 9

Growing Conditions: Full sun to partial shade. Humus-rich, well-drained, moist, acid soil. Fall colors are best in trees planted in full sun.

PAXISTIMA
CLIFF-GREEN,
MOUNTAIN-LOVER
Paxistima canbyi

Low evergreen shrub that creeps along the surface of the ground. The small (1/4- to 3/4-in.), narrow, evergreen leaves are lustrous and dark green.

Flower Color: ●

Height & Spread: Height: 6–15" Spread: 3–5'

Ornamental Features: Evergreen ground cover, low hedge, or rock garden shrub. Lustrous, dark green leaves.

Hardiness Zones: 4 to 8

Growing Conditions: Full sun to partial shade; needs more shade in zones 7–8. Well-drained, moist, humus-rich soil; tolerates alkaline soil. Cliff-green grows best where summers are cool. Scale insects can be a problem.

◀ *Indicates species shown*

Trees and Shrubs for American Gardens

		Flower Color	Height & Spread	Ornamental Features	Hardiness Zones	Growing Conditions
PHILADELPHUS SWEET MOCK ORANGE *Philadelphus coronarius*	An upright, vigorous, decid-uous shrub with a round crown and small clusters of white, 4-petaled, fragrant, 1-in. flowers. Pairs of oppos-ing oval leaves are 2- to 4-in. long. Older bark peels away to reveal red-brown and tan hues.	○	Height: 10–12' Spread: 10–12'	Border or screen shrub. Fragrant white flowers for several weeks in mid- to late spring.	4 to 8	Full sun to light shade. Moist, humus-rich, well-drained soil. Prune this fast-growing shrub in early sum-mer after flowering; remove deadwood and large shoots to promote more flowers. Overgrown plants may be pruned to the ground.
PHOTINIA RED TIP *Photinia × fraseri*	Small evergreen tree or large shrub with glossy leaves emerging bright red and turning deep green as they mature. The lance-shaped leaves, with finely toothed edges, reach 4–6 in. Flat clusters of small, white, mal-odorous flowers.	○	Height: 10–15' Spread: 5–8'	Fast-growing hedge or screen tree. Bright red foliage that turns deep green as leaves mature.	8 to 10	Full sun to light shade. Well-drained, humus-rich soil. Plants will not tolerate waterlogged conditions. ' Fertilize and prune annually to maintain vigorous growth. To avoid mildew and leaf spot, provide good air circulation.
PICEA NORWAY SPRUCE *Picea abies*	Conical, coniferous, ever-green trees with stiff, sharp-pointed needles. This is a large tree with graceful branches, drooping branch-lets, and deep green, 1-in. needles. Cylindrical cones are 4–6 in. long.		Height: 60–100' Spread: 25–40'	Specimen tree, screen, or hedge. Graceful form with pendant branches. Large, attrac-tive cones.	2 to 8	Full sun. Moist, well-drained, acid soil. Norway spruce grows rapidly where summers are cool and can be pruned into a hedge. Bagworms and aphids may be problems.
PICEA SERBIAN SPRUCE *Picea omorika*	Slender, dense, coniferous, evergreen tree. Needles are $3/4$ in. long, with white undersides and dark green upper surfaces. Russet, oblong cones are $1^1/2$–2 in. long.		Height: 50–80' Spread: 15–25'	Specimen or screen with spire shape. Unusual white-green foliage and narrow pyra-midal form.	4 to 8	Full sun. Moist, well-drained, acid soil. Trees are more tolerant of alkaline soil than other spruces. Trees grow slowly and may winter burn in cold, windy sites.
PICEA BLUE SPRUCE, COLORADO BLUE SPRUCE *Picea pungens* var. glauca	Popular evergreen conifer native to the Rocky Moun-tains and the Southwest, grown for its $3/4$- to $1^1/2$-in., stiff, silvery blue needles. Its outline is strongly conical. The soft, papery, cylindrical cones are 2–4 in. long.		Height: 50–120' Spread: 15–30'	Specimen tree for large set-tings. Silvery blue, sharp-pointed nee-dles. Inter-esting tan, papery cones.	3 to 7	Full sun. Humus-rich, moist, well-drained, acid soil; more tolerant of dry, rocky soils than other spruces. Older trees tend to lose lower branches and lose the youth-ful pyramidal form.

		Flower Color	Height & Spread	Ornamental Features	Hardiness Zones	Growing Conditions
PIERIS JAPANESE ANDROMEDA, LILY-OF-THE-VALLEY BUSH *Pieris japonica*	Evergreen shrub with lustrous, 1- to 3-in., finely toothed, dark green leaves. Spreading branches bear 3- to 6-in., drooping clusters of ¼-in., white, urn-shaped flowers.	○	Height: 9–12' Spread: 6–8'	Evergreen specimen or border shrub. Pleasant flowers in early to mid-spring.	5 to 8	Full sun to partial shade. Moist, acid, well-drained, humus-rich soil. Shelter from drying winter winds. Prune in late spring after flowering.
PINUS AUSTRIAN PINE *Pinus nigra*	Evergreen conifer with a broad, open crown, thick, 4- to 6-in., dark green needles in groups of 2, and stout branches. Bark has yellow-tan plates with black grooves in between. The 2- to 3-in. cones are round.		Height: 50–75' Spread: 20–40'	Specimen tree useful as a windbreak in open areas. Bold branches with bushy needles. Attractive patterned bark.	4 to 7	Full sun. Ordinary, moist, well-drained soil. Austrian pine tolerates a range of soils, from clayey and alkaline soil to better drained and acid soils. It is also heat and drought tolerant.
PINUS WHITE PINE *Pinus strobus*	Evergreen tree with soft, 3- to 5-in., narrow, white-lined needles in clusters of 5. The straight trunk supports a graceful, oval crown with whorls of strongly horizontal branches. Cones are 4–6 in. long and lack spines.		Height: 60–100' Spread: 30–40'	Specimen, shade, or screen tree. Soft, delicate foliage. Interesting cones.	3 to 8	Full sun. Fertile, well-drained, humus-rich, evenly moist soil. White pine adapts to both dry and soggy conditions and grows best where summers are cool. It is sensitive to salt spray (even from road salt).
PINUS LOBLOLLY PINE *Pinus taeda*	Evergreen tree with an irregularly open growth form. The 6- to 10-in. needles come in clusters of 3. Red-brown, scaly bark breaks into plates with age. Tapered cones are 3–6 in. long. Trees invade old fields in the Southeast.		Height: 50–75' Spread: 20–25'	Fast-growing screen or shade tree. Red-brown bark.	7 to 9	Full sun. Deeply moist, acidic soil. This fast-growing species tolerates even poor soils and bad drainage.
PISTACIA CHINESE PISTACHIO *Pistacia chinensis*	Deciduous tree related to the pistachio tree but grown for its spectacular autumn foliage, not for nuts. Foot-long, dark green compound leaves turn brilliant red orange in autumn. Trees bear red-violet, ¼-in., berry-like fruits.	●	Height: 30–60' Spread: 25–35'	Specimen or shade tree. Brilliant autumn color. Showy fruits. Scaly gray and salmon pink bark.	7 to 9	Full sun. Moist, well-drained soil of average fertility. Chinese pistachio adapts to dry, poor soil, even drought conditions, once established.

◀ *Indicates species shown*

Trees and Shrubs for American Gardens

		Flower Color	Height & Spread	Ornamental Features	Hardiness Zones	Growing Conditions
PLATANUS AMERICAN PLANE TREE, SYCAMORE *Platanus occidentalis*	Large deciduous tree with a thick trunk and irregular branches. Broad leaves are 4–9 in. long, with 3–5 pointed lobes. Fruits are 1-in., fuzzy balls that break apart in winter. Bark flakes off, leaving white, tan, and olive patches.	● ●	Height: 75–100' Spread: 50–75'	Big, bold specimen tree. Broad foliage. Bark white when young, multicolored in middle age.	4 to 9	Full sun. Deep, moist, humus-rich soil. This eastern bottomland native also tolerates well-drained sites. Anthracnose may be a problem. Fruit and leaves can be messy.
POPULUS EASTERN COTTON-WOOD, EASTERN POPLAR *Populus deltoides* QUAKING ASPEN ◄ *P. tremuloides*	Deciduous native trees with fluttering, flat-stemmed leaves and small, tufted, wind-borne seeds. P. deltoides *can grow to massive size, has stout branches and furrowed bark. P. tremuloides has creamy green bark and smaller leaves.*	●	*P. delt.* Height: 75–100' Spread: 50–75' *P. trem.* Height: 40–50' Spread: 20–30'	Clump-forming shade trees. Yellow foliage in autumn in P. tremuloides.	*P. delt.* 3 to 9 *P. trem.* 2 to 6	Full sun. Well-drained soil. Both prefer moist, even wet, soil, but will adapt to dry situations once established. Wood is not strong; trees are unsuited to areas with high winds. These are short-lived trees (50–70 years).
POTENTILLA SHRUBBY CINQUE-FOIL *Potentilla fruticosa*	Bushy, deciduous shrub with gray-green, palmately compound leaves that turn dark green by late summer, then yellow in autumn. Bright yellow, 5-petaled, 1-in. flowers look like small roses.	●	Height: 1–4' Spread: 2–5'	Border or massing shrub. Flowers from late spring to early autumn. Attractive foliage.	2 to 7	Full sun to very light shade. Well-drained, moist, humus-rich soil. Reduce mildew problems by planting where air circulation is good. Plants flower best in full sun.
PRUNUS DWARF FLOWERING ALMOND ◄ *Prunus glandulosa* FLOWERING ALMOND *P. triloba*	Deciduous shrubs grown for their 1- to 1½-in., pink or white flowers in single or double forms. P. glandulosa *has 1- to 3-in., lance-shaped leaves; those of the larger P. triloba are 1–2 in. long and have 3 lobes.*	○ ●	*P. gland.* Height: 4–5' Spread: 3–5' *P. triloba* Height: 12–15' Spread: 12–15'	Border or massing shrubs. Abundant pink or white flowers in spring.	*P. gland.* 4 to 9 *P. triloba* 3 to 8	Full sun. Well-drained, average soil. Flowering almond adapts to many conditions. These relatively short-lived species should be pruned after flowering. Tent caterpillars and scale insects can be a problem.
PRUNUS JAPANESE FLOWER-ING CHERRY *Prunus serrulata* HIGAN CHERRY ◄ *P. subhirtella*	Deciduous flowering trees with 2- to 5-in., pointed, toothed, oval leaves and abundant pink or white flowers borne in the spring. P. subhirtella *is the earliest blooming cherry. P. serrulata 'Kwanzan' is the hardiest of double-flowering types.*	○ ●	*P. serrul.* Height: 25–50' Spread: 20–40' *P. subhirt.* Height: 20–30' Spread: 15–30'	Specimen trees or large multistemmed shrubs. Pink or white flowers in mid-spring. Shiny, russet bark.	5 to 8	Full sun. Well-drained, average soil. Trees adapt to many conditions. These relatively short-lived species (30–50 years) may be pruned after flowering. Tent caterpillars and scale insects can be a problem.

		Flower Color	Height & Spread	Ornamental Features	Hardiness Zones	Growing Conditions
PSEUDOTSUGA DOUGLAS FIR *Pseudotsuga menziesii*	Large coniferous evergreen tree native to the West. This important timber tree makes a good specimen or shade tree. The 1-in., blue-green needles are flattened and somewhat soft. The 3-in. cones have forked bracts showing between scales.		Height: 50–100' Spread: 15–25'	Stately specimen tree. Pungent blue-green foliage. Interesting cones.	4 to 6	Full sun. Well-drained, moist, acid soil. Douglas fir grows best where humidity is high; protect from drying winds. Coastal varieties grow more rapidly than inland varieties.
PYRACANTHA SCARLET FIRETHORN *Pyracantha coccinea*	Evergreen shrub with narrow, dark green 1- to 2-in. leaves, grown as a free-standing shrub or espaliered to walls or trellises. Stems bear ¹⁄₂-in. spines and clusters of white, ¹⁄₃-in. flowers that produce red-orange, ¹⁄₄-in., berrylike fruits.	○	Height: 5–20' Spread: 5–10'	Border or wall-climbing shrub. Lustrous, evergreen leaves. Bright orange-red fruits from autumn into winter.	6 to 9	Full sun. Well-drained, acid soil. Firethorn grows best where humidity is high but air circulation is good. Fire blight, leaf blight, and fruit scab can be problems. Prune regularly in late winter to keep diseases under control.
PYRUS BRADFORD PEAR *Pyrus calleryana* 'Bradford'	Deciduous tree with a pear-shaped crown grown for its autumn color and abundant spring flowers. Leathery, lustrous, 2- to 3-in., egg-shaped leaves turn red or purple in autumn. Clusters of white, ¹⁄₃-in. flowers produce ¹⁄₂-in., applelike fruits.	○	Height: 25–40' Spread: 15–30'	Small lawn or street tree. White flowers in early to mid-spring. Red or purple autumn foliage.	4 to 8	Full sun. Ordinary, well-drained garden soil. This grows in a wide range of soil conditions. Prune in winter or early spring. Bradford pear is relatively resistant to fire blight.
QUERCUS WHITE OAK *Quercus alba*	Stately trees with broad crowns. This eastern native has highly variable, 6-in., round-lobed leaves that are dark green above and pale green below and turn brown in autumn. Bark is light gray and when mature has flaky, blocky ridges.	◐	Height: 50–80' Spread: 50–80'	Large shade or specimen tree. Attractive green foliage turns russet in autumn.	3 to 9	Full sun. Deep, moist, well-drained soil that is slightly acid. This large tree is difficult to transplant and grows slowly. Transplant when small as a balled-and-burlapped tree.
QUERCUS BUR OAK, MOSSY-CUP OAK *Quercus macrocarpa*	Massive tree native to the East and Midwest and bearing 4- to 10-in., irregularly lobed, wavy-edged, leathery leaves that are dark green above and gray below. The 1-in. acorns have a deep, fringed cap. Bark is dark and deeply furrowed.	◐	Height: 70–100' Spread: 75–90'	Large shade or specimen tree suitable for a spacious setting. Dark, grooved bark.	3 to 8	Full sun. Well-drained, even sandy, soil. This slow-growing tree tolerates limestone and alkaline soil. It also tolerates air pollution better than most oaks.

◀ *Indicates species shown*

Trees and Shrubs for American Gardens

			Flower Color	Height & Spread	Ornamental Features	Hardiness Zones	Growing Conditions
QUERCUS WILLOW OAK *Quercus phellos*	Deciduous tree with narrow, 2- to 5-in., willowlike leaves that turn from bright green to yellow in autumn. Leaves may persist into winter where it is mild.		●	Height: 40–80' Spread: 30–40'	Shade tree. Fine, bright green foliage in summer, golden yellow in autumn.	5 to 9	Full sun. Poorly drained, moist, acid soil. Loamy-clay soil is ideal. Willow oak grows faster than most other oaks and is relatively easy to transplant.
QUERCUS RED OAK *Quercus rubra*	Deciduous tree with 5- to 8-in., sharp lobed, spine-tipped leaves. The crown is rounded when grown in the open, but flat-topped with a more columnar trunk when grown in groups. Acorns take 2 seasons to mature. Autumn foliage is red.		●	Height: 60–80' Spread: 40–50'	Shade or specimen tree. Lustrous russet or red foliage in autumn, sometimes remaining over winter.	3 to 9	Full sun. Well-drained, evenly moist, acid soil. Sandy loam is ideal. This is the most rapid-growing of all the oaks. It is easy to transplant.
QUERCUS LIVE OAK *Quercus virginiana*	Massive, evergreen oak with broadly spreading crown and leathery 1- to 3-in., narrowly oval leaves that are glossy, dark green above and lighter beneath. Dark bark breaks into rectangular plates with age.		●	Height: 40–80' Spread: 60–100'	Shade or specimen tree of considerable grandeur. Lustrous, evergreen leaves.	8 to 10	Full sun. Well-drained, ordinary garden soil. Live oak adapts to many soil conditions; it is native to the sandy soils of the southern Atlantic and Gulf coasts. It grows best where climate is hot and humid and tolerates salt spray.
RHODODEN-DRON CAROLINA RHODODENDRON *Rhododendron carolinianum* ROSEBAY RHODODENDRON *R. maximum*	Leathery-leaved evergreen shrubs that bear rounded clusters (trusses) of cup-shaped flowers. Both species have cultivars with flower colors in white, pink, rose, or lilac. R. carolinianum is low and rounded. R. maximum is quite tall.		○ ● ● ●	R. carolin. Height: 3–6' Spread: 4–8' R. maxim. Height: 4–20' Spread: 4–30'	Specimen or screen shrubs. Attractive flowers from mid-spring (R. carolinianum) to early summer (R. maximum).	R. carolin. 5 to 8 R. maxim. 4 to 7	Partial shade (in the North) to full shade (in the South). Both species require evenly moist, well-drained, acid soil that is rich in humus. Mulch to maintain even moisture. Protect from drying winter winds.
RHODODEN-DRON DEXTER HYBRID RHODODENDRON *Rhododendron* hybrids	Evergreen shrubs that are hybrids of R. fortunei and R. catawbiense and produce denser and larger, more fragrant flowers than most rhododendron species. Flowers generally are lavender, white, or pink. The elliptical leaves are leathery.		○ ● ●	Height: 6–10' Spread: 5–8'	Specimen or screen shrubs. Large clusters of attractive flowers in late spring.	5 to 8	Partial shade (in the North) to full shade (in the South). These hybrids require evenly moist, well-drained, acid soil that is rich in humus. Mulch to maintain even moisture. Protect from drying winter winds.

		Flower Color	Height & Spread	Ornamental Features	Hardiness Zones	Growing Conditions
RHODODEN-DRON KURUME AZALEA *Rhododendron* hybrids	Azalea hybrids with lustrous, evergreen leaves. (Most azaleas are deciduous shrubs.) Some cultivars have reddish leaves in winter. Funnel-shaped, 1- to 1½-in. flowers are rose, pink, salmon, white, or coral.	○ ● ● ●	Height: 3–6' Spread: 5–8'	Compact evergreen specimen or border shrubs with dense crowns. Small, tidy flowers in mid-spring.	6 to 9	Full sun (in the North) to partial shade (in the South). Evenly moist, well-drained, acid soil that is rich in humus. Mulch to maintain even moisture. Protect from drying winter winds. Old leaves are shed in spring.
RHODODEN-DRON EXBURY HYBRID AZALEA, KNAP HILL AZALEA *Rhododendron* hybrids	Deciduous shrubs with upright form and leaves that turn yellow, orange, or red in autumn. Many cultivars are available with 2- to 3-in. clusters of trumpet-shaped white, pink, yellow, orange, or red unscented flowers.	○ ● ○ ● ●	Height: 4–8' Spread: 4–8'	Specimen or border shrub with upright form. Abundant flowers in late spring. Autumn leaf color.	5 to 7	Full sun (in the North) to partial shade (in the South). Both types require evenly moist, well-drained, acid soil that is rich in humus. Mulch to maintain even moisture. Protect from dry winter winds.
RHODODEN-DRON GHENT HYBRID AZALEA *Rhododendron × gandavense*	Deciduous shrubs encompassing more than 300 cultivars. Most have long-tubed, fragrant, 1½- to 2½-in. flowers in pink, orange, yellow, red, white, or in combinations.	○ ● ○ ● ●	Height: 6–10' Spread: 6–8'	Specimen or tall border shrub. Fragrant flowers in early summer. Autumn leaf color.	5 to 7	Full sun (in the North) to partial shade (in the South). Requires evenly moist, well-drained, acid soil that is rich in humus. Mulch to maintain even moisture. Protect from drying winter winds. Grows best in cooler regions.
RHODODEN-DRON INDICA HYBRID AZALEA, SOUTHERN INDIAN HYBRID AZALEA *Rhododendron* hybrids	Relatively tender, evergreen shrubs often grown in greenhouses as winter potted plants for their 2- to 3-in., funnel-shaped flowers in red, white, or lavender. Cultivars are available in single- or double-flowered forms.	○ ● ●	Height: 6–10' Spread: 8–10'	Specimen or border shrub. Large, showy, colorful flowers in early to mid-spring.	8 to 9	Full sun (in cool areas) to partial shade (in hot areas). These require evenly moist, well-drained, acid soil that is rich in humus. Mulch to maintain even moisture. Protect from drying winter winds.
RHUS SMOOTH SUMAC *Rhus glabra* STAGHORN SUMAC ◄ *R. typhina*	Small native trees or large shrubs with smooth, stout twigs that bear 6- to 12-in., compound, toothed leaves. Leaves and twigs turn bright red in autumn. Both plants bear spires of showy, red-purple berries in autumn.	●	Height: 10–20' Spread: 6–12'	Rapid-growing screen or hedge. Brilliant crimson or orange autumn color. Spires of crimson berries in autumn.	2 to 9	Full sun to partial shade. Ordinary, well-drained, garden soil. Plants spread by root sprouts; with time they can become weedy.

◄ *Indicates species shown*

Trees and Shrubs for American Gardens

		Flower Color	Height & Spread	Ornamental Features	Hardiness Zones	Growing Conditions
ROSA MEIDILAND SHRUB ROSE *Rosa* hybrid RUGOSA ROSE *R. rugosa*	Shrubby roses with leathery, deciduous foliage and 3½-in., 5-petaled, fragrant, magenta, pink, or white flowers with bright gold centers. R. rugosa is an old-fashioned species. Meidilands are modern patented ones.	○ ◐ ●	Height: 3–6' Spread: 1–3'	Barrier hedge or border. Summer-long season of magenta, white, or pink flowers.	4 to 9	Full sun to light shade. Well-drained soil with ample moisture and organic matter. However, plants tolerate windy and salty environments and are among the best roses for seaside plantings.
SALIX GOLDEN WEEPING WILLOW *Salix alba* var. *tristis* WEEPING WILLOW *S. babylonica*	Deciduous trees with thin, drooping branches that sweep to the ground. Branches of the hardier S. alba var. tristis are distinctly yellow gold. Narrow, 3- to 6-in. leaves emerge in mid-spring simultaneously with yellow catkin flowers.		S. alba Height: 50–75' Spread: 40–60' S. babyl. Height: 30–40' Spread: 30–40'	Specimen tree or screen. Drooping, fountain form of branches. Golden yellow branches of S. alba.	S. alba 4 to 9 S. babyl. 7 to 9	Full sun. Moist, acid soil. Both species adapt to all but alkaline conditions. Roots travel far and can break sewer or septic tank lines; be careful where you site trees. Weak wood is prone to storm damage.
SALIX PUSSY WILLOW *Salix discolor*	Deciduous shrub or small tree native to eastern wetlands. In late winter to early spring flower buds burst, producing attractive, short, fuzzy catkins. Force in winter by bringing twigs indoors. Undersides of the 3-in. leaves are blue green.	◐	Height: 10–20' Spread: 6–12'	Border or screen shrub or tree. Attractive, fuzzy catkin flowers in late winter or early spring.	3 to 7	Full sun. Moist, humus-rich soil. A native of very wet conditions, pussy willow also tolerates evenly moist, well-drained conditions.
SARCOCOCCA SWEET BOX *Sarcococca hookerana*	Evergreen shrub with glossy, 2- to 4-in., pointed, narrow leaves borne on slender green twigs and branches. Like its relative, boxwood, it has a sharply aromatic odor when bruised. Small, white fragrant flowers produce ¼-in. black fruits with pits.	○	Height: 2–6' Spread: 4–6'	Evergreen ground cover or hedge (depending on cultivar). Lustrous dark green foliage. Fragrant spring flowers.	6 to 9	Partial to full shade. Well-drained, fertile, humus-rich, evenly moist soil. Prune deadwood in early spring.
SASSAFRAS SASSAFRAS *Sassafras albidum*	Deciduous eastern native tree often grown in naturalized settings. The aromatic 3- to 7-in. leaves may be unlobed or have 1 or 2 side lobes. Leaves turn bright red orange in autumn. Red-brown bark becomes furrowed with age.	◐	Height: 30–60' Spread: 20–40'	Specimen or woodland edging tree. Handsome red foliage in autumn. Attractive bark.	5 to 9	Full sun. Moist, well-drained, humus-rich soil. Prune deadwood in winter. With time these trees will spread by root sprouts, which should be pruned to the ground if a thicket is not desired.

			Flower Color	Height & Spread	Ornamental Features	Hardiness Zones	Growing Conditions
	SKIMMIA SKIMMIA *Skimmia japonica*	Evergreen, domed shrub having 2½- to 5-in., oblong leaves clustered at the ends of twigs. Leaves are medium green above, yellow green below. Female plants bear terminal clusters of small, fragrant, white flowers that produce ⅓-in. red fruits.	○	Height: 3–4' Spread: 3–4'	Small border or massing shrub. Glossy evergreen foliage. White flowers. Small red fruits.	7 to 8	Partial shade to full shade. Moist, humus-rich, well-drained, acid soil. Purchase male and female plants to guarantee fruit production.
	SOPHORA JAPANESE PAGODA TREE *Sophora japonica*	Deciduous flowering tree with rounded crown. Twigs bear lustrous, 6- to 10-in., compound leaves and 8- to 12-in. clusters of creamy white, pealike flowers. Pod fruits are 2–4 in. long. Gray bark becomes deeply furrowed with age.	○	Height: 50–75' Spread: 50–60'	Specimen or shade tree. Interesting foliage. Spectacular white flowers in summer.	5 to 8	Full sun. Well-drained, evenly moist, humus-rich, loamy soil. Once established, this tree is quite drought tolerant.
	SORBUS KOREAN MOUNTAIN ASH *Sorbus alnifolia*	Deciduous tree with rich green, 2- to 4-in., oval, toothed leaves that turn yellow orange in autumn. The 2- to 3-in. clusters of ¾-in., white, 5-petaled flowers produce clusters of ¼-in., vermilion or scarlet fruits that persist into winter.	○	Height: 40–50' Spread: 20–30'	Specimen tree for lawns. Flower clusters in mid-spring. Good autumn color. Attractive fruits autumn into winter.	3 to 7	Full sun. Average, well-drained, slightly acid soil. This tree is quite adaptable but will not tolerate air pollution. Prune in late winter or early spring.
	SPIRAEA BUMALDA SPIREA *Spiraea × bumalda* 'Anthony Waterer' JAPANESE SPIREA ◀ *S. japonica*	Compact deciduous shrubs that bear 4- to 6-in. clusters of tiny, 5-petaled, pink or white flowers resembling miniature roses. Low-growing S. × bumalda 'Anthony Waterer' has deep pink flowers; larger S. japonica has white to rose blooms.	○ ●	S. × bum. Height: 2–4' Spread: 4–6' S. jap. Height: 4–5' Spread: 4–6'	Massing or border shrubs. Lovely flower clusters in late spring (S. japonica) or summer (S. × bumalda).	3 to 8	Full sun to light shade. Moist, fertile, well-drained soil. These shrubs adapt to most conditions as long as drainage is adequate.
	STEWARTIA TALL STEWARTIA ◀ *Stewartia monadelpha* JAPANESE STEWARTIA *S. pseudocamellia*	Deciduous shrubs or small trees with fragrant, white, 5-petaled, camellia-like flowers. Leaves turn red purple in autumn. S. monadelpha has smaller leaves and flowers and smooth, red, peeling bark. S. pseudocamellia has red, flaking bark.	○	S. monad. Height: 30–40' Spread: 15–25' S. pseud. Height: 40–50' Spread: 25–35'	Specimen trees. Beautiful white flowers from mid- to late summer. Red-purple foliage in autumn.	6 to 8	Full sun to partial shade. Moist, well-drained, humus-rich, acid soil. Neither species grows well in poorly drained soil.

◀ *Indicates species shown*

Trees and Shrubs for American Gardens

		Flower Color	Height & Spread	Ornamental Features	Hardiness Zones	Growing Conditions
STYRAX JAPANESE SNOWBELL *Styrax japonicus* FRAGRANT SNOWBELL *S. obassia*	Small deciduous trees that bear fragrant, white, bell-shaped flowers. S. japonicus has individual ³/₄-in. flowers. S. obassia has larger leaves, and its highly fragrant flowers are gathered into 6- to 8-in. erect clusters. Smooth bark cracks with age.	○	Height: 20–30' Spread: 20–30'	Specimen or border trees. White flowers in late spring to early summer. Attractive gray bark.	5 to 8	Full sun to partial shade. Moist, well-drained, humus-rich, acid soil. Prune to shape desired in late winter.
SYRINGA JAPANESE TREE LILAC, TREE LILAC *Syringa reticulata*	Large shrub or small deciduous tree with dark green, pointed, oval, 2- to 5-in. leaves and 6- to 12-in. clusters of white flowers with a pungent fragrance reminiscent of privet. Bark is red brown and cherrylike, with horizontal streaks.	○	Height: 20–30' Spread: 15–20'	Specimen or border tree. White flowers in early summer. Attractive bark.	3 to 7	Full sun to light shade. Loose, well-drained, acid soil. Plant in well-ventilated site to lessen mildew and blight problems. Prune old wood and excess sprouts in late winter; prune old flowers after they have withered.
SYRINGA COMMON LILAC *Syringa vulgaris*	A very popular, old-fashioned deciduous shrub bearing fragrant, tubular flower clusters in 4- to 8-in. panicles. Dark green, 2- to 4-in., heart-shaped leaves are attached in pairs to gray twigs. Hundreds of cultivars are available.	○ ●	Height: 10–15' Spread: 5–10'	Border or mass planting shrub. Fragrant, mid-spring flowers in many colors.	3 to 7	Full sun to light shade. Neutral soil rich in humus. Plant in well-ventilated site to lessen mildew problems. Prune old wood and excess sprouts in late winter; prune old flowers after they have withered.
TABEBUIA GOLDEN TRUMPET TREE *Tabebuia chrysotricha*	Small, tropical, semievergreen tree with a rounded crown and a profusion of golden yellow, 3- to 4-in., tubular flowers in mid-spring during the brief period when the tree is leafless. The palmately compound leaves are fuzzy underneath.	●	Height: 25–30' Spread: 25–30'	Specimen tree. Abundant golden flowers streaked with maroon in mid-spring.	10 to 11	Full sun. Sandy, well-drained soil. Golden trumpet tree responds well to fertilizer and periodic moisture, but is quite drought tolerant once established.
TAXUS ENGLISH YEW *Taxus baccata* JAPANESE YEW *T. cuspidata*	Large, multistemmed coniferous evergreen shrubs or trees with ¹/₂- to 1-in., flat needles that are dark green above and lime green below. Female trees bear bright red, fleshy fruits surrounding a poisonous black seed. Bark is red brown and flaky.		T. bacca. Height: 4–40' Spread: 5–15' T. cuspid. Height: 4–20' Spread: 10–20'	Hedge or screen trees. Handsome evergreen foliage.	T. bacca. 6 to 7 T. cuspid. 4 to 7	Sun or shade. Fertile, evenly moist, well-drained, acid soil. Yews will not tolerate soggy soil. Protect from drying winter winds. Deer browsing may be a problem.

			Flower Color	Height & Spread	Ornamental Features	Hardiness Zones	Growing Conditions
	THUJA AMERICAN ARBOR-VITAE ◄ *Thuja occidentalis* ORIENTAL ARBOR-VITAE *T. orientalis (Platycladus orientalis)*	Evergreen coniferous trees with dense crowns of scale-like leaves in flattened sprays. Leaves are dark olive green above and yellow green below; they are pungent when bruised. T. orientalis is smaller with finer foliage.		T. occi. Height: 40–50' Spread: 10–15' T. orien. Height: 15–25' Spread: 8–12'	Screen or hedge trees. Attractive sprays of flattened, evergreen foliage. Fibrous, shaggy bark.	T. occi. 3 to 7 T. orien. 6 to 9	Full sun. Deep, moist, well-drained soil. Trees tolerate alkaline soil. Prune to remove any winter-killed foliage. Don't plant next to buildings; spreading roots can crack masonry. Bagworms and leaf miners can be problems.
	TILIA LITTLELEAF LINDEN ◄ *Tilia cordata* SILVER LINDEN *T. tomentosa*	Deciduous shade or avenue trees with heart-shaped leaves and fragrant, light yellow flowers that attract bees. T. tomentosa has 2- to 5-in. leaves that are white below. T. cordata has 2- to 3-in. leaves that turn yellow in autumn.	○ ●	Height: 50–70' Spread: 25–40'	Shade or hedge tree. Fragrant flowers in late spring. Yellow autumn foliage in T. cordata.	T. corda. 3 to 8 T. tomen. 5 to 8	Full sun. Moist, well-drained, fertile, alkaline, humus-rich soil. Both species respond well to additions of lime. T. tomentosa is drought tolerant once established. Aphids and foliage-feeding insects can be problems.
	TSUGA CANADA HEMLOCK, EASTERN HEMLOCK *Tsuga canadensis*	Graceful, coniferous evergreen tree native to the East. The branches of this loosely pyramidal species droop slightly with age. Small ($\frac{1}{2}$-in.), flat, very dark green needles have white stripes below. Cones are oval and $\frac{1}{2}$ in. long.		Height: 50–80' Spread: 20–40'	Magnificent screen, or hedge specimen tree. Beautiful sprays of green foliage.	3 to 7	Full sun to shade. Well-drained, moist soil rich in humus. Hemlock does not tolerate excessively dry soil or windy sites. Trees are susceptible to woolly adelgid insect attack.
	ULMUS CHINESE ELM, LACEBARK ELM *Ulmus parvifolia*	Deciduous tree with mottled, peeling bark and thick, 1- to $2\frac{1}{2}$-in., pointed, oval, toothed leaves with fuzzy undersides. Inconspicuous late-summer flowers produce $\frac{1}{3}$-in., flat, light green fruits in early autumn.	●	Height: 40–50' Spread: 40–50'	Shade and specimen tree. Peeling, lacy bark with various colored patches.	5 to 9	Full sun. Moist, well-drained, fertile soil. This tough, beautiful tree is fairly resistant to Dutch elm disease and elm leaf and Japanese beetles.
	VIBURNUM FRAGRANT VIBURNUM, KOREAN SPICE VIBURNUM *Viburnum carlesii*	Deciduous flowering shrub whose pairs of velvety, dark green, 1- to 4-in., heart-shaped leaves have irregularly toothed edges. Perfumed flowers in 2- to 3-in. clusters are pink in bud, but open to display tubular white petals.	○ ●	Height: 4–6' Spread: 4–6'	Border or foundation planting. Very fragrant, tidy white flower clusters in mid-spring.	4 to 8	Full sun to partial shade. Well-drained, evenly moist, slightly acid soil. To reduce root rot, avoid soggy soils. Prune after flowering in early summer. This is a slow-growing shrub.

◄ Indicates species shown

Trees and Shrubs for American Gardens

			Flower Color	Height & Spread	Ornamental Features	Hardiness Zones	Growing Conditions
	VIBURNUM LINDEN VIBURNUM *Viburnum dilatatum*	Deciduous flowering shrub. Lustrous, dark green, 2- to 5-in. leaves turn russet in autumn. Flat, 3- to 5-in.-wide clusters of white flowers produce 1/3-in., bright red fruits that persist into winter.	○	Height: 8–10' Spread: 6–8'	Specimen and border shrub. White flowers in late spring. Bright red fruits in autumn. Russet autumn foliage.	5 to 8	Full sun to partial shade. Slightly acid, moist, well-drained soil. Avoid water-logged soil; viburnums are prone to rot and diseases if drainage is inadequate.
	VIBURNUM DOUBLEFILE VIBURNUM *Viburnum plicatum var. tomentosum*	Deciduous shrub with horizontal branches and small, white tubular flowers in flat, lacy clusters. Flowers precede the midsummer appearance of black, berry-like fruits. Pairs of dark green leaves turn reddish purple in autumn.	○	Height: 7–10' Spread: 9–12'	Specimen, screen, and border shrub. Showy clusters of flowers in mid-spring. Berrylike fruits in summer.	5 to 8	Full sun to partial shade. Well-drained soil that is moist and fertile. Avoid waterlogged soil; viburnums are prone to rot and diseases if drainage is inadequate.
	VITEX CHASTE TREE *Vitex agnus-castus*	Deciduous shrub or small tree with 6- to 8-in., palmately compound, sometimes toothed, dull green leaves that are aromatic when bruised. Dense spikes of lilac-blue, white, pink, or lavender flowers are fragrant and up to 12 in. long.	○ ◐ ◐ ●	Height: 5–15' Spread: 8–15'	Specimen or border tree. Showy, perfumed flower clusters all summer long.	6 to 7	Full sun. Average garden soil. Chaste tree is very adaptable to even poor, infertile soil, but responds well to additional fertilizer. It can withstand severe pruning.
	WEIGELA WEIGELA *Weigela florida*	Deciduous shrub with a spreading form. Pairs of 2- to 4-in., lance-shaped leaves have finely toothed edges. Branches bear a profusion of 1-in., rosy pink, funnel-shaped flowers with pale pink throats. Cultivars come with red or white flowers.	○ ◐ ●	Height: 6–9' Spread: 9–12'	Border or specimen shrub. Showy pink flowers bloom abundantly in late spring, sporadically into autumn.	5 to 9	Full sun to partial shade. Well-drained, evenly moist soil. Avoid waterlogged soil. Prune in early spring to remove dead wood and keep shrub growing vigorously.
	ZELKOVA JAPANESE ZELKOVA *Zelkova serrata*	Medium-sized deciduous tree with a vase-shaped crown and sharp-toothed, oval leaves that turn from deep green to deep golden orange in autumn. The gray bark is smooth at first and becomes cracked with age.	◐	Height: 50–75' Spread: 20–40'	Shade or specimen tree. Yellow-orange autumn foliage. Attractive bark texture.	5 to 8	Full sun to light shade. Moist, well-drained, ordinary garden soil. Tree needs moisture to become established, but thereafter is quite tolerant of drought and wind.

Plant Hardiness Zone Map

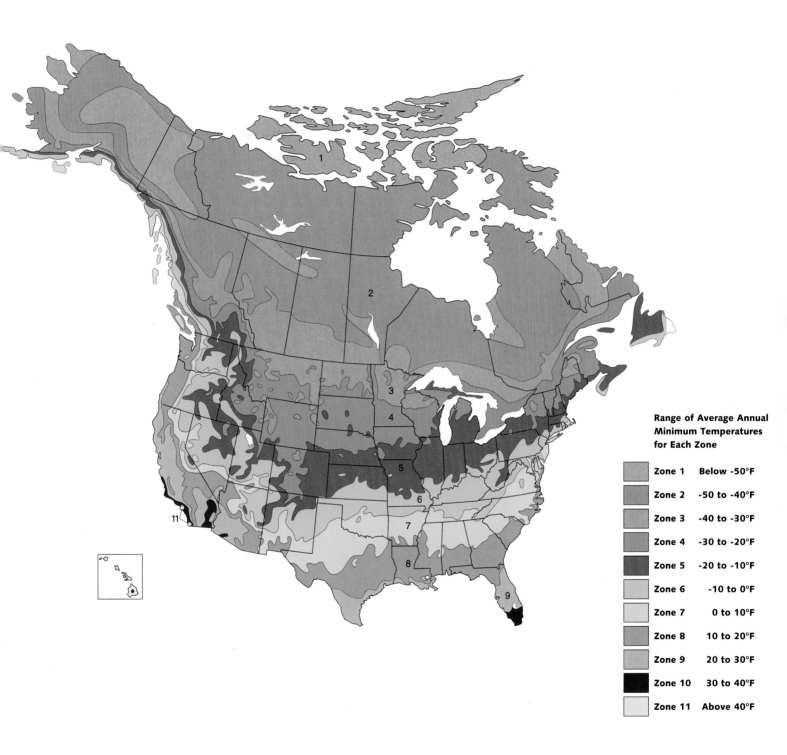

Range of Average Annual Minimum Temperatures for Each Zone

Zone	Range
Zone 1	Below -50°F
Zone 2	-50 to -40°F
Zone 3	-40 to -30°F
Zone 4	-30 to -20°F
Zone 5	-20 to -10°F
Zone 6	-10 to 0°F
Zone 7	0 to 10°F
Zone 8	10 to 20°F
Zone 9	20 to 30°F
Zone 10	30 to 40°F
Zone 11	Above 40°F

Resources for Trees and Shrubs

There are many dependable mail-order suppliers that can be helpful for landscaping with trees and shrubs. A selection is included here. Most have catalogues available upon request (some charge a fee). An excellent source of further resources is Gardening by Mail by Barbara J. Barton. Updates on each edition are provided three times a year, available through subscription (forms provided in back of book); a new edition comes out every few years. To obtain this book check your local bookstore or contact the publisher: Houghton Mifflin Co., 222 Berkeley Street, Boston, MA 02116. Telephone: (617) 351-5000.

Nurseries

Appalachian Gardens
P.O. Box 82
Waynesboro, PA 17268
717-762-4312
Many unusual trees and shrubs for your landscape.

W. Atlee Burpee
300 Park Avenue
Warminster, PA 18974
215-674-4900
Wide variety of shrubs and trees.

Famous & Historic Trees
8555 Plummer Road
Jacksonville, FL 32219
800-320-8733
Specializes in trees propagated from historical stock.

Forestfarm
990 Thetherow Road
Williams, OR 97544-9599
503-846-7269
Extensive selection of nursery-grown trees and shrubs.

Gurney's Seed & Nursery Co.
110 Capital Street
Yankton, SD 57079
605-665-1930
Large selection of fruit and nut trees as well as some ornamentals.

Henry Field's Seed & Nursery Co.
415 N. Burnett Street
Shenandoah, IA 51602
605-665-4491
Hedges, trees, shrubs, and supplies.

J.L. Hudson, Seedsman
P.O. Box 1058
Redwood City, CA 94064
No telephone calls.
Seeds for hundreds of varieties of flowering shrubs and trees. Also seed exchanges.

Inter-State Nurseries
1800 Hamilton Road
Bloomington, IL 61704
309-663-9551
Fruit trees, hedges, roses, ornamental trees and shrubs.

Kelly Nurseries
1706 Morrissey Drive
Bloomington, IL 61704
309-663-9551
General nursery stock, including fruit and nut trees.

Lake County Nursery, Inc.
Route 84
P.O. Box 122
Perry, OH 44081-0122
216-259-5571
Wide selection of nursery stock for specific features and growing conditions.

Henry Leuthardt
Nurseries, Inc.
P.O. Box 666
Montauk Highway
East Moriches,
NY 11940-0666
516-878-1387
Espaliered apple and pear trees, and other fruits.

Mellinger's Inc.
2310 W. South Range Road
North Lima, OH 44452
800-321-7444
Ornamental trees and shrubs, fruit trees, and supplies.

Miller Nurseries
5060 West Lake Road
Canandaigua, NY 14424
800-836-9630
Fruit trees and ornamental trees and shrubs.

Northwoods Retail Nursery
27635 S. Oglesby Road
Canby, OR 97013-9528
503-266-5432
Fruit trees and unique ornamental trees and shrubs.

Owen Farms
Route 3, Box 158A
Ripley, TN 38063
901-635-1588
Trees, shrubs, and perennials, including bonsai.

Roslyn Nursery
211 Burrs Lane
Dix Hills, NY 11746
516-643-9347
Azaleas, rhododendrons, conifers, and rare trees and shrubs.

F.W. Schumacher Co.
36 Spring Hill Road
Sandwich,
MA 02563-1023
508-888-0659
Large selection of tree and shrub seeds.

Spring Hill Nurseries
6523 N. Galena Road
Peoria, IL 61632
309-689-3828
Trees and flowering shrubs as well as perennials.

Stark Bro's Nurseries
P.O. Box 10
Louisiana,
MO 63353-0010
800-325-4180
Many fruit varieties, also flowering shrubs and ornamental trees.

Wayside Gardens
1 Garden Lane
Hodges, SC 29695-0001
800-845-1124
Ornamental trees and flowering shrubs as well as ground covers and perennials.

White Flower Farm
P.O. Box 50
Litchfield,
CT 06759-0050
203-496-9600
Assorted flowering shrubs
along with bulbs, annuals,
and perennials. Espaliered
apple trees.

Woodlanders, Inc.
1128 Colleton Avenue
Aiken, SC 29801
803-648-7522
Nursery-grown trees and
shrubs, both native and
exotic.

Evergreen Specialties

Camellia Forest Nursery
125 Carolina Forest
Chapel Hill, NC 27516
No telephone calls.
Hardy camellias, ever-
greens, and dwarf
conifers.

Siskiyou Rare
Plant Nursery
2825 Cummings Road
Medford, OR 97501-1524
503-772-6846
Special selection of dwarf
conifers.

Vans Pines, Inc.
7550 144th Avenue
West Olive, MI 49460
800-888-7337
Large selection of ever-
green trees, some decidu-
ous trees and shrubs.

Regional Specialties

The Banana Tree
715 Northampton Street
Easton, PA 18042
215-253-9589
Rare and unusual tropical
seeds.

Baycreek Gardens
P.O. Box 339
Grayson, GA 30221
404-339-1600
Rhododendrons, azaleas,
conifers, and shrubs for
the southern landscape.

Brudy's Exotics
P.O. Box 820874
Houston, TX 77282-0874
800-926-7333
Seeds and stock for tropical and exotic trees and
shrubs.

Corn Hill Nursery, Ltd.
R.R. 5
Petitcodiac, N.B.,
Canada E0A 2H0
506-756-3635
Hardy trees and shrubs
for cooler regions.

Crockett's Tropical Plants
P.O. Box 2746
Harlingen, TX 78551
210-423-1747
Tropical flowering shrubs.

Musser Forests, Inc.
P.O. Box 340
Indiana, PA 15701-0340
412-465-5685
Northern-grown evergreen
and hardwood seedlings,
ornamental shrubs, and
ground covers.

Supplies & Accessories

Country Home Products
P.O. Box 89
Ferry Road
Charlotte, VT 05445
800-446-8746
Mowers, trimmers, clip-
pers, composters, and var-
ious garden tools.

Earth-Rite
Zook & Ranck, Inc.
RD 1, Box 243
Gap, PA 17527
800-332-4171
Fertilizers and soil amend-
ments for landscapes.

Garden Way, Inc.
102nd St. & 9th Avenue
Troy, NY 12180
800-833-6990
Rotary tillers, power
equipment, and garden
carts.

Gardener's Eden
P.O. Box 7303
San Francisco, CA 94120
800-822-9600
Many items appropriate
for gardeners, including
outdoor containers, tools,
and accessories.

Gardener's Supply Co.
128 Intervale Road
Burlington, VT 05401
800-876-5520
A wide selection of gar-
dening products.

Gardens Alive!
5100 Schenley Place
Lawrenceburg, IN 47025
812-537-8650
Beneficial insects and a
complete line of supplies
for organic gardening.

Kemp Company
160 Koser Road
Lititz, PA 17543
800-441-5367
Shredders, chippers, and
other power equipment.

Kinsman Company, Inc.
River Road
Point Pleasant,
PA 18950
800-733-5613
Stakes, supports, arbors,
tools, and supplies.

A.M. Leonard, Inc.
P.O. Box 816
Piqua, OH 45356-0816
800-543-8955
Nursery and landscape
tools and supplies.

Walt Nicke Co.
P.O. Box 433
36 McLeod Lane
Topsfield, MA 01983
800-822-4114
Over 300 tools and
products.

Plow & Hearth
P.O. Box 830
Orange, VA 22960
800-866-6072
Gardening tools and prod-
ucts as well as garden
ornaments and furniture.

Ringer Corporation
9959 Valley View Road
Eden Prairie, MN 55344
612-941-4180
Organic soil amendments,
beneficial insects, and garden tools.

Smith & Hawken
2 Arbor Lane
Box 6900
Florence, KY 41022-6900
800-776-3336
Well-crafted tools as well
as containers, supplies,
and furniture.

Index

Photo Credits

200
Slow Cooker
Creations

Stephanie Ashcraft and Janet Eyring

GIBBS SMITH
TO ENRICH AND INSPIRE HUMANKIND

This book is dedicated to busy women everywhere!
—S.A. and J.E.

First Edition
14 13 12 11 10   10 9 8 7 6 5 4 3 2

Published by
Gibbs Smith
P.O. Box 667
Layton, Utah 84041

Orders: 1.800.748.5439
www.gibbs-smith.com

Designed by Debra McQuiston
Printed and bound in China
Gibbs Smith books are printed on either recycled, 100% post-consumer waste, FSC-certified papers or on paper produced from a 100% certified sustainable forest/controlled wood source.

Library of Congress Cataloging-in-Publication Data
Ashcraft, Stephanie.
  200 slow cooker creations / Stephanie Ashcraft and Janet Eyring. — 1st ed.
      p. cm.
  ISBN-13: 978-1-4236-1702-0
  ISBN-10: 1-4236-1702-9
  1. Electric cookery, Slow. I. Eyring, Janet. II. Title. III. Title: Two hundred slow cooker creations.
  TX827.A84 2010
  641.5'884—dc22
                                                    2010006854

Contents

Helpful
Hints

1. For healthier versions of slow cooker meals, use reduced-fat soups and reduced-fat or light sour cream and cream cheese. Ground turkey can be used in place of ground beef.

2. Ground beef or turkey should be browned and drained before adding to slow cooker.

3. Fresh milk, cream, sour cream, and cream cheese should be added during the last hour of cooking to prevent curdling. Evaporated milk does not curdle and can be substituted for fresh milk in most recipes.

4. Long-grain converted rice is recommended for rice dishes. Do not overcook these recipes or rice will become mushy.

5. To test the cooking temperature of a slow cooker, fill it $3/4$ full of water, cover, and turn on high heat for 4 hours. With an instant heat thermometer, test water immediately after lid is removed. Temperature should be at least 180 degrees. If it is lower, we recommend replacing the slow cooker. If it is higher, check all recipes for doneness after 3 hours of cooking.

6. As a general rule, lifting the lid off the slow cooker lengthens the cooking time by 15 to 30 minutes.

7. Stirring is generally not necessary until time to serve.

8. Your slow cooker should be at least half full to ensure proper cooking. If over $3/4$ full, additional cooking time may be needed.

9. Recipes that contain raw poultry or beef should cook a minimum of 3 hours on high heat. Combinations of raw meat and fresh vegetables should cook at least 4 hours on high heat.

10. To make cleanup easier, spray the inside of the slow cooker stoneware with nonstick cooking spray before adding ingredients.

11. At cleanup, cool the stoneware liner somewhat before adding water; this will prevent cracking.

12. Adapting favorite oven recipes to a slow cooker:

Conventional Oven Baking Time	Slow Cooker High Cooking Time	Slow Cooker Low Cooking Time
15–30 mins.	$1\frac{1}{2}$–2 hours	4–6 hours
35–40 mins.	3–4 hours	6–10 hours
50 mins. – 3 hours	4–6 hours	8–18 hours

One hour on high heat is equal to 2–$2\frac{1}{2}$ hours on low heat. (High heat = 275 degrees; low heat = 200 degrees. Heat varies from brand to brand.)

13. If your stoneware is removable, never place it on a hot stovetop burner.

14. Root vegetables (onions, carrots, potatoes, turnips) take longer to cook than meat. Place vegetables around sides of slow cooker so they get the most direct heat.

15. Tough, inexpensive meat cuts work well. The moist, gentle heat slowly tenderizes these cuts as they cook.

16. Don't add more liquid than a recipe calls for, as liquid is retained. It there's too much liquid at the end of cooking time and you want to thicken it, stir in some instant mashed potato flakes, instant tapioca, flour, or cornstarch mixed with water.

17. Prepared jarred garlic may be substituted for minced garlic.

18. Fresh chopped onion can be used in place of dried minced onion. One medium fresh onion equals ½ cup dried.

19. Recipes can be assembled and stored in the refrigerator the night before (unless they call for uncooked pasta). In the morning, place cold stoneware in cold electrical base. DO NOT PREHEAT ELECTRICAL BASE. Once stoneware is in place, turn to preferred heat setting, and cook for maximum recipe cooking time.

20. To remove scratches from stoneware, use Bon Ami or vinegar and baking soda. Baking soda also works well to clean the electrical base. DO NOT SUBMERGE ELECTRICAL BASE IN WATER.

21. When baking breads or cakes, place 6–8 paper towels across the top of the slow cooker stoneware and then place the lid on top. This prevents the breads or cakes from becoming soggy.

22. Searing meat before adding it to the slow cooker isn't necessary, but it does add a richer taste.

Happy slow cooking!

Beverages

Hot Chocolate

Makes 10–15 servings

4–5 cups nonfat dry milk
$1/2$–$3/4$ cup baking cocoa
$3/4$–1 cup sugar
2 teaspoons vanilla
11 cups water
Whipped cream
    (optional)
Mini chocolate chips
    (optional)

Combine all ingredients except whipped cream and chocolate chips in a $4^1/_2$- to 6-quart slow cooker. Cover and cook on low heat for 3–4 hours, stirring occasionally. Serve each cup topped with whipped cream and chocolate chips, if desired.

Mallow-Mint Hot Chocolate

Makes 10–15 servings

4–5 cups nonfat dry milk
$1/2$–$3/4$ cup baking cocoa
$3/4$–1 cup sugar
2 teaspoons mint extract
11 cups water
Miniature marshmallows

Combine all ingredients except marshmallows in a $4^1/_2$- to 6-quart slow cooker. Cover and cook on low heat for 3–4 hours, stirring occasionally. Serve each cup with marshmallows sprinkled over top.

Almond Hot Chocolate

Makes 10–15 *servings*

4–5 cups nonfat dry milk
$^1/_2$–$^3/_4$ cup baking cocoa
$^3/_4$ cup sugar
2 teaspoons almond
    extract
11 cups water
Whipped cream
    (optional)
Cinnamon (optional)

Combine all ingredients except whipped cream and cinnamon in a $4^1/_2$- to 6-quart slow cooker. Cover and cook on low heat for 3–4 hours, stirring occasionally. Serve each cup topped with whipped cream and a dash of cinnamon, if desired.

Rich Holiday Cocoa

Makes 12 *servings*

10 cups milk
$^3/_4$ cup sugar
$^3/_4$ cup cocoa
$^1/_2$ teaspoon salt
2 cups hot water
Candy canes
Miniature marshmallows

Pour milk into a $4^1/_2$- to 6-quart slow cooker and turn on high heat. Mix together the sugar, cocoa, salt, and hot water in a heavy saucepan. Boil for 3 minutes, stirring often. Pour into milk and stir. Cover and cook on high heat for 2–$2^1/_2$ hours, stirring occasionally. Serve each cup with a candy cane and marsh-mallows sprinkled over top.

Strawberry-Banana Apple Cider

Makes 16 servings

**1 gallon apple cider or
apple juice
2 cinnamon sticks
1 small box strawberry-
banana gelatin**

Pour apple cider into a 4$\frac{1}{2}$- to 6-quart slow cooker. Add the cinnamon sticks. Cover and cook on high heat for 3 hours. Stir in the gelatin until dissolved. Cover and cook on high heat for 1 hour more. Turn to low heat to keep warm and remove cinnamon sticks before serving.

NOTE: Try strawberry, raspberry, or peach gelatin in place of the strawberry-banana for more great tastes.

Tropical Delight

Makes 9 servings

1 (64-ounce) bottle
   Hawaiian Punch
1 (8-ounce) can
   pineapple slices,
   juice reserved
1 whole nutmeg
2 cinnamon sticks

Pour punch into a 3½- to 5-quart slow cooker. Add pineapple juice from can; set pineapple slices aside. Add the nutmeg and cinnamon sticks to juice. Cover and cook on low heat for 3–4 hours. Before serving, float pineapple slices on top of punch.

Spicy Peach Punch

Makes 9 servings

1 (46-ounce) bottle
   peach nectar
2½ cups orange juice
1 cinnamon stick
5 whole cloves
²/₃ cup light brown sugar
1 tablespoon lime juice

Combine peach nectar and orange juice in a 2½- to 4-quart slow cooker. Tie cinnamon stick and cloves in a cheesecloth and add to the juices. Cover and cook on low heat for 4 hours or high heat for 2 hours. Stir in brown sugar and lime juice until sugar dissolves. Turn to low heat to keep warm and remove cheesecloth before serving.

Hot Cranberry Punch

Makes 8–10 servings

4 cups unsweetened
   pineapple juice
4 cups cranberry juice
   cocktail
1/2 cup firmly packed
   brown sugar
1/2 teaspoon ground
   cloves
1 cinnamon stick
1 cup water

Combine all ingredients in a 3¹/2- to 5-quart slow cooker. Cover and cook on low heat for at least 4 hours, stirring occasionally. When ready to serve, remove cinnamon stick.

Sweet Cherry Cider

Makes 10–15 servings

3½ quarts apple cider
2 cinnamon sticks
1 small box cherry
    gelatin

Pour cider in a 4½- to 6-quart slow cooker. Add the cinnamon sticks. Cover and cook on high heat for 3 hours. Stir in the gelatin. Cover and leave on high heat for 1 hour more, until gelatin dissolves, stirring once or twice. Turn to low heat to keep warm and remove cinnamon sticks before serving.

NOTE: For a more intense cherry flavor, add a second box of gelatin.

Autumn Brew

Makes 16 servings

1 gallon apple juice
1 cup orange juice
2 cinnamon sticks
5 whole cloves
4–5 orange slices,
    without seeds

Pour juices into a 4½- to 6-quart slow cooker. Add the cinnamon sticks, cloves, and orange slices. Cover and cook on high heat for 3–4 hours. Turn to low heat to keep warm and remove cinnamon sticks, cloves, and orange slices before serving.

Fruity Holiday Wassail

Makes 12–15 *servings*

3 (3-inch) sticks
   cinnamon
2 teaspoons ground
   cloves
8 cups water
3/4 cup frozen cranberry
   juice cocktail
   concentrate
3/4 cup frozen raspberry
   juice concentrate
3/4 cup frozen apple
   juice concentrate
1/2 cup sugar
1/3 cup lemon juice
1 orange, sliced
   (optional)

In a 3½- to 5-quart slow cooker, combine all ingredients except the orange slices. Cover and cook on high heat for 2–3 hours or on low heat for 5–6 hours. Float orange slices in slow cooker during the last hour of cooking.

Dips &
Fondues

Cheesy Beef and Bean Dip

Makes 12–15 servings

½–1 pound ground beef, browned and drained

2 (15-ounce) cans refried beans

2 (14.5-ounce) cans diced tomatoes and chiles, with liquid

1 envelope taco seasoning

1 pound Velveeta cheese, cubed

Combine all ingredients in a greased 4½- to 6-quart slow cooker. Cover and cook on low heat for 3–4 hours or on high heat for 1½ hours, stirring every 30 minutes until cheese is melted. Set on low heat to serve.

NOTE: This dip is also tasty as filling for burritos or soft tacos.

Bodacious Bean Dip

Makes 4–8 *servings*

**1 (20-ounce) can
refried beans**
**½ cup chopped
green onion**
¼ teaspoon salt
**1½ tablespoons taco
seasoning**
**1 cup grated medium or
sharp cheddar cheese**

Combine all ingredients except
cheese in a greased 2- to 3½-quart
slow cooker. Cover and cook on low
heat for 2–3 hours or on high heat
for 30 minutes and then on low heat
for 30 minutes more. If using the
high heat method, add the cheese
when heat is turned to low. If using
the low heat method, add cheese
the last hour of cooking.

Spicy Southwestern Dip

Makes 12–15 *servings*

1–1½ pounds ground turkey, browned and drained

1 large onion, chopped

1 (14.5-ounce) can black beans, rinsed and drained

1 (15-ounce) can tomato sauce

1 (4-ounce) can chopped green chiles, with liquid

1 (3-ounce) can chopped jalapeños, with liquid

2 pounds Velveeta cheese, cubed

Combine all ingredients in a greased 4½- to 6-quart slow cooker. Cover and cook on low heat for 3–4 hours or on high heat for 1½–2 hours, stirring every 30 minutes until cheese is melted.

Chili-Cheese Dip

Makes 6–8 *servings*

1/2–1 pound ground beef,
   browned and drained
1 (15-ounce) can chili
1 pound Mexican
   Velveeta cheese,
   cubed

Combine all ingredients in a greased 3- to 4 1/2-quart slow cooker. Cover and cook on low heat for 3–4 hours or on high heat for 1 1/2–2 hours, stirring every 30 minutes until cheese is melted.

Salsa Cheese Dip

Makes 10–15 *servings*

1 (16-ounce) jar chunky
   salsa or picante
   sauce
1 pound mild Velveeta
   cheese, cubed

Combine the salsa and cheese in a greased 3 1/2- to 4-quart slow cooker. Cover and cook on low heat for 1 1/2–3 hours, stirring every 30 minutes until cheese is melted.

Italian Sausage Fondue

Makes 8–10 *servings*

½ pound Italian
   sausage, browned
   and drained
2 (14-ounce) jars
   pizza sauce
2 teaspoons Italian
   seasoning
1 tablespoon cornstarch
1–1½ cups grated
   Italian-blend cheese

Combine all ingredients except the cheese in a greased 2½- to 4-quart slow cooker. Cover and cook on low heat for 2–3 hours. Stir in cheese before serving.

Pizza Fondue

Makes 8–10 *servings*

1 (26- to 28-ounce) jar
   spaghetti sauce
2 teaspoons Italian
   seasoning
1 tablespoon cornstarch
½ cup sliced pepperoni,
   quartered
1 cup grated mozzarella
   cheese

Combine all ingredients except the cheese in a greased 2- to 3½-quart slow cooker. Cover and cook on low heat for 2–3 hours. Add cheese the last hour of cooking and stir to combine. Stir again just before serving.

Cheese Fondue

2 (10.75-ounce) cans
   cheddar cheese
   soup, condensed
1 tablespoon
   Worcestershire sauce
1 teaspoon lemon juice
2 tablespoons dried
   chopped chives
   (optional)
2 cups grated sharp
   cheddar cheese

Combine all ingredients except the cheese in a greased 2- to 3½-quart slow cooker. Cover and cook on low heat for 2–2½ hours. Add cheese the last hour of cooking, stirring to combine.

NOTE: Any leftover fondue can be used as a sauce for white fish, Brussels sprouts, or baked potatoes.

Easy Chocolate Fondue

Makes 6–8 servings

2 cups milk chocolate chips

²/₃ cup half-and-half

Stir ingredients together in a greased 1- to 2-quart slow cooker. Cover and cook on low heat for 1 hour. Stir halfway through cooking time and again when done.

Caramel Fondue

Makes 6–8 servings

½ cup butter
½ cup light corn syrup
1 cup brown sugar
1 (14-ounce) can sweetened condensed milk

In a saucepan, mix together all of the ingredients and bring to a boil. Transfer to a preheated, greased 1- to 2½-quart slow cooker and set on low heat to serve.

Peanut Butter Fondue

Makes 8–10 servings

1/2 cup butter
1/2 cup light corn syrup
1 cup brown sugar
1 (14-ounce) can sweet-
    ened condensed milk
1/2 cup peanut butter

In a saucepan, mix together all of
the ingredients and bring to a boil.
Transfer to a preheated, greased
1- to 2 1/2-quart slow cooker and
set on low heat to serve.

Chocolate Raspberry Fondue

Makes 6–8 *servings*

½ **cup seedless raspberry jam or preserves**
1 **(12-ounce) bag semisweet chocolate chips**
1 **(12-ounce) jar caramel ice cream topping**

Combine all of the ingredients in a greased 1- to 1½-quart slow cooker. Cover and cook on low heat for 1½ hours, stirring every 30 minutes until melted and smooth. Cover and keep warm for serving up to 2 hours. If fondue is too thick, add some evaporated milk by the tablespoon until desired consistency is reached.

Rocky Road Fondue

Makes 6–8 servings

1½ tablespoons butter
    or margarine
1 (10-ounce) bar
    chocolate with
    almonds, broken
1½ cups miniature
    marshmallows
3 tablespoons milk
½ cup heavy whipping
    cream

Place the butter, chocolate, marsh-mallows, and milk in a greased 1- to 1½-quart slow cooker. Cover and cook on low heat for 1½ hours, stirring every 30 minutes until melted and smooth. Gradually stir in the whipping cream. Cover and keep warm for serving up to 2 hours.

NOTE: This chocolaty fondue is delicious over ice cream!

Soups, Stews, & Sides

Easy Bean Soup

Makes 6–8 servings

1 (15.5-ounce) can
  cannellini beans,
  drained
1 (16-ounce) can pinto
  or red beans, drained
1 (15-ounce) can black
  beans, drained
2 (10-ounce) cans diced
  tomatoes with green
  chiles, with liquid
1/2 onion, chopped, or
  1/4 cup dried minced
  onion
1 (14-ounce) can
  chicken broth

Combine all ingredients in a greased 3¹/₂- to 5-quart slow cooker. Cover and cook on low heat for 6–8 hours or on high heat for 3–4 hours.

NOTE: Use diced Italian tomatoes in place of diced tomatoes with green chiles for a milder soup.

Sweet Baked
Bean Soup

Makes 4–6 servings

**2 (16-ounce) cans baked
beans with molasses**
**1 (14.5-ounce) can
beef broth**
**1 (15-ounce) can diced
stewed tomatoes,
with liquid**
**1 tablespoon dried
minced onion**
Salt and pepper

Combine all ingredients in a lightly greased 2- to 3½-quart slow cooker. Cover and cook on low heat for 4–6 hours.

Fall Harvest Chowder

Makes 8–10 *servings*

½ **pound ground beef,**
   browned and drained
½ **cup chopped onion or**
   ¼ **cup dried minced**
   onion
4 **cups water**
1 **cup diced carrots**
1 **cup diced celery**
1 **cup peeled and**
   cubed potatoes
1 **(28-ounce) can**
   diced tomatoes
1 **(8-ounce) can**
   tomato puree
1 **teaspoon salt**
¼ **teaspoon black**
   pepper
¼ **teaspoon crushed bay**
   leaves
1½ **teaspoons Italian**
   seasoning

Combine all ingredients in a greased 4½- to 6-quart slow cooker. Cover and cook on low heat for 6–8 hours or on high heat for 3–4 hours. For a thicker soup, cook on low heat for 8–10 hours.

Three-Bean Chowder

Makes 8–10 *servings*

1 (16-ounce) can kidney
    beans, with liquid
1 (16-ounce) can
    fat-free refried
    beans
1 (15-ounce) can black
    beans, with liquid
1 (14-ounce) can
    vegetable broth
1 (14.5-ounce) can diced
    stewed tomatoes,
    with liquid
1 medium onion,
    chopped, or ½ cup
    dried minced onion
¾ cup chunky salsa
1 teaspoon minced
    garlic
2 teaspoons chili
    powder
¼ teaspoon cumin

Combine all ingredients in a greased 4- to 5-quart slow cooker. Cover and cook on low heat for 6–8 hours.

Simple Chili

Makes 6–8 servings

2 pounds ground beef,
   browned and drained
1 large onion, chopped,
   or ½ cup dried
   minced onion
1 (28-ounce) can diced
   tomatoes, with liquid
2 (8-ounce) cans
   tomato puree
1 (16-ounce) can kidney
   beans, with liquid
1 (4-ounce) can
   diced green chiles,
   with liquid
1 cup water
1 teaspoon minced
   garlic
2 tablespoons chili
   powder
2 teaspoons salt
1 teaspoon pepper

Combine all ingredients in a greased 4½- to 6-quart slow cooker. Cover and cook on low heat for 4–6 hours or on high heat for 2–3 hours.

Southwestern Chili

Makes 6–8 servings

½ **pound ground beef,
    browned and drained**
1 **green bell pepper,
    diced**
½ **cup chopped onion or
    ¼ cup dried minced
    onion**
3 **cups water**
1 **(16-ounce) can pinto
    beans, with liquid**
1 **(16-ounce) can black
    beans, with liquid**
1 **(10-ounce) can
    tomatoes with green
    chiles, with liquid**
1½ **teaspoons chili
    powder**
½ **teaspoon cumin**
1 **teaspoon salt**
¼ **teaspoon pepper**

Combine all ingredients in a greased 4½- to 6-quart slow cooker. Cover and cook on low heat for 6–8 hours or on high heat for 3–4 hours.

Beefy Chili

Makes 4–6 *servings*

1 pound ground beef,
   browned and drained
1/2 large onion, chopped,
   or 1/4 cup dried
   minced onion
1 (14.5-ounce) can diced
   tomatoes with green
   chiles, with liquid
1 (8-ounce) can
   tomato sauce
1/2 cup water
1 tablespoon chili
   powder
1 teaspoon salt
1/2 teaspoon pepper
1/2 teaspoon minced
   garlic

Combine all ingredients in a greased 2 1/2- to 4 1/2-quart slow cooker. Cover and cook on low heat for 4–6 hours or on high heat for 2–3 hours.

Chili Con Pollo

Makes 8–10 *servings*

3 large boneless,
   skinless chicken
   breasts
1 (16-ounce) jar
   chunky salsa
1 (15.8-ounce) can great
   Northern beans, with
   liquid
1 (15-ounce) can black
   beans, with liquid
1 (14.5-ounce) can diced
   tomatoes, with liquid
2 teaspoons cumin

Place chicken in a greased 3½-
to 5-quart slow cooker. Pour salsa,
beans, tomatoes, and cumin over
top. Cover and cook on low heat
for 6–9 hours. Break chicken into
bite-size pieces with two forks
before serving.

NOTE: Use hot salsa and diced
tomatoes with green chiles for a
spicier version.

Vegetable Beef Stew

1–1½ pounds cubed
   stew beef
1 (8-ounce) bag baby
   carrots, cut in thirds
2 medium potatoes,
   diced
1 (15.25-ounce) can
   whole kernel corn,
   drained
1 (14.5-ounce) can green
   beans, drained
2 (12-ounce) jars
   beef gravy
1 (11.5-ounce) can
   V8 juice

Combine all ingredients in a
greased 4½- to 6-quart slow
cooker. Cover and cook on low
heat for 6–8 hours or on high
heat for 4 hours.

Hungry Man Stew

Makes 8–10 *servings*

1 pound ground beef,
   turkey, or sausage
1 medium onion, sliced
2 cups diced carrots or
   baby carrots, halved
3 red or russet potatoes,
   diced
1 (16-ounce) can dark
   kidney beans,
   drained
1/4 cup uncooked white
   long-grain converted
   rice (not instant)
1 (8-ounce) can
   tomato sauce
4 cups water
1/4 teaspoon chili powder
1/4 teaspoon
   Worcestershire sauce

In a frying pan, brown the meat with the onion; drain and pour into a greased 3 1/2- to 5-quart slow cooker. Add remaining ingredients. Cover and cook on low heat for 6–8 hours or until potatoes and rice are tender.

Four-Hour Stew

Makes 4–6 servings

2 pounds cubed
   stew beef
2 cups quartered new or
   white potatoes
20 baby carrots, cut
   in thirds
1 (10.75-ounce) can
   cream of celery soup,
   condensed
1 (10.75-ounce) can
   cream of mushroom
   soup, condensed
1 soup can water
1 envelope dry onion
   soup mix

Combine all ingredients in a
greased 3½- to 5-quart slow
cooker. Cover and cook on low
heat for 6–8 hours or on high
heat for 4 hours.

Chunky Beef Stew

Makes 4–6 servings

**2 pounds cubed
stew beef**
15 baby carrots, halved
**$\frac{1}{2}$ cup dried minced
onion**
3 large potatoes, cubed
**1 (10.75-ounce) can
tomato soup,
condensed**
1 soup can water
1 teaspoon salt
2 tablespoons vinegar
Black pepper

Combine all ingredients in a greased 3½- to 5-quart slow cooker. Cover and cook on low heat for 10–12 hours or on high heat for 5–6 hours. If the liquid seems too thin, thicken by stirring in small amounts of instant potato flakes until desired thickness is reached.

Chicken Noodle Soup

Makes 4–6 servings

5 cups hot water
2 tablespoons instant
   chicken bouillon
   granules
1 (16-ounce) can
   chicken broth
2 cups cooked and
   chopped chicken
1 teaspoon salt
15 baby carrots, cut
   in thirds
3 cups uncooked
   egg noodles

Combine all ingredients except egg noodles in a greased 3½- to 5-quart slow cooker. Cover and cook on low heat for 4–6 hours. About 30 minutes before serving, stir in the noodles. Do not overcook or noodles will become mushy.

Chicken and Wild Rice Soup

Makes 6–8 servings

1 (10.75-ounce) can cream of chicken soup, condensed
2 cups cooked chopped chicken
1 cup shredded carrots
1 cup diced celery
2 (4-ounce) boxes long-grain and wild rice mix, with seasoning packets
5 cups chicken broth
5 cups water

Combine all ingredients in a greased 4½- to 6-quart slow cooker. Cover and cook on low heat for 4–6 hours, or until rice is done. Do not overcook or rice will become mushy.

Turkey and Rice Soup

Makes 4–6 servings

1 small onion, chopped
1 cup diced celery
2–3 cups cooked diced
   turkey
1 cup converted white
   rice, uncooked
4 cups water
1 (12-ounce) jar
   turkey gravy
$1/2$ teaspoon salt
$1/4$ teaspoon pepper

Combine all ingredients in a greased 3$1/2$- to 5-quart slow cooker. Cover and cook on low heat for 5–7 hours, or until rice is done. Do not overcook or rice will become mushy.

Hearty Vegetable Soup

Makes 4–6 *servings*

1 pound round steak,
   cut into 1-inch cubes
1 (14.5-ounce) can diced
   tomatoes, with liquid
2 cups water
2 new or white potatoes,
   cubed
$3/4$ cup dried minced
   onion
15 baby carrots, cut
   in thirds
1 (15-ounce) can green
   beans, with liquid
1 (15-ounce) can whole
   kernel corn, with
   liquid
3 cubes beef bouillon
$1/2$ teaspoon dried basil
$1/2$ teaspoon dried
   oregano
1 teaspoon salt
$1/4$ teaspoon pepper

Combine all ingredients in a
greased $3^1/_2$- to 5-quart slow
cooker. Cover and cook on low
heat for 6–8 hours or on high
heat for 3–4 hours.

Easy Minestrone

Makes 4–6 *servings*

$1/2$–1 pound ground beef,
   browned and drained
2 (10.75-ounce) cans
   minestrone soup,
   condensed
2 cups water
2 (15-ounce) cans pork
   and beans
1 cup shredded carrots
$1/2$ cup dried minced
   onion or 1 large
   onion, chopped
$1 1/2$ tablespoons
   Worcestershire sauce
$1/2$ teaspoon oregano

Combine all ingredients in a
greased $4 1/2$- to 6-quart slow
cooker. Cover and cook on low
heat for 3–5 hours.

Zesty Minestrone

Makes 4–6 *servings*

3 cups water
1½ pounds cubed stew
  beef, browned
¼ cup dried minced
  onion
20 baby carrots, cut
  in thirds
1 (14.5-ounce) can diced
  tomatoes, with liquid
1 teaspoon salt
1 tablespoon dried basil
½ cup dried vermicelli
1½ tablespoons dried
  oregano
1 (10-ounce) bag frozen
  mixed vegetables
¼ cup grated Parmesan
  cheese

Combine all ingredients except frozen vegetables, cheese, and vermicelli in a greased 3½- to 5-quart slow cooker. Cover and cook on low heat for 6–8 hours or on high heat for 3–4 hours. About 30 minutes before serving, add the frozen vegetables and vermicelli. Top individual servings with the cheese.

Alphabet Soup

Makes 4–6 *servings*

1/2 pound cubed
   stew beef
1 (14.5-ounce) can
   stewed tomatoes,
   with liquid
1 (8-ounce) can
   tomato sauce
1 cup water
1 envelope dry onion
   soup mix
1 (10-ounce) bag frozen
   mixed vegetables,
   partially thawed
1/2 cup uncooked
   alphabet pasta

Combine all ingredients except the vegetables and pasta in a greased 3 1/2- to 5-quart slow cooker. Cover and cook on low heat for 6–8 hours. About 30 minutes before serving, stir in the vegetables and pasta. Cover and cook on high heat for 30 minutes. Add more water if mixture seems too dry or too thick.

Tomato Beef Soup

Makes 4–6 *servings*

1 pound ground beef,
    browned and drained
1/2 cup dried minced
    onion
1 (26-ounce) jar
    spaghetti sauce
3 1/2 cups water
1 (14.5-ounce) can diced
    tomatoes with green
    chiles, with liquid
1 cup sliced celery
1 teaspoon beef bouillon
    granules or 1 cube
    beef bouillon
1 teaspoon pepper

Combine all ingredients in a
greased 3 1/2- to 5-quart slow
cooker. Cover and cook on low
heat for 5–6 hours or on high
heat for 3–4 hours.

Spicy Potato Soup

Makes **10–12** *servings*

1 pound ground beef or
   sausage, browned
   and drained
4 potatoes, peeled and
   cubed
1 small onion, chopped
5–6 cups water
3 (8-ounce) cans
   tomato sauce
$1/2$ teaspoon salt
1 teaspoon black pepper
1 teaspoon hot pepper
   sauce

Combine all ingredients in a
greased $4^1/2$- to 6-quart slow
cooker. Cover and cook on low
heat for 7–9 hours or on high
heat for 3–4 hours.

NOTE: For a more mild soup, omit
the black pepper and hot pepper
sauce and replace with 1 teaspoon
Italian seasoning.

Cheesy Potato Soup

Makes 10–12 servings

6 cups potatoes, peeled
   and diced
5 cups water
2 cups chopped onions
4 chicken bouillon
   cubes or 4 teaspoons
   instant chicken
   bouillon granules
6 slices bacon, cooked
   and crumbled
1 (12-ounce) can
   evaporated milk
2 cups grated cheddar
   cheese

Combine the potatoes, water, onions, and bouillon in a greased 5- to 7-quart slow cooker. Cover and cook on low heat for 6–8 hours or until potatoes are tender. Stir in the bacon, milk, and cheese. Cover and cook 20 minutes more, or until cheese is melted.

NOTE: Add 1/2 cup diced celery and 1/2 cup chopped carrots at the beginning of cook time to make a little more hearty.

Cheesy Vegetable Soup

Makes 6–8 servings

1 (10.75-ounce) can
   cream of mushroom
   or celery soup,
   condensed
1 (12-ounce) can
   evaporated milk
$^3/_4$ cup water
1 tablespoon dried
   minced onion
1 cup Cheez Whiz
4 cups frozen mixed
   or California-blend
   vegetables, thawed

Combine all ingredients in a greased 3$^1/_2$- to 5-quart slow cooker. Cover and cook on low heat for 3–4 hours. Stir well before serving.

Vegetable Cheese Soup

Makes 4–6 *servings*

1 (15-ounce) can
    cream-style corn
3–4 new or red potatoes,
    quartered
1/2 cup shredded carrots
1/2 cup chopped onion or
    1/4 cup dried minced
    onion
1/4 teaspoon pepper
2 (14.5-ounce) cans
    vegetable broth
1 1/2 cups grated cheddar
    cheese

Combine all ingredients except
cheese in a greased 3 1/2- to 5-quart
slow cooker. Cover and cook on low
heat for 6–8 hours or on high heat
for 4–5 hours. Just before serving,
stir in the cheese until melted.

Broccoli-Cheese Soup

Makes 4–6 *servings*

2 (16-ounce) packages
   frozen chopped
   broccoli
2 (10.75-ounce) cans
   cheddar cheese soup,
   condensed
2 (12-ounce) cans
   evaporated milk
1/4 cup dried minced
   onion
1/2 teaspoon salt
1/4 teaspoon pepper

Combine all ingredients in a greased 4$\frac{1}{2}$- to 6-quart slow cooker. Cover and cook on high heat for 2–3 hours or on low heat for 4–5 hours.

NOTE: This is also delicious as a topping for baked potatoes.

Santa Fe Cheese Soup

1 pound Velveeta
   cheese, cubed
1 pound ground beef,
   browned and drained
1 (15.25-ounce) can
   whole kernel corn,
   with liquid
1 (15-ounce) can kidney
   beans, with liquid
1 (14.5-ounce) can diced
   tomatoes with green
   chiles, with liquid
1 (14.5-ounce) can
   stewed tomatoes,
   diced, with liquid
1 envelope taco
   seasoning mix

Combine all ingredients in a greased 4½- to 6-quart slow cooker. Cover and cook on high heat for 3 hours or on low heat for 4–5 hours.

Cowboy Soup

Makes 4–6 *servings*

1 pound ground beef,
    browned and drained
1 (14.5-ounce) can
    crushed tomatoes
1 (14.5-ounce) can diced
    tomatoes with green
    chiles or jalapeños,
    with liquid
1 (15-ounce) can whole
    kernel corn, drained
1/2 cup dried minced
    onion
6 cups water
1 (6.8-ounce) box
    Spanish rice, with
    seasoning packet

Combine all ingredients in a greased 4 1/2- to 6-quart slow cooker. Cover and cook on low heat for 4–5 hours. Do not over-cook or rice will become mushy.

Easy Tortilla Soup

Makes 6–8 servings

1 pound ground beef,
   browned and drained
1/2 teaspoon minced
   garlic
2 (14-ounce) cans
   chicken broth
2 (14-ounce) cans
   stewed tomatoes,
   chopped, with liquid
1 cup medium salsa
2 tablespoons dried
   cilantro
1 tablespoon ground
   cumin
3–4 flour or corn
   tortillas, cut into
   1/2-inch strips
Grated Monterey Jack or
   cheddar cheese

Combine all ingredients except tortilla strips and cheese in a greased 4 1/2- to 6-quart slow cooker. Cover and cook on high heat for 4–6 hours or on low heat for 8–10 hours. Ladle hot soup into individual serving bowls over the tortilla strips and cheese.

Chicken Tortilla Soup

Makes **8–10** *servings*

1 pound boneless,
   skinless chicken,
   cooked and shredded
1 (15-ounce) can
   crushed tomatoes
1 (10-ounce) can
   enchilada sauce
1 medium onion,
   chopped, or ½ cup
   dried minced onion
1 (4-ounce) can chopped
   green chiles
2 cloves garlic, minced
2 cups water
1 (14.5-ounce) can
   chicken broth
1 (15-ounce) can whole
   kernel corn
1 teaspoon cumin
1 teaspoon chili powder
¼ teaspoon crushed bay
   leaves
1 tablespoon dried
   chopped cilantro
1 bag tortilla strips

Combine all ingredients except chips in a greased 4½- to 6-quart slow cooker. Cover and cook on low heat for 6–8 hours or on high heat for 3–4 hours. Serve with crushed tortilla strips sprinkled over top.

NOTE: Add 1 cup shredded carrots or shredded zucchini at the beginning of cook time for extra veggies.

Easy Taco Soup

Makes 4–6 servings

1 (15-ounce) can chili
    with beans and meat
1 (15-ounce) can whole
    kernel corn, with
    liquid
1 (14.5-ounce) can diced
    tomatoes, with liquid
1 (8-ounce) can
    tomato sauce
1 (15-ounce) can black
    beans, with liquid
1½–3 tablespoons taco
    seasoning mix

Combine all ingredients in a greased 3½- to 4½-quart slow cooker. Cover and cook on low heat for 6–8 hours.

Salsa Fever Soup

Makes 6–8 servings

3 cups chunky salsa
6 cups beef broth
½ cup long-grain white
    rice, uncooked

Combine all ingredients in a greased 4½- to 6-quart slow cooker. Cover and cook on low heat for 4–6 hours, or until rice is done. Do not overcook or rice will become mushy.

Corn on the Cob

Makes 6–8 servings

6–8 ears corn, in husks
3¼ cups water

Remove silk from corn but leave husks on. (If husks fall off, tie back on with kitchen twine.) Lay corn on its side in a 4½- to 6-quart slow cooker. Add water. Cover and cook on high heat for 2–3 hours.

Creamy Potato Casserole

Makes 8–10 servings

7 medium potatoes, peeled and quartered
1/2 cup butter or margarine, melted and divided
1 small onion, chopped
1 teaspoon salt
1 cup sour cream
1 (10.5-ounce) can cream of mushroom soup, condensed
2 cups grated cheddar cheese
1 (6-ounce) package herb-seasoned stuffing mix

Place potatoes in a greased 4 1/2- to 6-quart slow cooker. Pour 1/4 cup butter over top. Add the onion, salt, sour cream, soup, and cheese; mix well. Pour stuffing mix evenly over potatoes and drizzle with remaining butter. Cover and cook on low heat for 6–8 hours or on high heat for 3–4 hours.

Broccoli-Cheese Casserole

Makes 4–6 servings

1 (10-ounce) package
    frozen chopped
    broccoli, thawed
3 cups cooked
    long-grain white rice
1/4 cup chopped celery
    (optional)
1 (10.5-ounce) can
    cream of mushroom
    soup, condensed
1 cup Cheez Whiz
1/2 teaspoon salt
1/8 teaspoon black
    pepper
1/8 teaspoon garlic
    powder

Combine all ingredients in a greased 2- to 3 1/2-quart slow cooker. Cover and cook on low heat for 1 1/2–2 hours or until heated through.

Cheesy Cauliflower Florets

Makes 5 servings

1 (16-ounce) package
    frozen cauliflower
    florets
1 (10.75-ounce) can
    cheddar cheese soup,
    condensed

Place frozen cauliflower in a 3½-
to 4-quart slow cooker. Pour soup
over top. Cover and cook on low
heat for 4–5 hours.

NOTE: Frozen broccoli or a blend
of broccoli, cauliflower, and carrots
can also be used.

Sweet Autumn Carrots

Makes 8–10 *servings*

2 pounds baby carrots
⅓ cup brown sugar
⅓ cup orange juice
2 tablespoons butter or
    margarine, melted
⅔ teaspoon cinnamon
⅛ teaspoon nutmeg

Place carrots in a greased 2- to 3½-quart slow cooker. Combine remaining ingredients and pour over carrots. Cover and cook on low heat for 3–4 hours or until carrots are tender.

NOTE: For a thicker sauce, remove carrots from slow cooker with a slotted spoon when done and keep warm. Pour drippings from slow cooker into a small saucepan and bring to a boil. Add a mixture of ⅓ cup water and 2 tablespoons cornstarch to saucepan. Bring to a boil and pour over carrots before serving.

Thanksgiving Stuffing

Makes 10–12 *servings*

½ cup butter or
    margarine, melted
1½ cups chopped onion
1½ cups chopped celery
2 (6-ounce) packages
    seasoned stuffing mix
1 (14.5-ounce) can
    vegetable broth
2 eggs, beaten

In a large bowl, mix together all of the ingredients. Pour mixture in a greased 3½- to 5-quart slow cooker. Cover and cook on low heat for 4–5 hours.

NOTE: This recipe can be doubled and cooked in a greased 6- to 7-quart slow cooker.

Pasta

Cajun Chicken Pasta

Makes 6–8 *servings*

1 pound boneless,
   skinless chicken
   tenders
1 (15-ounce) can
   crushed tomatoes
1 (6-ounce) can
   tomato paste
$\frac{1}{2}$ cup chopped
   red bell pepper
$\frac{1}{2}$ cup chopped onion or
   $\frac{1}{4}$ cup dried minced
   onion
1 tablespoon minced
   garlic
$1\frac{1}{2}$ teaspoons Cajun
   seasoning
$\frac{1}{4}$ teaspoon crushed bay
   leaves
Cooked penne pasta, or
   other favorite pasta

Combine all ingredients except pasta in a greased $3\frac{1}{2}$- to 5-quart slow cooker. Cover and cook on low heat for 6–8 hours. Serve over hot cooked pasta.

Broccoli-Cheese and Chicken Pasta

Makes 6 servings

6 boneless, skinless
   chicken breasts
2 (10.75-ounce) cans
   broccoli cheese soup,
   condensed
2 cups milk
1/2 cup dried minced
   onion
1/2 teaspoon dried basil
Salt and pepper
Cooked angel hair pasta

Place chicken in a greased 4½- to 6-quart slow cooker. Combine all of the remaining ingredients except pasta and pour over the chicken. Cover and cook on high heat for 1 hour and then reduce to low heat and cook for 5–6 hours. Serve over hot cooked pasta.

Stuffed Pasta Shells

Makes 4–6 *servings*

1/2 pound ground beef,
   browned and drained
1/2 cup chopped onion
1 cup grated mozzarella
   cheese
1/4 cup seasoned
   breadcrumbs
1 teaspoon minced
   garlic
1 1/2 teaspoons dried
   parsley
1 egg, beaten
18 jumbo pasta shells,
   partially cooked*
2 (15.5-ounce) jars
   spaghetti sauce
1/2 cup grated Parmesan
   cheese

Combine the beef, onion, mozzarella, breadcrumbs, garlic, parsley, and egg. Stuff partially cooked pasta shells with spoonful of meat mixture. Pour 1 jar spaghetti sauce in a greased 4 1/2- to 6-quart slow cooker. Place stuffed shells on top of sauce. Pour remaining sauce evenly over top. Sprinkle with the cheese. Cover and cook on low heat for 4–5 hours. Do not overcook or the pasta shells will become mushy.

*Only cook jumbo shells for 7 minutes in boiling water. They will become mushy if overcooked.

Hearty Beef
and Cheddar Mac

Makes 6–8 servings

**1 pound ground beef,
   browned and drained**
**1 medium onion,
   chopped**
1½ cups diced potatoes
**1½ cups baby carrots,
   cut in thirds**
½ teaspoon salt
**1 (10.5-ounce) can
   cream of mushroom
   soup, condensed**
½ cup milk
**1½ cups elbow
   macaroni, cooked**
**2 cups grated cheddar
   cheese**

Combine all ingredients except the milk, macaroni, and cheese in a greased 3½- to 5-quart slow cooker; stir to combine. Cover and cook on low heat for 6–8 hours or on high heat for 3–4 hours. Stir in the milk and macaroni during the last 30 minutes of cooking if on low heat, or the last 15 minutes if on high heat. Sprinkle the cheese over top.

Cheesy Chicken and Noodles

Makes 8–10 servings

4–6 boneless, skinless
   chicken breasts
2 (10.75-ounce) cans
   cream of chicken
   soup, condensed
1 (10.75-ounce) can
   cheddar cheese soup,
   condensed
1 teaspoon dried
   rosemary or dill
Hot cooked egg noodles

Place chicken in a greased 4½-
to 6-quart slow cooker. Combine
all of the remaining ingredients
except noodles and pour over
chicken. Cover and cook on low
heat for 6–8 hours or on high heat
for 3–4 hours. Serve over
hot cooked noodles.

Pork Chop Stroganoff

Makes 4–6 servings

4 boneless pork chops
Salt and pepper, to taste
1 (8-ounce) package
   sliced mushrooms
1 (10.5-ounce) can
   cream of mushroom
   soup, condensed
1 cup sour cream
1 (8-ounce) bag wide egg
   noodle pasta, cooked

Place pork chops in a greased 3½-
to 5-quart slow cooker. Sprinkle
with salt and pepper. Layer mushrooms over meat. Spread soup over
top, then cover and cook on low
heat for 6–8 hours. Remove pork
chops from slow cooker and cut
into bite-sized pieces. Return pork
to slow cooker and then stir in sour
cream. Stir the cooked noodles into
the sauce and then serve.

Simple Beef Stroganoff

Makes 4–6 servings

1 pound cubed stew beef
½ cup dried minced
    onion
1 (10.75-ounce) can
    cream of mushroom
    soup, condensed
1 (4-ounce) can mush-
    rooms, drained
¼ teaspoon garlic salt
1 cup sour cream
1 cup frozen peas
Hot cooked egg noodles

Combine all ingredients except the sour cream, peas, and noodles in a greased 3½- to 5-quart slow cooker. Cover and cook on low heat for 6–8 hours. Add sour cream and peas the last hour of cooking. Serve over hot cooked noodles.

NOTE: For a richer taste, substitute 1 (8-ounce) package cream cheese for the sour cream.

Chicken Stroganoff

Makes 4–6 servings

2–3 boneless, skinless
   chicken breasts
2 (4-ounce) cans
   mushroom pieces,
   drained
1 (10.5-ounce) can
   cream of mushroom
   soup, condensed
Black pepper
1 tablespoon soy sauce
1 (16-ounce) container
   sour cream
Hot cooked wide
   egg noodles

Place chicken in a greased 2½-
to 4-quart slow cooker. Pour
mushrooms, soup, pepper, and
soy sauce over top. Cover and
cook on low heat for 6–8 hours
or on high heat for 3–4 hours.
Break up chicken with two forks.
Stir in the sour cream. Cover
and cook on low heat for 15–30
minutes. Serve over hot cooked
noodles.

Easy Lasagna

Makes 6–8 servings

12 lasagna noodles,
   uncooked
1 pound ground beef,
   browned and drained
1 teaspoon Italian
   seasoning
1 (28-ounce) jar
   spaghetti sauce
¼ cup water
1 (16-ounce) container
   cottage cheese
2 cups grated
   mozzarella cheese

Break noodles in half. Place half of the noodles in the bottom of a greased 4-quart slow cooker. Stir the Italian seasoning into meat and then spread half of the meat over the noodles in the slow cooker. Spoon half of the sauce over the meat. Pour half of the water over top. Layer half of the cottage cheese and half of the mozzarella over the beef. Repeat layers. Cover and cook on low heat for 4–5 hours. Do not overcook or the noodles will become mushy.

Supreme Pizza Lasagna

Makes **10–12** *servings*

12 lasagna noodles
1 teaspoon Italian
seasoning
12 ounces sausage,
browned and drained
24 pepperoni slices
2 (26–28-ounce) jars
chunky spaghetti
sauce
¼ cup water
1 (16-ounce) container
ricotta cheese
2 cups grated
mozzarella cheese

Break 4 noodles to fit in the bottom of a greased 6- to 7-quart slow cooker. Stir Italian seasoning into the sausage and then spread half of the meat over the noodles in the slow cooker. Lay 12 pepperoni slices over sausage. Over the pepperoni, layer one-third of the sauce, half of the water, half of the ricotta cheese, and one-third of the mozzarella. Top with another layer of noodles, sausage, pepperoni, and another third of the sauce. Spread remaining water and ricotta cheese over sauce, then another third of the mozzarella. Top with the remaining noodles, sauce, and mozzarella. Cover and cook on low heat for 4–5 hours. Do not overcook or the noodles will become mushy.

Chicken Alfredo Lasagna

Makes 10–12 *servings*

12 lasagna noodles,
    uncooked
2 (16-ounce) jars
    Alfredo sauce
1/3 cup water
1½ cups cooked and
    diced chicken
1 (16-ounce) container
    ricotta or cottage
    cheese
2 cups grated
    mozzarella cheese

Break 4 noodles to fit in the bottom of a greased 6- to 7-quart slow cooker. Layer one-third of the sauce, half of the water, and half of the chicken over the noodles in the slow cooker. Spread half of the ricotta cheese and one-third of the mozzarella over top. Add another layer of noodles. Layer another third of sauce, remaining chicken, water, ricotta cheese, and another third of the mozzarella. Top with the remaining noodles, sauce, and mozzarella. Cover and cook on low heat for 4–5 hours. Do not overcook or the noodles will become mushy.

NOTE: Add 1 (2.25-ounce) can of sliced olives between layers.

Veggie Lasagna

Makes 10–12 *servings*

12 lasagna noodles, uncooked
¼ cup water
1 (2.25-ounce) can sliced olives, drained
1 (4-ounce) can mushroom pieces, drained
½ cup shredded carrots
½ cup shredded zucchini
2 (26–28-ounce) jars chunky vegetable spaghetti sauce
1 (16-ounce) container ricotta or cottage cheese
2 cups grated mozzarella cheese

Break 4 noodles to fit in the bottom of a greased 6- to 7-quart slow cooker. Sprinkle half of the olives, mushrooms, carrots, and zucchini over the noodles in the slow cooker. Layer one-third of the sauce, half of the water, half of the ricotta cheese, and one-third of the mozzarella over top. Add another layer of noodles and all the remaining vegetables. Spread another third of the sauce and the remaining water and ricotta cheese over top. Sprinkle with another third of the mozzarella. Top with the remaining noodles, sauce, and mozzarella. Cover and cook on low heat for 4–5 hours. Do not overcook or noodles will become mushy.

Vegetable Spaghetti

Makes 8–10 *servings*

1 large onion, chopped
8–10 baby carrots, cut
   in thirds
1 (8-ounce) package
   sliced mushrooms
1 green bell pepper,
   seeded and chopped
2 (14.5-ounce) cans
   diced Italian
   tomatoes, with liquid
1 (15-ounce) can tomato
   sauce
1 (6-ounce) can
   Italian-style
   tomato paste
2 teaspoons sugar
$1/2$ teaspoon salt
$1/2$ teaspoon Italian
   seasoning
Cooked spaghetti
Freshly grated
   Parmesan cheese

Combine all ingredients except the pasta and cheese in a greased 3$1/2$- to 5-quart slow cooker. Cover and cook on low heat for 6–8 hours; stir well. Serve over hot cooked spaghetti garnished with the cheese.

NOTE: For a thicker sauce, drain one of the cans of Italian tomatoes before adding to slow cooker.

Poultry

Chicken Cordon Bleu

Makes 4–6 *servings*

4–6 slices ham
4–6 slices Swiss or
mozzarella cheese
4–6 boneless, skinless
chicken breasts,
flattened to ¼ inch
1 (10.75-ounce) can
cream of chicken
soup, condensed
½ cup milk
½ cup Italian seasoned
breadcrumbs

Roll a slice of ham and cheese inside each flattened chicken breast. Secure with a toothpick. Place chicken rolls in a greased 2½- to 3½-quart slow cooker. Combine the soup and milk and then pour over the chicken. Sprinkle breadcrumbs over top. Cover and cook on low heat for 6–8 hours.

Chicken Parmesan

Makes 4–6 *servings*

4–6 boneless, skinless chicken breasts

1 envelope dry onion soup mix

2 (10.75-ounce) cans cream of mushroom soup, condensed

1½ cups evaporated milk

1 cup apple juice

1 cup uncooked converted white rice

¼ teaspoon pepper

⅓ cup grated Parmesan cheese

Place chicken breasts in the bottom of a greased 3½- to 5-quart slow cooker. Combine all of the remaining ingredients except the cheese and pour over the chicken. Sprinkle with cheese over top. Cover and cook on low heat for 8–10 hours or on high heat for 4–6 hours.

NOTE: Watch cooking time so rice doesn't become mushy.

Mama's Italian Chicken

Makes 4–6 *servings*

4 frozen boneless, skinless chicken breasts

1 envelope Italian salad dressing mix

1 (10.75-ounce) can cream of chicken soup, condensed

Place chicken in a greased 3¹/₂- to 4¹/₂-quart slow cooker. Sprinkle with the dry dressing mix. Pour soup over top. Cover and cook on low heat for 8–10 hours or on high heat for 4–5 hours.

NOTE: For a lighter version, substitute 1 (14-ounce) can chicken broth for the cream soup.

Creamy Chicken with Mushrooms

Makes 4–6 *servings*

4 boneless, skinless chicken breasts
1 envelope Italian salad dressing mix
¼ cup water
1 (8-ounce) package cream cheese, softened
1 (10.75-ounce) can cream of chicken soup, condensed
1–2 (4-ounce) cans mushroom pieces, drained

Place chicken in a greased 3½- to 5-quart slow cooker. Combine the dressing mix and water; pour over chicken. Cover and cook on high heat for 3 hours.

In a bowl, beat the cream cheese and soup until blended. Stir in the mushrooms. Pour over chicken and cook 2 hours longer on high heat, or until chicken juices run clear.

Citrus-Glazed Chicken

Makes 4 *servings*

4 boneless, skinless
   chicken breasts
1/3 cup orange juice
1 (14-ounce) can
   chicken broth
3 tablespoons brown
   sugar
1/8 teaspoon salt
1 tablespoon cornstarch

Place chicken in a greased 3- to 4½-quart slow cooker. Pour the orange juice and chicken broth over the chicken. Sprinkle brown sugar and salt over top. Cover and cook on low heat for 6–9 hours. Remove chicken with a slotted spoon or spatula; set aside.

Pour liquid from the slow cooker into a small saucepan. Stir in the cornstarch with a whisk. Bring to a boil over medium heat, stirring until sauce thickens. Pour glaze over chicken.

Lemon Honey Chicken

Makes 2–3 *servings*

2 boneless, skinless
    chicken breasts
3/4 teaspoon ginger
1/4 cup lemon juice
1/2 cup honey
1 (14-ounce) can
    chicken broth

Place chicken in a greased 1½- to 2½-quart slow cooker. Combine the ginger, lemon juice, honey, and chicken broth and then pour over the chicken. Cover and cook on low heat for 6–8 hours or on high heat for 3–4 hours.

NOTE: Sauce can be thickened by adding small amounts of instant potato flakes until the desired consistency is reached.

Chicken Cacciatore

Makes 4 servings

2–4 frozen boneless, skinless chicken breasts

1 (26-ounce) jar chunky vegetable spaghetti sauce

1/2 teaspoon minced garlic

Place chicken in a greased 3- to 4^1/$_2$-quart slow cooker. Pour spaghetti sauce over top. Sprinkle with the garlic. Cover and cook on low heat for 10–12 hours or on high heat for 5–6 hours.

Apricot Chicken

Makes 4–6 servings

4–6 boneless, skinless chicken breasts
1 cup Catalina salad dressing
1 envelope dried onion soup mix
1 cup apricot jam or preserves

Place chicken in a greased 3½- to 5-quart slow cooker. Combine the dressing, dry soup mix, and preserves and then pour over the chicken. Cover and cook on low heat for 6–8 hours. Do not cook on high heat.

Cranberry BBQ Chicken

Makes 4–6 *servings*

3–4 pounds boneless chicken pieces
¼ cup dried minced onion
1 (16-ounce) can whole cranberry sauce*
1 cup barbecue sauce
Salt and pepper

Combine all ingredients in a greased 3½- to 5-quart slow cooker. Cover and cook on high heat for 4 hours or on low heat for 6–8 hours.

*Do not use jellied cranberry sauce.

Hawaiian BBQ Chicken

Makes 4–6 servings

4–6 boneless, skinless
   chicken breasts
1 (8-ounce) can crushed
   pineapple
1 (16-ounce) bottle
   barbecue sauce
Hot cooked rice

Place chicken in a greased 3½- to
5-quart slow cooker. Combine the
pineapple and barbecue sauce and
then pour over the chicken. Cover
and cook on low heat for 6–8 hours
or on high heat for 3–4 hours.
Serve over the hot cooked rice.

Pineapple Chicken

Makes 4–6 servings

4–6 boneless, skinless chicken breasts
1/8 teaspoon pepper
Paprika
1 (20-ounce) can pineapple tidbits, drained
2 tablespoons Dijon mustard
2–3 tablespoons soy sauce
1/4 teaspoon minced garlic

Place chicken in a greased 3 1/2- to 5-quart slow cooker. Sprinkle with the pepper and paprika. Combine the pineapple, mustard, soy sauce, and garlic and then pour over the chicken. Cover and cook on low heat for 7–9 hours or on high heat for 3–4 hours.

Hawaiian Haystacks

Makes 4–6 *servings*

10–12 chicken tenders, cut in chunks
1 cup chicken broth
2 (10.75-ounce) cans cream of chicken soup, condensed
1 (12-ounce) can evaporated milk
6 cups cooked rice
Toppings such as grated cheese, peas, pineapple, coconut, Chinese noodles, sliced olives, diced tomatoes, diced bell peppers, and sliced green onions, etc.

Place chicken in a greased $3\frac{1}{2}$- to 5-quart slow cooker. Combine all remaining ingredients except rice and toppings and then pour over the chicken. Cover and cook on low heat for 6–8 hours or on high heat for 3–4 hours. Put all desired toppings into individual bowls. Serve individual plates of chicken gravy over hot cooked rice and sprinkle toppings of choice over top.

Orange Chicken

**6 boneless, skinless
   chicken breasts**
¼ cup molasses
**2 tablespoons cider
   vinegar**
**2 tablespoons orange
   juice**
**2 tablespoons
   Worcestershire sauce**
**2 teaspoons Dijon
   mustard**
**⅛ to ¼ teaspoon
   hot pepper sauce
   (optional)**

Place chicken in a greased 4½- to 6-quart slow cooker. Combine all of the remaining ingredients and then pour over the chicken. Cover and cook on low heat for 7–9 hours or on high heat for 3–4 hours.

Lemonade Chicken

Makes 4 servings

4 boneless, skinless chicken breasts
1 (6-ounce) can frozen lemonade, thawed
3 tablespoons brown sugar
1 tablespoon vinegar
¼ cup ketchup
1 (14-ounce) can chicken broth

Place chicken in a greased 3- to 4½-quart slow cooker. Combine the remaining ingredients and then pour over the chicken. Cover and cook on low heat for 6–8 hours or on high heat for 3–4 hours.

Chicken Teriyaki

Makes 4–6 servings

10–12 boneless, skinless chicken tenders, cut into thirds
1 (16-ounce) bag frozen oriental vegetables
1 (18-ounce) bottle teriyaki sauce

Place chicken in a greased 3- to 4½-quart slow cooker. Combine the frozen vegetables and teriyaki sauce and then pour over the chicken. Cover and cook on low heat for 4–6 hours or on high heat for 3 hours.

Sweet-and-Sour Chicken

Makes 4–6 servings

4–6 boneless, skinless
chicken breasts, cut
into 1-inch pieces
1 (18-ounce) jar
sweet-and-sour
sauce
1 (16-ounce) bag frozen
Szechuan stir-fry
vegetables
$\frac{1}{2}$ teaspoon salt
6 cups cooked rice
$\frac{1}{4}$ to $\frac{1}{2}$ cup chopped
toasted almonds
(optional)

In a greased $3\frac{1}{2}$- to 5-quart slow
cooker, combine the chicken,
sauce, frozen vegetables, and
salt. Cover and cook on low heat
for 5–6 hours or on high heat for
$2\frac{1}{2}$–3 hours. Serve over the rice
and sprinkle with almonds.

Honey-Mustard Chicken Stir-Fry

Makes 4–6 *servings*

2 large boneless, skinless chicken breasts
1½ cups teriyaki marinade
⅓ cup water
1 (18-ounce) bottle honey-mustard barbecue sauce
1 (16-ounce) bag frozen California-blend vegetables
Cooked brown or white rice

Marinate the chicken overnight in the teriyaki marinade. Place marinated chicken and water in a greased 3- to 4½-quart slow cooker; discard the used marinade. Cover and cook on low heat for 6–8 hours. Break chicken into chunks with a knife and then pour barbecue sauce over the chicken. Stir in the frozen vegetables. Cover and cook on high heat for 30–60 minutes more, or until vegetables are heated completely through. Serve over hot cooked rice.

NOTE: To shorten preparation time, buy pre-marinated chicken breasts from the meat department of your local grocery store.

Almond Chicken

1 (14-ounce) can
    chicken broth
2 strips bacon, cooked
    and crumbled
2 tablespoons butter
3–4 boneless, skinless
    chicken breasts
1/4 cup dried minced
    onion
1 (4-ounce) can sliced
    mushrooms, drained
2 tablespoons soy sauce
1/2 teaspoon salt
1 1/2 cups diagonally
    sliced celery
    (optional)
Cooked rice
1 cup toasted slivered
    almonds

Combine all ingredients except the rice and almonds in a greased 3 1/2- to 4 1/2-quart slow cooker. Cover and cook on low heat for 6–8 hours or on high heat for 3–4 hours. Serve over hot cooked rice and sprinkle with the almonds.

Creamy Black Bean Salsa Chicken

Makes 3–5 servings

- 2–4 boneless, skinless chicken breasts
- 1 cup chicken broth
- 1 cup salsa
- 1 (15-ounce) can corn, drained
- 1 (15-ounce) can black beans, drained
- 1 envelope taco seasoning
- 1/2 cup sour cream
- 1 cup grated cheddar cheese

Place chicken in a greased 3$\frac{1}{2}$- to 5-quart slow cooker. Pour the broth, salsa, corn, beans, and taco seasoning over the chicken. Cover and cook on low heat for 6–8 hours or on high heat for 3–4 hours. Remove the chicken with a slotted spoon and place on a serving dish. Add the sour cream and cheese to the sauce in the slow cooker and then pour over the chicken.

Sweet 'n' Salty Chicken

Makes 4–6 *servings*

4–6 boneless, skinless
   chicken breasts
1 cup soy sauce
1 cup sugar
1 teaspoon garlic salt
½ cup chopped onion

Place chicken in a greased 4½- to 6-quart slow cooker.

In a saucepan, combine the soy sauce, sugar, garlic salt, and onion. Bring to a boil and then pour over the chicken. Cover and cook on low heat for 6–8 hours or on high heat for 3–4 hours.

All-Day Salsa Chicken

Makes 4–6 servings

3–4 boneless, skinless chicken breasts

1 (16-ounce) jar chunky salsa

1 (10.5-ounce) can cream of chicken soup, condensed

Place chicken in a greased 3- to 4½-quart slow cooker. Combine the salsa and soup and then pour over the chicken. Cover and cook on low heat for 6–8 hours.

Chicken and Green Chiles

Makes 6–8 servings

4–6 boneless, skinless
   chicken breasts
1½ cups chopped onion
1 (10.75-ounce) can
   cream of chicken
   soup, condensed
2 (4-ounce) cans
   chopped green
   chiles, with liquid

Place chicken in a greased 4½- to
6-quart slow cooker. Combine all of
the remaining ingredients and pour
over the chicken. Cover and cook
on low heat for 6–8 hours or on
high heat for 3–4 hours.

Creamy Chicken Soft Tacos

Makes 6–8 servings

4 frozen boneless, skin-less chicken breasts
1 (16-ounce) jar salsa
1 cup sour cream
6–8 flour tortillas
Shredded romaine lettuce (optional)
Grated cheddar cheese (optional)

Place chicken in a greased 3½- to 4½-quart slow cooker. Pour salsa over the chicken. Cover and cook on low heat for 10–12 hours or on high heat for 6–8 hours. During the last hour of cooking, shred the chicken using two forks and then stir in the sour cream. Fold mixture inside warm tortillas with lettuce and cheese, if desired.

Chicken Enchiladas

Makes 4–6 *servings*

2 dozen corn tortillas

3–4 boneless, skinless
   chicken breasts,
   cooked and shredded

1 (10-ounce) bottle
   green taco sauce

$\frac{1}{4}$ cup dried minced
   onion

1 (10.75-ounce) can
   cream of mushroom
   soup, condensed

1 (4-ounce) can diced
   green chiles, with
   liquid

2 cups grated cheddar
   cheese

Salt and pepper

In a greased $3\frac{1}{2}$- to $4\frac{1}{2}$-quart slow cooker, layer half of each ingredient in the order listed. Repeat with a second layer. Cover and cook on high heat for 30 minutes and then on low heat for 3 hours more.

Chicken Fajitas

Makes 8–10 servings

4–6 frozen boneless, skinless chicken breasts
2½ cups chunky salsa
1 green bell pepper, thinly sliced
1 red bell pepper, thinly sliced
½ cup chopped onion
1 large onion, thinly sliced
Soft flour tortillas

Place all ingredients except tortillas in a greased 4- to 6-quart slow cooker. Cover and cook on low heat for 10–12 hours or on high heat for 5–6 hours. Just before serving, remove fajita mixture with a spoon and shred chicken using two forks. Scoop chicken mixture into flour tortillas and serve.

NOTE: Serve the fajitas with guacamole, sour cream, shredded lettuce, grated cheese, and fresh salsa.

Easy Chicken Bake

Makes 4–6 *servings*

4–6 boneless, skinless chicken breasts
2 (10.75-ounce) cans cream of chicken soup, condensed
1 envelope dry onion soup mix
1 cup sour cream

Place chicken in a greased 3½- to 5-quart slow cooker. Combine all of the remaining ingredients except the sour cream and then pour over the chicken. Cover and cook on low heat for 6–8 hours or on high heat for 4 hours. About 1 hour before serving, stir in the sour cream.

NOTE: For a richer taste, substitute 1 (8-ounce) package cream cheese for the sour cream.

Wild Rice and Chicken

Makes 4–6 servings

2 (10.75-ounce) cans
    cream of chicken
    soup, condensed
2 cups water
2 (4.3-ounce) boxes
    seasoned long-grain
    and wild rice, with
    seasoning packets
4 boneless, skinless
    chicken breasts

Combine the soup, water, rice, and seasoning packets. Pour half of the rice mixture into a greased 3½- to 4½-quart slow cooker. Lay the chicken on top. Pour remaining rice mixture over chicken. Cover and cook on low heat for 6–7 hours or on high heat for 3–4 hours. Do not overcook or the rice will become mushy.

NOTE: Rice will expand during cooking time. Do not cook this recipe in a slow cooker smaller than 3½ quarts.

Chicken and Potatoes

Makes 4–6 servings

½ cup butter or
    margarine, melted
¼ cup dried minced
    onion
1 (16-ounce) package
    frozen hash brown
    potatoes
1 (8-ounce or larger)
    can cooked chicken,
    drained
1 (10.75-ounce) can
    cream of mushroom
    soup, condensed
1½ cups milk
1 cup grated cheddar
    cheese
¼ teaspoon black
    pepper
1 cup cheese cracker
    crumbs, divided

In a large bowl, mix together all of the ingredients except half of the cracker crumbs. Transfer to a greased 3½- to 5-quart slow cooker and then top with remaining cracker crumbs. Cover and cook on low heat for 6–8 hours or on high heat for 3–4 hours.

Chicken and Rice Casserole

Makes 2–4 servings

- 1 (10.75-ounce) can cream of celery soup, condensed
- 1 (4-ounce) can sliced mushrooms, with liquid
- 1/2 cup uncooked long-grain converted white rice
- 2 boneless, skinless chicken breasts, cooked and cubed
- 1 tablespoon dry onion soup mix

Combine the soup, mushrooms, and rice in a greased 2- to 3½-quart slow cooker. Place the chicken on top of mixture and sprinkle with the soup mix. Cover and cook on low heat for 4–6 hours.

Chicken and Dressing

Makes 4–6 servings

4–6 boneless, skinless
   chicken breasts
1 (10.75-ounce) can
   cream of chicken
   soup, condensed
1/3 cup milk
1 (6-ounce) package
   chicken-flavored
   stuffing mix
1 2/3 cups water

Place the chicken in a greased 4 1/2-
to 6-quart slow cooker. Combine
the soup and milk and then pour
over the chicken. Combine the
stuffing mix and water and then
spoon over top. Cover and cook on
low heat for 6–8 hours.

Scalloped Chicken

Makes 4–6 servings

1 (5-ounce) box
   scalloped potatoes,
   including seasoning
   packet
1 (8-ounce or larger) can
   white meat chicken
3 3/4 cups water

Put potatoes in a greased 2 1/2- to
3 1/2-quart slow cooker. Top with
the seasoning packet and chicken
and then pour water over top.
Cover and cook on low heat for
4–5 hours or on high heat for
1 1/2–2 hours.

Tater Tot Casserole

Makes 4–6 servings

1 (32-ounce) bag frozen
   tater tots
1 (8-ounce) can chicken,
   drained*
1/2 teaspoon salt
1/4 teaspoon pepper
1 (14.5-ounce) can green
   beans, drained
1 (10.75-ounce) can
   cream of mushroom
   soup, condensed
1 tablespoon dried
   minced onion
1/2 cup milk
1/2 cup grated cheddar
   cheese

Pour the frozen tater tots on the bottom of a greased 4 1/2- to 6-quart slow cooker. Combine all of the remaining ingredients except the cheese and then pour over the tater tots. Cover and cook on low heat for 4 1/2–5 hours or on high heat for 3 hours. About 30 minutes before serving, sprinkle cheese over top.

*Tuna may be substituted.

Chicken for Everything!

Makes 6–8 servings

6–8 boneless, skinless
    chicken breasts
2 teaspoons garlic
    powder
4 cups water
1/2 teaspoon crushed
    dried bay leaf
1 tablespoon dried
    minced onion

Place all of the ingredients in a lightly greased 4 1/2- to 6-quart slow cooker. Cover and cook on low heat for 6–8 hours or on high heat for 3–4 hours. Remove chicken from slow cooker and shred or chop to use in casseroles, soups, or other dishes. Chicken can be frozen in individual freezer bags for easy use later.

BBQ Chicken Sandwiches

Makes 4–6 servings

4–6 boneless, skinless
    chicken breasts
1/2 to 1 onion, sliced or
    chopped
1 (16-ounce) bottle
    barbecue sauce
Hamburger or hoagie
    buns

Put chicken and onion in a greased 3 1/2- to 5-quart slow cooker. Pour the barbecue sauce over top. Cover and cook on low heat for 8–10 hours or on high heat for 4–6 hours. Shred chicken with two forks and serve on buns.

NOTE: If chicken is too dry, add chicken broth by the tablespoon, until desired texture is reached.

Greek Pita Chicken Sandwiches

Makes 6–8 servings

2–4 boneless, skinless chicken breasts

1 medium sweet onion, thinly sliced

1/2 teaspoon minced garlic

1 1/2 teaspoons lemon pepper seasoning

1/2 teaspoon dried oregano

1/4 teaspoon allspice

1/2 cup plain yogurt

Pita bread rounds, cut in half

1–2 Roma tomatoes, diced

1 cucumber, sliced

Place the chicken in a greased 2 1/2- to 3 1/2-quart slow cooker. Lay the onion over the chicken and then sprinkle with the seasonings. Cover and cook on low heat for 6–8 hours. Break chicken apart with two forks and then stir in the yogurt. Spoon into warm pita bread halves. Garnish with the tomato and cucumber.

Honey-Mustard Chicken Wings

Makes 10–15 *servings*

3 pounds chicken wings
1 (18-ounce) bottle
   honey-mustard
   barbecue sauce*
1 teaspoon minced
   garlic
1 teaspoon dried
   rosemary
2–3 tablespoons
   cornstarch
2–3 tablespoons brown
   sugar
Ranch and/or blue
   cheese dressing

Place the chicken wings in a greased 3$\frac{1}{2}$- to 4$\frac{1}{2}$-quart slow cooker. Pour the barbecue sauce over the chicken. Sprinkle the garlic and rosemary over top. Cover and cook on low heat for 6–8 hours or on high heat for 3–4 hours. Remove chicken wings with a slotted spoon. Pour the sauce into a 2-quart saucepan and then whisk in the cornstarch and brown sugar; bring to a boil. Return the chicken to the slow cooker and then drizzle the glaze over top. Wings can be kept on warm or low setting and served directly from the slow cooker. Serve with ranch and blue cheese dressing for dipping.

*Original or honey-flavored barbecue sauce can be substituted.

Cranberry Turkey

Makes 8–10 servings

**3–4 pounds boneless
turkey breast**
**1 envelope onion and
herb soup mix**
**1 (16-ounce) can whole
cranberry sauce***
¼ cup water

Place the turkey breast inside a greased 3½- to 5-quart slow cooker. Combine all of the remaining ingredients and spread over top. Cover and cook on low heat for 8–10 hours or on high heat for 3–4 hours. Internal temperature will be 190 degrees when done.

NOTE: A turkey breast with bone can be used by increasing the cook time to 10–12 hours on low heat. Check the internal temperature for doneness.

*Do not use jellied cranberry sauce.

Apple Cider Turkey

Makes 8–10 *servings*

3–4 pounds boneless
    turkey breast
Salt and pepper
1/3 cup apple cider or
    juice

Place the turkey inside a greased 3½- to 5-quart slow cooker. Season with salt and pepper. Pour the juice over top. Cover and cook on low heat for 8–10 hours. Internal temperature will be 190 degrees when done.

NOTE: A turkey breast with bone can be used by increasing the cook time to 10–12 hours on low heat. Check the internal temperature for doneness.

Creamy Turkey and Mushrooms

Makes 10–12 *servings*

3–4 pounds boneless
   turkey breast
2 (10.5-ounce) cans
   cream of mushroom
   soup, condensed
1/2 cup sliced fresh
   mushrooms
1 envelope dry onion
   soup mix
1 cup sour cream

Place the turkey in a greased 4½- to 6-quart slow cooker. Combine all of the remaining ingredients except the sour cream and then spoon over top. Cover and cook on low heat for 8–10 hours. Internal temperature will be 190 degrees when done. About 1 hour before serving, break turkey breast into large chunks with two forks. Stir in the sour cream. Cover and cook for remaining hour.

Fresh Onion Turkey Breast

Makes **8–10** *servings*

3–4 pounds boneless turkey breast
1 envelope dry onion soup mix
1/2 medium onion, thinly sliced

Place the turkey inside a greased 3½- to 5-quart slow cooker. Sprinkle the soup mix over the turkey. Lay the onion over top. Cover and cook on low heat for 8–10 hours. Internal temperature will be 190 degrees when done.

NOTE: A turkey breast with bone can be used by increasing the cooking time to 10–12 hours on low heat. Check the internal temperature for doneness.

Turkey Olé

Makes 4–6 servings

4 cups shredded cooked
    turkey*
1 (1-ounce) envelope
    enchilada sauce mix
2 (6-ounce) cans
    tomato paste
1/2 cup water
1 cup grated Monterey
    Jack cheese

Stir the turkey, enchilada sauce mix, tomato paste, and water together in a greased 3- to 4½-quart slow cooker. Cover and cook on low heat for 3–4 hours or on high heat for 1½–2 hours. Before serving, sprinkle the cheese over top.

NOTE: The turkey can be used as a filling for tacos, enchiladas, or tostadas.

*Chicken can be substituted.

Beef

Beefy Corn Bread Casserole

Makes 6–8 servings

1 pound lean ground
beef, browned and
drained
1 medium onion,
chopped
1 (10.75-ounce) can
tomato soup,
condensed
1 (15.25-ounce) can
whole kernel corn,
drained
1–2 tablespoons chili
powder
1 teaspoon salt
1/2 cup water

Topping

1 (6.5-ounce) package
corn bread mix
1 egg
2 tablespoons butter or
margarine, melted
1/3 cup milk
1/2 cup grated cheddar
cheese

Place the beef and onion in a greased 3- to 4$\frac{1}{2}$-quart slow cooker. Stir in the soup, corn, chili powder, salt, and water.

In a bowl, mix together the corn bread mix, egg, butter, and milk. Spread the batter evenly over the meat mixture. Cover and cook on low heat for 5–6 hours, or until a toothpick inserted into the center comes out clean. Sprinkle the cheese over top for last the 15 minutes of cooking.

NOTE: This recipe can be doubled using a 6- to 7-quart slow cooker.

Spicy Frito Pie

Makes 6–8 *servings*

½ **pound ground beef,
  browned and drained**
2 **(16-ounce) cans pork
  and beans, pork
  removed**
1 **(4-ounce) can chopped
  green chiles**
1 **(8-ounce) can tomato
  sauce**
4–6 **drops Tabasco sauce**
1 **bag Fritos corn chips**

Combine all of the ingredients
except the chips in a greased 3- to
4½-quart slow cooker. Cover and
cook on low heat for 6–8 hours or
on high heat for 3–4 hours. Scoop
over a handful of Fritos.

NOTE: Try serving with some
shredded lettuce, diced tomato,
sour cream, and grated cheddar
cheese on top!

Shepherd's Pie

Makes 4–6 *servings*

1 pound ground beef,
    browned and drained
1 (10.75-ounce) can
    tomato soup,
    condensed
1 (15-ounce) can whole
    kernel corn, drained
1 (15-ounce) can
    French-cut green
    beans, drained
$1/2$ teaspoon dried basil
2 cups mashed potatoes
2 cups grated cheddar
    cheese

Combine the beef, soup, corn, beans, and basil in a greased $3^1/2$- to 5-quart slow cooker. Spread the potatoes over top. Cover and cook on low heat for 5–6 hours. The last hour of cooking, sprinkle cheese over the potatoes.

Beef and Mushrooms with Rice

Makes 4–6 *servings*

3 pounds cubed stew beef
1 (10.75-ounce) can cream of mushroom soup, condensed
2 (4-ounce) cans mushrooms, with liquid
½ cup apple juice
1 envelope dry onion soup mix
Cooked rice

Combine all of the ingredients except the rice in a greased 3½- to 5-quart slow cooker. Cover and cook on low heat for 10 hours. Serve in bowls, ladled over warm rice.

Easy Swiss Steak

Makes 4–6 servings

1½ pounds round steak,
   cut into serving-size
   pieces
1 pound baby carrots
1 envelope dry onion
   soup mix
1 (8-ounce) can
   tomato sauce
½ cup water

Place the carrots in a greased
3½- to 5-quart slow cooker. Top
with the steak pieces. Combine
the dry soup mix, tomato sauce,
and water and then pour over the
steak. Cover and cook on low heat
for 8–10 hours.

Saucy Burritos

Makes 4–6 servings

1 pound ground beef,
   cooked and drained
2 (16-ounce) cans
   refried beans
1 envelope taco
   seasoning
1 (8-ounce) can
   tomato sauce
½ cup water
Flour tortillas

Combine all of the ingredients
except the tortillas in a greased
3½- to 5-quart slow cooker. Cover
and cook on low heat for 6–8
hours. Spread hot beef mixture
on warm tortillas and fold like
a burrito.

Zesty Beef
and Bean Burritos

Makes 6–8 servings

- ½ pound ground beef, browned and drained
- 2 (15-ounce) cans pinto beans, with liquid
- 1 medium onion, chopped
- 1 teaspoon chili powder
- 1 teaspoon ground cumin
- ¼ teaspoon cayenne pepper
- 6–8 flour tortillas

Combine all of the ingredients except the tortillas in a greased 2- to 3½-quart slow cooker. Cover and cook on low heat for 5–7 hours. Slightly mash the beans with a potato masher. Spoon beef and bean mixture onto center of warm tortillas and fold like a burrito.

NOTE: For a different taste, make a vegetarian version and leave out the beef.

Green Chile Flank Steak

Makes 4–6 servings

1½ pounds flank steak,
    cut to fit in slow
    cooker
⅓ cup water
1 (4-ounce) can chopped
    green chiles
2 tablespoons vinegar
1¼ teaspoons chili
    powder
1 teaspoon garlic
    powder
½ teaspoon sugar
½ teaspoon salt
¼ teaspoon pepper

Place the steak in a greased 3½-
to 5-quart slow cooker. Combine
all of the remaining ingredients
and sprinkle over top. Cover and
cook on low heat for 8–10 hours.

Easy Meat Loaf

Makes 6–8 servings

2 pounds extra-lean
   ground beef
1/3 cup chopped green
   bell pepper
1/3 cup chopped onion or
   1/4 cup dried minced
   onion
1 (8-ounce) can
   tomato sauce
1 egg, beaten
1 cup quick oats

In a mixing bowl, combine all of the ingredients. Shape into a loaf and then place in a greased 3 1/2- to 5-quart slow cooker. Cover and cook on low heat for 6–8 hours, or until a meat thermometer reaches 165 degrees. Turn off slow cooker and wait 10–15 minutes before serving.

BBQ Meat Loaf

Makes 10–12 servings

3 pounds ground beef
1½ cups quick oats
2 eggs, beaten
1¼ cups milk
½ teaspoon black
   pepper
½ cup dried minced
   onion
1 (16-ounce) bottle
   barbecue sauce,
   divided

In a large bowl, combine the beef, oats, eggs, milk, pepper, onion, and half of the barbecue sauce. Press meat mixture into a greased 5- to 7-quart slow cooker. Spread the remaining barbecue sauce over top. Cover and cook on low heat for 6–8 hours, or until a meat thermometer reaches 165 degrees.

Grandma's Saucy Meat Loaf

Makes 4-6 servings

1½ pounds ground beef
¾ cup quick oats
1 egg, beaten
¾ cup milk
¼ teaspoon black
   pepper
¼ cup dried minced
   onion

Topping
⅔ cup ketchup
1 tablespoon brown
   sugar
1 tablespoon mustard

In a large bowl, combine the beef, oats, egg, milk, pepper, and onion. Shape into a loaf and place in a greased 2½- to 3½-quart slow cooker. Combine the ketchup, brown sugar, and mustard and then spread over top. Cover and cook on low heat for 6–8 hours, or until a meat thermometer reaches 165 degrees.

Ginger Ale Pot Roast

Makes 6–8 servings

1 (16-ounce) bag baby
    carrots
4–6 russet potatoes,
    peeled and cubed
3–4-pound rump roast
1/2 medium onion, thinly
    sliced
1 envelope brown
    gravy mix
1 envelope onion
    soup mix
2 cups ginger ale*

Place the carrots and potatoes in
a greased 4 1/2- to 6-quart slow
cooker. Place the roast over top.
Lay the onion over the roast. Dissolve the dry mixes in the ginger
ale and then pour over meat.
Cover and cook on low heat for
8–10 hours.

*Do not use diet ginger ale.

Spicy Salsa Roast

Makes 6–8 *servings*

3-pound roast, any kind
2 tablespoons taco
**   seasoning**
1 (16-ounce) jar salsa

Place the meat in a greased 3½-to 5-quart slow cooker. Sprinkle the taco seasoning over the roast. Pour the salsa over top. Cover and cook on low heat for 10–12 hours or on high heat for 5–6 hours.

NOTE: Shred any leftovers to use in tacos, burritos, or enchiladas for another tasty meal! This recipe also freezes well.

Roast and Red Potatoes

Makes 6–8 servings

1 (16-ounce) bag baby
  carrots
1 cup chopped onion or
  $1/2$ cup dried minced
  onion
8–10 red potatoes,
  quartered
3–4-pound rump roast
1 envelope dry onion
  soup mix
1 cup water

Place the carrots, onion, and potatoes in a greased 4- to 5-quart slow cooker. Place the roast on top. Dissolve the soup mix in the water and then pour over the roast. Cover and cook on low heat for 8–10 hours.

NOTE: If using a frozen roast, cook on low heat 2–4 hours more.

Cola Roast

Makes 4–6 servings

3-pound beef roast
1 envelope dry onion
    soup mix
2 (12-ounce) cans cola*

Place the roast in a greased 4- to 5-quart slow cooker. Sprinkle with the dry soup mix. Pour soda over top. Cover and cook on low heat for 7–8 hours.

*Diet soda cannot be substituted.

Italian Beef Roast

Makes 6–8 servings

1 (16-ounce) bag baby
    carrots
4–6 russet potatoes,
    peeled and cubed
2–3-pound beef roast
1/2 onion, thinly sliced
1 cup Italian salad
    dressing

Place the carrots and potatoes in a greased 4$\frac{1}{2}$- to 6-quart slow cooker. Place the roast over top. Lay the onion over the roast. Pour the dressing over top. Cover and cook on low heat for 8–10 hours.

Easy Mexican Roast

Makes 4–6 servings

3-pound chuck roast
1 envelope taco
seasoning
$^1/_2$ cup water

Place the roast in a greased $3^1/_2$- to 5-quart slow cooker. Combine the taco seasoning and water and then pour over top. Cover and cook on low heat for 10–12 hours.

Tri-Tip Roast

Makes 4–6 servings

3–4-pound tri-tip roast
Salt and pepper
1 (10.75-ounce) can
cream of celery soup,
condensed
1 (10.75-ounce) can
cream of mushroom
soup, condensed
1 (14-ounce) can beef
broth

Season the roast with salt and pepper and then place in a greased $3^1/_2$- to 5-quart slow cooker. Combine the soups and broth and then pour over the roast. Cover and cook on low heat for 8–10 hours or on high heat for 4–6 hours.

Unbelievably Simple Brisket

Makes 6–8 servings

4–5 pounds fresh beef brisket
1 envelope dry onion soup mix
1 (4-ounce) can mushrooms, with liquid

Trim all excess fat from the brisket. Combine the soup mix and mushrooms. Place the brisket in a greased 4$1/2$- to 6-quart slow cooker, cutting to fit if necessary. Spread the soup mixture over top. Cover and cook on low heat for 10–14 hours. Remove meat and cut across the grain into thin slices. Serve with the sauce from the slow cooker poured over top.

Family Favorite Brisket

Makes 4–6 servings

4 pounds fresh beef
   brisket
1 teaspoon salt
2 teaspoons dry mustard
2 teaspoons paprika
$1/2$–1 teaspoon garlic
   powder
Black pepper

Trim all excess fat from the brisket. Combine the seasonings until well blended; rub into brisket. Place brisket in a greased $4^{1}/_{2}$- to 6-quart slow cooker, with the more fatty side on top, cutting to fit if necessary. Cover and cook on low heat for 10–12 hours. Remove meat from liquid and cut across the grain into thin slices.

Sweet-and-Tangy Twisted Beef

Makes 6–8 servings

2 pounds stew beef*
1/4 cup brown sugar
1/4 cup soy sauce
1 cup salsa
Cooked rice

Combine all of the ingredients except the rice in a greased 3 1/2- to 5-quart slow cooker. Cover and cook on low heat for 7–9 hours or on high heat for 4 hours. Serve over warm rice.

NOTE: Try adding 3/4 cup frozen kernel corn during the last 30–40 minutes of cooking for another fun twist!

*Pork or chicken stew meat can be substituted.

Mandarin Orange Steaks

Makes 4–6 *servings*

2 pounds boneless
    beef steaks
1½ cups orange juice
½ cup fresh lemon juice
1 teaspoon hot sauce
1 (11-ounce) can
    mandarin oranges,
    drained and chilled
Cooked rice

Place the steaks in a greased 2-
to 3½-quart slow cooker. Combine
the orange juice, lemon juice, and
hot sauce and then pour over the
steaks. Cover and cook on low
heat for 8–10 hours. Serve topped
with chilled mandarin oranges over
warm rice.

NOTE: If meat is too dry, add beef
broth by the tablespoon until
desired consistency is reached.

Sweet-and-Sour Beef

Makes 4–6 *servings*

**2 pounds cubed
    stew beef**
**1 (10-ounce) bottle
    sweet-and-sour
    sauce**
1 cup shredded carrots
Cooked rice

Combine all of the ingredients except the rice in a greased 2- to 3½-quart slow cooker. Cover and cook on low heat for 6–8 hours. Ladle over warm rice.

Italian Shredded Beef Sandwiches

Makes 8–10 *servings*

2-pound frozen chuck
   roast
1 envelope dry Italian
   salad dressing mix
1 tablespoon minced
   garlic
Hamburger buns

Place roast in a greased 3½- to
4½-quart slow cooker. Sprinkle
the dry dressing mix and minced
garlic over top. Cover and cook on
low heat for 14–18 hours or on high
heat for 6–8 hours. Before serving,
remove fat and shred meat with
two forks. Serve warm on hamburger buns.

French Dip Sandwiches

Makes 4–6 servings

2–3-pound rump roast
2 (14.5-ounce) cans beef consommé
4–6 hoagie buns

Place the roast in a greased 3½- to 5-quart slow cooker. Pour the consommé over top. Cover and cook on low heat for 8–10 hours or on high heat for 5–7 hours. Remove roast and save extra juice. With a fork, break apart the roast and serve on hoagies. Serve the juice on the side for dipping.

Sweet BBQ Beef Sandwiches

Makes 10–12 servings

3–4-pound extra-lean
  boneless beef roast
1 (12-ounce) can
  root beer*
1½ cups barbecue sauce
Hamburger buns

Place the roast in a greased 3½-
to 5-quart slow cooker. Combine
the root beer and barbecue sauce
and then pour over the roast.
Cover and cook on low heat for
8–10 hours. Shred the cooked roast
with two forks. Serve warm on
hamburger buns.

*Do not use diet root beer.

Hot Meatball Subs

1 (18-ounce) bag frozen
  cooked meatballs*
1 (26-ounce) jar
  chunky garden-style
  spaghetti sauce
1/2 teaspoon minced
  garlic (optional)
Hoagie buns
Monterey Jack or
  mozzarella cheese,
  sliced

Combine the meatballs, spaghetti sauce, and garlic, if desired, in a greased 2- to 3½-quart slow cooker. Cover and cook on low heat for 4–6 hours. Place meatballs and desired amount of sauce on buns. Lay cheese slices over top and let melt slightly.

*Can use 25–28 frozen precooked homemade meatballs instead.

Chili Dogs

Makes 8–10 servings

1/2–1 pound ground beef,
   browned and drained
2 (15-ounce) cans chili
   with beans
1 cup chopped onion or
   1/2 cup dried minced
   onion
1 teaspoon oregano
1 teaspoon chili powder
1 teaspoon cumin
1/2 teaspoon minced
   garlic
1 (16-ounce) package
   hot dogs
Hot dog buns
Grated cheddar cheese
   and chopped onion

Combine the beef, chili, onion, and remaining seasonings in a greased 3- to 4½-quart slow cooker. Cover and cook on low heat for 6–8 hours or on high heat for 3–4 hours. Cook hot dogs immediately before serving. Spoon chili mixture over the hot dogs in buns. Sprinkle the cheese and onion over top.

BBQ Meatballs

Makes 4–6 *servings*

**2 (18-ounce) bags frozen
    cooked meatballs***
**1 (16-ounce) bottle
    barbecue sauce**
⅓ cup chopped onions

Combine all of the ingredients in a greased 3½- to 4-quart slow cooker. Cover and cook on low heat for 3–4 hours.

NOTE: Meatballs can be served with toothpicks as appetizers, or on toasted hoagies with cheese.

*Cocktail sausages can be substituted.

Sweet-and-Sour Meatballs

Makes 10–15 *servings*

2 (18-ounce) bags frozen
   cooked meatballs
1 (14-ounce) can
   crushed pineapple,
   with juice
1 cup brown sugar
3 tablespoons soy sauce
1 tablespoon cornstarch
1 tablespoon water

Place the frozen meatballs in a greased 3½- to 4-quart slow cooker.

In a saucepan, combine the pineapple, sugar, and soy sauce. Bring mixture to a boil, stirring frequently.

In a small bowl, mix together the cornstarch and water and then add to the simmering sauce to thicken. Pour sauce over meatballs. Cover and cook on low heat for 3–4 hours.

NOTE: Meatballs can be served on a platter with toothpicks as appetizers, or over hot cooked white rice garnished with chow mein noodles as a main dish.

Meatballs and Onion Gravy

Makes 4–6 servings

2 (18-ounce) bags frozen cooked meatballs

1 (12-ounce) jar beef gravy

1 envelope dry onion soup mix

Combine all of the ingredients in a greased 3½- to 4-quart slow cooker. Cover and cook on low heat for 3–4 hours.

NOTE: Meatballs can be served on a platter with toothpicks as appetizers, or on toasted hoagies with provolone cheese.

Pork

Orange-Glazed Pork Ribs

Makes 4–6 servings

2 pounds country-style boneless pork ribs
1 large onion, thinly sliced
1 cup orange marmalade
$1/3$ cup chopped green bell pepper
$1/4$ cup soy sauce
1 teaspoon minced garlic
$1/2$ teaspoon ground ginger

Place the ribs in a greased $3^{1}/_{2}$- to 5-quart slow cooker. Lay the onion slices over the ribs. Combine all of the remaining ingredients and then pour over top. Cover and cook on low heat for 6–8 hours or on high heat for 3–4 hours.

BBQ Pork Ribs

Makes 4–6 servings

3–4 pounds boneless
   pork ribs
1 large onion, sliced
2 cups barbecue sauce
2 teaspoons lemon juice

Combine all of the ingredients in a greased 3$\frac{1}{2}$- to 5-quart slow cooker. Cover and cook on low heat for 8–10 hours.

NOTE: This recipe can be doubled and cooked in a 6- to 7-quart slow cooker.

Sweet Pork Ribs

Makes 2–4 servings

1 pound baby back
   pork ribs
1 cup barbecue sauce
1 (18-ounce) jar cherry
   jam or preserves
1$\frac{1}{2}$ tablespoons Dijon
   mustard
$\frac{1}{2}$ teaspoon salt
$\frac{1}{2}$ teaspoon pepper

Place the ribs in a greased 2- to 3$\frac{1}{2}$-quart slow cooker. Combine all of the remaining ingredients and then pour over the ribs. Cover and cook on low heat for 6–8 hours or on high heat for 3–4 hours.

Aloha Pork Chops

Makes 4–6 *servings*

4–5 boneless pork chops
1/2 green bell pepper,
    seeded and diced
1 medium onion,
    chopped
1 (20-ounce) can
    crushed pineapple,
    drained
1 (18-ounce) bottle
    honey-mustard
    barbecue sauce

Place the pork chops in a greased 4 1/2- to 6-quart slow cooker. Sprinkle the bell pepper and onion over the pork chops. Spread the pineapple over top. Pour the barbecue sauce evenly over the pineapple. Cover and cook on low heat for 6–8 hours or on high heat for 3–4 hours. Break the meat into chunks.

Pork Chops and Mushrooms

Makes 4 servings

4 boneless pork chops,
    about 1/2-inch thick
2 medium onions, sliced
1 (4-ounce) can sliced
    mushrooms, drained
1 envelope dry onion
    soup mix
1/2 cup water
1 (10.75-ounce) can
    cream of mushroom
    soup, condensed

Place the pork chops in a greased
3 1/2- to 4 1/2-quart slow cooker. Top
with the onions and mushrooms.
Combine the remaining ingredients
and then pour over top. Cover and
cook on low heat for 6–8 hours.

Honey-Mustard Pork Chops

Makes 4–5 *servings*

4–5 boneless pork chops
½ cup flour
¼ teaspoon black
   pepper
1 teaspoon mustard
1 (10.75-ounce) can
   chicken with rice
   soup, condensed
1 soup can water

Dip the pork chops in the flour and then place in a greased 4½- to 6-quart slow cooker. Sprinkle the pepper over top. Combine all of the remaining ingredients and then pour over top. Cover and cook on low heat for 6–8 hours or on high heat for 3–4 hours. Remove the pork chops with a slotted spoon and place on a serving tray and cover with foil to keep warm.

In a blender, puree the liquid from the slow cooker for 30–60 seconds to make gravy.

Apple-Cranberry Pork Chops

Makes 4 *servings*

4 boneless pork chops
1 (16-ounce) can whole cranberry sauce
³/₄ cup applesauce

Place the pork chops in a greased 2- to 3¹/₂-quart slow cooker. Spread the cranberry sauce over top and then pour in the apple-sauce. Cover and cook on low heat for 6–8 hours or on high heat for 3–4 hours.

BBQ'd Pork Chops

6 boneless pork chops
1 (16-ounce) bottle
barbecue sauce
½ cup dried minced
onion

Brush each pork chop with the barbecue sauce and then place in a greased 3½- to 5-quart slow cooker. Sprinkle the onion over the pork chops and then pour the remaining sauce over top. Cover and cook on low heat for 6–8 hours.

Polynesian Pork Chops

Makes 4–6 servings

4–6 lean boneless pork chops

1 (8-ounce) can crushed pineapple

1 cup barbecue sauce

Place the pork chops in a greased 3½- to 5-quart slow cooker. Combine the pineapple and barbecue sauce and then pour over the pork chops. Cover and cook on low heat for 6–8 hours or on high heat for 3–4 hours.

Italian Pork Chops

Makes 6 servings

6 boneless pork chops
1 (14.5-ounce) can
   Italian diced
   tomatoes, drained
½ (16-ounce) bottle
   Italian salad dressing
Grated Parmesan cheese

Place the pork chops in a greased 3½- to 5-quart slow cooker. Pour the tomatoes and dressing over top. Cover and cook on low heat for 6–8 hours or on high heat for 3–4 hours. Serve with the cheese sprinkled over top.

Easy Pork Chop Casserole

Makes 4–6 *servings*

4–6 boneless pork chops
3 cups water
1 cup uncooked long-
    grain converted rice
1 (10.75-ounce) can
    cream of mushroom
    soup, condensed
1 teaspoon salt
1 teaspoon dried parsley
¼ teaspoon pepper

Place the pork chops in a greased 3½- to 5-quart slow cooker. Combine all of the remaining ingredients and then pour over top. Cover and cook on low heat for 6–8 hours or on high heat for 3–4 hours. Do not overcook or the rice will become mushy.

Pineapple Ham Steaks

Makes 4–6 *servings*

2 slices fully cooked
   boneless ham (about
   ³/₄-inch thick each)
2 tablespoons brown
   sugar
1 tablespoon Dijon
   mustard
6 pineapple slices

Place the ham in a greased 2¹/₂- to 3¹/₂-quart slow cooker. Combine the brown sugar and mustard and then spread over the ham. Lay the pineapple slices over top. Cover and cook on low heat for 6 hours or on high heat for 3 hours.

NOTE: This recipe can be doubled using a 4¹/₂- to 6-quart slow cooker.

Potato, Stuffing, and Ham Casserole

Makes **10–12** *servings*

- 1 (32-ounce) package frozen cubed hash browns
- 1 tablespoon dried chopped onion
- 1 teaspoon salt
- 1 (8-ounce) container sour cream
- 1 (10.75-ounce) can cream of chicken soup, condensed
- 2 cups grated cheddar cheese
- 2 cups chopped cooked ham
- 1 (6-ounce) package herb-seasoned stuffing mix
- 1/4 cup butter or margarine, melted

Combine all of the ingredients except the stuffing mix and butter in a greased 4$^1/_2$- to 6-quart slow cooker. Sprinkle stuffing mix over top and then drizzle with the butter. Cover and cook on low heat for 5–6 hours or on high heat for 2$^1/_2$–4 hours.

Cheesy Ham and Potato Bake

Makes 4–6 *servings*

1 (32-ounce) package
frozen shredded hash
browns
1 teaspoon salt
1/2 teaspoon pepper
1 (l0.75-ounce) can
cream of chicken
soup, condensed
1 (12-ounce) can
evaporated milk
1 1/2 cups chopped
cooked ham
2 cups grated cheddar
cheese, divided

Mix all of the ingredients except
1 cup cheese in a greased 3 1/2-
to 5-quart slow cooker. Cover and
cook on low heat for 5–6 hours.
About 30 minutes before serving, sprinkle the remaining cheese
over top.

Ranch Potatoes and Ham

Makes 2–4 *servings*

2 pounds red potatoes, quartered or halved

2 cups chopped or diced cooked ham

1 (10.75-ounce) can cream of potato soup, condensed

½–1 envelope ranch salad dressing mix

1 (8-ounce) package cream cheese, softened

Place the potatoes and ham in a greased 3½- to 5-quart slow cooker. Combine the soup and dry salad dressing mix and then stir into the potatoes and ham. Cover and cook on low heat for 8 hours. Add the cream cheese during the last hour of cooking. Stir before serving.

Sweet Apricot Pork Roast

Makes 4–6 *servings*

2½–3-pound boneless pork roast

1 medium onion, thinly sliced

1 (16-ounce) jar apricot jam or preserves

3 tablespoons Dijon mustard

Place the roast in a greased 2- to 3½-quart slow cooker. Lay the onion slices over the roast. Combine the jam and mustard and then spread over top. Cover and cook on low heat for 6–8 hours or on high heat for 3–4 hours, or until the internal temperature reaches 165 degrees.

Savory Pork Roast

Makes 8–10 servings

4–5-pound pork loin
   roast
1/2 cup dried minced
   onion
2 tablespoons soy sauce
1/4 teaspoon crushed
   dried bay leaf
1 tablespoon garlic
   powder

Place the roast in a greased 4 1/2-
to 5-quart slow cooker. Add the
remaining ingredients. Cover and
cook on low heat for 7–9 hours.

Cranberry Pork Roast

Makes 4–6 *servings*

2½–3-pound boneless rolled pork loin
½ teaspoon salt
¼ teaspoon pepper
1 (16-ounce) can whole cranberry sauce*
¼ cup honey
1 teaspoon grated fresh orange peel
⅛ teaspoon ground cloves
⅛ teaspoon ground nutmeg

Place the roast in a greased 4½- to 6-quart slow cooker. Season with the salt and pepper. Combine all of the remaining ingredients and then pour over top. Cover and cook on low heat for 6–8 hours, or until the internal temperature reaches 165 degrees. For extra-tender meat, cook an additional 2 hours. Let stand 10 minutes before slicing.

*Do not use jellied cranberry sauce as it adds too much liquid.

Holiday Honey Ham

Makes 8–10 *servings*

3-5-pound ham
24–36 whole cloves
½ cup pineapple juice
¼ cup honey

Pierce the ham with the cloves and cover the entire ham. Place in a greased 4- to 6-quart slow cooker. Pour the juice and honey over top. Cover and cook on low heat for 6–9 hours. Remove cloves before slicing and serving.

Sweet-and-Sour Pork

Makes 2–4 *servings*

1 pound pork
   tenderloin, cut into
   1-inch pieces
1 (20-ounce) can
   pineapple chunks,
   drained
1 cup sweet-and-sour
   sauce
1/4 teaspoon ground
   ginger

Place all of the ingredients in the
order listed in a greased 2- to
3½-quart slow cooker. Cover and
cook on low heat for 4–6 hours.

Sausage, Peppers, and Rice

Makes 8–10 *servings*

4 cups boiling water
4 beef bouillon cubes
1½ pounds pork sausage
1 teaspoon garlic
   powder
2 teaspoons ground
   cumin
4 medium onions,
   chopped
4 medium green bell
   peppers, chopped
1 (4-ounce) can chopped
   jalapeños, drained
2 (6.25-ounce) packages
   long-grain converted
   and wild rice mix,
   with seasoning
   packets

Pour the hot water into a greased 6- to 7-quart slow cooker already set on high heat. Stir in the bouillon cubes.

In a frying pan, brown the sausage, garlic powder, and cumin; drain. Add the onions and bell peppers and saute until tender, about 5–7 minutes. Transfer mixture to the slow cooker. Stir in the jalapeños, rice, and seasoning packets. Cover and cook on low heat for 4–5 hours. Do not overcook or the rice will become mushy.

Simple Sausage Casserole

Makes 6–8 servings

**1 pound pork sausage,
    browned and drained**
**1 envelope chicken
    soup mix**
**³/₄ cup uncooked
    long-grain white rice
    (not instant)**
2 stalks celery, diced
¹/₃ cup slivered almonds
4 cups water
Salt and pepper

Combine all of the ingredients in a greased 4¹/₂- to 6-quart slow cooker and stir well. Cover and cook on low heat for 4–5 hours or until rice is tender. Do not overcook or rice will become mushy.

Smoked Sausage Bake

Makes 2–4 servings

1 pound smoked or
   polish sausage,
   sliced
1 envelope dry chicken
   soup mix
1 cup uncooked long-
   grain converted rice
2 stalks celery, diced
1 (14.5-ounce) can diced
   tomatoes, drained
1 green bell pepper,
   chopped
4 cups water
$\frac{1}{2}$ teaspoon salt

Combine all ingredients in a
greased $3\frac{1}{2}$- to 5-quart slow
cooker and stir well. Cover and
cook on low heat for 4–5 hours or
until rice is tender. Do not overcook
or rice will become mushy.

Shredded Pork Burritos

Makes 4–6 *servings*

3½-pound boneless pork
    loin roast
1 teaspoon salt
½ teaspoon pepper
1½ teaspoons minced
    garlic
1 cup water
Flour tortillas

Place the roast in a greased 4- to 5-quart slow cooker. Sprinkle the salt, pepper, and garlic over top; add the water. Cover and cook on low heat for 8–9 hours, or until pork is tender. Remove pork with a slotted spoon and then discard the liquid in slow cooker. Shred the meat using two forks. Fill warm tortillas with meat and fold like a burrito.

Pork Chile Verde

Makes 4–6 servings

1 pound pork stew meat
1 (12-ounce) bottle
   green taco sauce or
   salsa verde
1 (14-ounce) can black
   beans, drained
1 (14-ounce) can great
   Northern beans,
   drained
1 (4-ounce) can chopped
   green chiles, drained

Combine all of the ingredients in a greased 3½- to 4½-quart slow cooker. Cover and cook on low heat for 6–8 hours or on high heat for 3–4 hours.

NOTE: Add ½ cup chopped onion for even more flavor.

Southwestern Pork Wraps

Makes 8–10 *servings*

2–3-pound boneless
   pork loin roast
3 (4-ounce) cans
   chopped green
   chiles, with liquid
1 (8-ounce) can
   tomato sauce
2/3 cup barbecue sauce
1 large sweet onion,
   thinly sliced
2–4 tablespoons chili
   powder
1 teaspoon ground
   cumin
1 teaspoon dried
   oregano
Flavored flour tortillas
Shredded lettuce and
   sour cream

Place the roast in a greased 3½-
to 4-quart slow cooker. Combine
all of the other ingredients except
the tortillas, lettuce, and sour
cream, and then spread over the
roast. Cover and cook on low heat
for 8–10 hours or on high heat for
4–5 hours. When done, shred roast
using two forks. Wrap the meat in
warm tortillas with the lettuce and
sour cream.

Asian Pork Wraps

Makes 8–10 *servings*

1½–3-pound boneless
    pork loin roast
²/₃ cup hoisin sauce*
2 teaspoons minced
    garlic
1 teaspoon ground
    ginger
½ teaspoon Chinese
    five-spice powder
Whole wheat tortillas
Sliced green onion,
    mandarin oranges,
    toasted slivered
    almonds, and
    shredded lettuce

Place the roast in a greased 3½-
to 5-quart slow cooker. Combine
all of the remaining ingredients
except the tortillas and toppings,
and then spread over roast. Cover
and cook on low heat for 6–8
hours. When done, shred roast
using two forks. Serve on warm
tortillas with green onion, mandarin oranges, almonds, and lettuce.

*Hoisin sauce can be found in the
Asian/Oriental section of most
grocery stores.

Shredded Ham Sandwiches

Makes 4–6 servings

2 pounds shredded ham
1 (20-ounce) bottle
cola*
1 (16-ounce) bottle
barbecue sauce
Hamburger buns

Combine all of the ingredients except the hamburger buns in a greased 3½- to 5-quart slow cooker. Cover and cook on low heat for 8–10 hours or on high heat for 4–5 hours. Using a slotted spoon, remove ham and serve on the hamburger buns.

*Do not substitute diet cola.

BBQ Pulled Pork Sandwiches

Makes 4–6 servings

2–3-pound boneless pork roast
3/4 cup dried minced onion
1 (12-ounce) bottle barbecue sauce
1/4 cup honey
Sandwich rolls

Place the roast in a greased 3½- to 5-quart slow cooker. Combine the onion, barbecue sauce, and honey and then pour over top. Cover and cook on low heat for 6–8 hours. When done, shred the roast using two forks. Serve warm on the sandwich rolls.

Cranberry-Sauced Cocktail Sausages

Makes 16 servings

2 (16-ounce) packages little smoked sausages
1 cup chili sauce
1 cup barbecue sauce
3/4 cup jellied cranberry sauce

Place the sausages in a greased 2½- to 3½-quart slow cooker. Combine all of the remaining ingredients and pour over top. Cover and cook on low heat for 1½–3 hours.

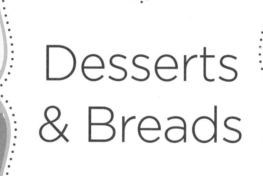

Desserts & Breads

Cherry Biscuit Cobbler

Makes 6–8 *servings*

1/3 **cup brown sugar**
1/2 **teaspoon cinnamon**
1/3 **cup melted butter or**
   margarine
2 **(8-ounce) packages**
   refrigerator biscuits,
   separated and
   quartered
1 **(21-ounce) can**
   cherry pie filling

Mix together the brown sugar, cinnamon, and butter. Mixture will be lumpy. Grease a 3 1/2- to 5-quart slow cooker and then layer 1 package of biscuits, half the cinnamon-and-sugar mixture, and then half of the pie filling. Add the second package of biscuits; cover with the remaining cinnamon-and-sugar mixture, and top with the remaining pie filling. Cover and cook on high heat for 2 1/2–3 hours, or until biscuits are done in the center.

Easy Cherry Cobbler

Makes 10–12 *servings*

2 **(21-ounce) cans**
   cherry pie filling
1 **yellow cake mix**
1/2 **cup melted butter or**
   margarine

Pour the pie filling in a greased 4 1/2- to 6-quart slow cooker. Sprinkle dry cake mix over top. Pour the melted butter over the cake mix. Cover and cook on high heat for 2 hours or on low heat for 4 hours.

Country Peach Cobbler

Makes 6–8 servings

1 (29-ounce) can peach
   slices, drained with
   juice reserved
2/3 cup old-fashioned
   oatmeal (not instant)
1 cup Bisquick
1/2 teaspoon cinnamon
1/2 cup firmly packed
   brown sugar

Pour the peaches into a greased
2 1/2- to 3 1/2-quart slow cooker. Mix
together the oatmeal, Bisquick, and
peach juice and then spoon over
the peaches. Sprinkle cinnamon
and brown sugar over top. Cover
and cook on low heat for 3 hours.

Coconut Peach Cobbler

Makes 10–12 servings

1 (21-ounce) can
   peach pie filling
1 (29-ounce) can peach
   slices, drained with
   juice reserved
1 white or yellow
   cake mix
1/2 teaspoon cinnamon
1/2 cup coconut
1/8 cup butter or
   margarine, thinly
   sliced

Spread the pie filling and peaches
in a greased 4 1/2- to 6-quart slow
cooker. Sprinkle the cake mix,
cinnamon, and coconut over top.
Pour peach juice over the dry
ingredients. Place butter slices
over any dry areas. Cover and
cook on low heat for 4 hours or
on high heat for 2 hours.

Apple Nut Cobbler

Makes 10–12 servings

2 (21-ounce) cans
   apple pie filling
1 white or yellow
   cake mix
$\frac{1}{2}$ cup butter or
   margarine, melted
$\frac{1}{3}$ cup chopped pecans

Spread the pie filling in a greased $4\frac{1}{2}$- to 6-quart slow cooker. Sprinkle the cake mix over top. Drizzle butter evenly over cake mix and then top with the nuts. Cover and cook on low heat for 4 hours or on high heat for 2 hours.

NOTE: Use $\frac{1}{4}$ cup melted butter and $\frac{1}{3}$ cup water in place of $\frac{1}{2}$ cup butter, for a low-fat version.

Cherry-Blackberry Cobbler

Makes 10–12 servings

1 (21-ounce) can
   cherry pie filling
1 (21-ounce) can
   blackberry pie filling
1 yellow or white
   cake mix
2 eggs
$\frac{1}{3}$ cup evaporated milk
1 teaspoon cinnamon

Spread the pie filling in a greased $4\frac{1}{2}$- to 6-quart slow cooker. Combine all of the remaining ingredients and then spoon over the pie filling. Cover and cook on low heat for 3 hours or on high heat for $1\frac{1}{2}$ hours. Turn off the slow cooker and let the cobbler cool for 20 minutes.

NOTE: Use 2 cans of one flavor of pie filling instead of two flavors.

Blackberry Walnut Cobbler

Makes 7–9 servings

2 (21-ounce) cans blackberry pie filling
1 yellow cake mix
1/2 cup butter or margarine, melted
2/3 cup chopped walnuts

Spread the pie filling in a greased 3- to 4 1/2-quart slow cooker. Combine the cake mix and butter. Mixture will be crumbly. Pour over the pie filling. Sprinkle nuts over top. Cover and cook on low heat for 4 hours or on high heat for 2 hours.

Easy Blueberry Crisp

Makes 6–8 servings

2 (21-ounce) cans blueberry pie filling
2 1/2 cups granola cereal
1 1/2 teaspoons cinnamon
1/3 cup sugar
1/3 cup melted butter or margarine

Place the pie filling in a greased 3- to 4 1/2-quart slow cooker. Sprinkle the remaining ingredients over top in the order listed. Cover and cook on low heat for 3 hours.

Apple Raisin Crisp

Makes 6–8 *servings*

2 (21-ounce) cans
   apple pie filling
2½ cups old-fashioned
   oats
2 tablespoons raisins
1/4 cup walnut gems
1½ teaspoons cinnamon
⅓ cup sugar
⅓ cup melted butter or
   margarine

Place the pie filling in a greased 3-
to 4½-quart slow cooker. Sprinkle
the remaining ingredients over top
in the order listed. Cover and cook
on low heat for 3 hours.

Peachy Cherry Crisp

Makes 6–8 servings

1 (21-ounce) can
   cherry pie filling
1 (15-ounce) can peach
   slices, drained
2½ cups granola cereal
1 teaspoon cinnamon
⅓ cup sugar
⅓ cup melted butter or
   margarine

Place the pie filling and peach slices in a greased 3- to 4½-quart slow cooker. Sprinkle the remaining ingredients over top in the order listed. Cover and cook on low heat for 3 hours.

Gooey Cherry Chocolate Cake

Makes **10–12** *servings*

2 (21-ounce) cans cherry pie filling
1 milk chocolate cake mix
½ cup butter or margarine, melted

Spread the pie filling in a greased 4½- to 6-quart slow cooker. Sprinkle the cake mix over top and then drizzle with butter. Cover and cook on low heat for 4 hours or on high heat for 2 hours. Turn off the slow cooker and let the cake sit, covered, for 30 minutes before serving.

NOTE: See tip 21 on page 7.

Triple Rich Chocolate Cake

Makes 8–10 *servings*

1 devil's food cake mix
4 eggs
1 cup light sour cream
¾ cup vegetable oil
1 cup water
1 small box instant
    chocolate pudding
1 cup chocolate chips

Combine all ingredients by hand in a 2-quart mixing bowl. Pour the batter in a greased 3½- to 5-quart slow cooker. Cover and cook on low heat for 5–6 hours, or until done in the center. Turn off the slow cooker and let the cake sit, covered, for 30 minutes before serving.

NOTE: See tip 21 on page 7.

Hot Fudge Brownie Cake

Makes 8–10 servings

2 cups packaged
brownie mix
1 large egg
1 tablespoon vegetable
oil
$\frac{1}{4}$ cup water
$\frac{1}{3}$ cup milk chocolate
chips
$\frac{1}{3}$ cup chopped nuts
$\frac{1}{2}$ cup brown sugar
2 tablespoons baking
cocoa
$\frac{3}{4}$ cup boiling water

Combine the brownie mix, egg, oil, water, chocolate chips, and nuts. Spread the batter in a greased 2$\frac{1}{2}$- to 3$\frac{1}{2}$-quart slow cooker. Combine the sugar, cocoa and boiling water, making sure the sugar is completely dissolved. Pour mixture over the batter. Cover and cook on high heat for 2 hours. Turn off the slow cooker and let the brownies sit, covered, for 30 minutes.

NOTE: See tip 21 on page 7.

Moist Chocolate Cake

Makes 6–8 servings

2 cups packaged
    brownie mix
1 large egg
1 tablespoon vegetable
    oil
1/4 cup water

Topping

1 cup boiling water
1/2 cup brown sugar
3 tablespoons baking
    cocoa

Combine the brownie mix, egg, oil, and water. Spread the batter in a greased 3 1/2- to 4-quart slow cooker. Combine the boiling water, sugar, and cocoa and then pour over top. Do not stir after sauce has been added. Cover and cook on high heat for 2–2 1/2 hours. Let cake cool, covered, for 30 minutes before serving.

NOTE: See tip 21 on page 7.

Sugar and Spice Cake

Makes 8–10 *servings*

1 yellow cake mix
4 eggs
1 cup light sour cream
3/4 cup vegetable oil
1 cup water
1 small box instant
   vanilla pudding
1/4 cup sugar
1 teaspoon cinnamon

Combine all of the ingredients except the cinnamon and sugar in a 2-quart mixing bowl; set aside. Combine the cinnamon and sugar and then sprinkle mixture in a greased 3½- to 5-quart slow cooker, making sure to cover the bottom and sides. Spread the batter in the slow cooker. Cover and cook on low heat for 5–6 hours, or until done in the center.

NOTE: See tip 21 on page 7.

Moist Carrot Cake

Makes 4–6 *servings*

1½ cups flour
3/4 cup sugar
2 large eggs
1/4 cup water
1/3 cup vegetable oil
1 teaspoon baking
   powder
1/2 teaspoon baking soda
3/4 teaspoon cinnamon
1/4 teaspoon nutmeg
1 cup grated carrots

Combine all of the ingredients in a 2-quart mixing bowl. Pour the batter in a greased 2- to 3½-quart slow cooker. Cover and cook on low heat for 2 hours, or until firm in the center. (You can lightly jiggle the covered slow cooker to check firmness.)

NOTE: See tip 21 on page 7.

Lemon Custard Cake

Makes 6–8 servings

1 (13.9-ounce) box
  lemon-poppy seed
  quick bread mix
1 egg
1 cup light sour cream
1¼ cups water, divided
1 tablespoon vegetable
  oil
½ cup sugar
¼ cup freshly squeezed
  lemon juice

Combine the bread mix, egg, sour cream, and ½ cup water in a 2-quart mixing bowl. Pour the batter in a greased 3½- to 4-quart slow cooker. Combine the remaining ingredients and then pour evenly over the batter. Do not stir after sauce has been added. Cover and cook on high heat for 2–2½ hours. Let cake cool for 30 minutes before serving.

NOTE: See tip 21 on page 7.

Pineapple Upside-Down Cake

Makes 8–10 *servings*

1 yellow cake mix
$\frac{1}{4}$ cup melted butter
$\frac{1}{8}$ cup brown sugar
1 (15-ounce) can
    crushed pineapple,
    with liquid
8–12 maraschino
    cherries, halved

Prepare cake mix according to package directions. Pour the butter in a greased $3\frac{1}{2}$- to 5-quart slow cooker and then sprinkle the brown sugar over top. Add the pineapple with juice and cherries. Pour the batter over the top. Cover and cook on low heat for 4–5 hours, or until cake is firm in the center. Let cool for 30 minutes and then invert onto a serving platter.

NOTE: See tip 21 on page 7.

Nutty Brownies

Makes 10–12 servings

1/4 cup butter or
   margarine, melted
3/4 cup chopped walnuts
   or pecans
1 (21-ounce) box
   brownie mix

Pour the butter in a greased 3 1/2-quart slow cooker. Sprinkle with half of the nuts. Prepare brownie mix according to package directions and then pour over the nuts. Sprinkle remaining nuts over top. Cover and cook on low heat for 3–3 1/2 hours, or until done. Let stand 5 minutes and then invert onto a serving platter.

NOTE: See tip 21 on page 7.

Caramel Rolls

Makes 6–8 servings

1/2 teaspoon cinnamon
1/2 cup brown sugar
2 (8-ounce) packages
   refrigerator biscuits
1/4 cup melted butter

Combine the cinnamon and sugar in a small bowl. Dip individual biscuits into the melted butter and then into cinnamon-sugar mixture. Place each coated biscuit in a greased 3 1/2- to 5-quart slow cooker. Cover and cook on high heat for 2 1/2–3 hours, or until rolls are done. You can check rolls in the center after 2 hours for doneness.

NOTE: See tip 21 on page 7.

Dulce de Leche

Makes 6 servings

**1 (14-ounce) can sweet-
    ened condensed milk**
Water

Remove the label from the milk can. Place the can on its side in a 2¹/₂- to 3¹/₂-quart slow cooker. Fill the slow cooker with water until it is 3–4 inches above the can. Cover and cook on low heat for 8–10 hours. Turn off the slow cooker and let the can cool for 40 minutes inside the slow cooker. Chill the caramel in the unopened can in the refrigerator until ready to serve.

NOTE: The caramel can be used as a dip for apple slices and banana chunks, or as a topping for pancakes, crepes, or ice cream. Warm caramel can also be spread in the bottom of a graham cracker crust and topped with whipped topping.

Honey Wheat Bread

Makes 10–15 servings

⅔ cup powdered milk

2 cups warm water

2 tablespoons canola or vegetable oil

¼ cup honey

¾ teaspoon salt

1 (0.25-ounce) envelope or 2¼ teaspoons active dry yeast

3 cups whole wheat flour, divided

1 cup flour, divided

In a bowl, dissolve the powdered milk in the warm water. Stir in the oil, honey, salt, yeast, and half of each flour. Beat with an electric mixer on low speed for 2 minutes. Add the remaining flour and beat on low until combined. Place the dough in a greased 4- to 5-quart slow cooker. Cover and cook on high heat for 2–3 hours. Remove the stoneware from the slow cooker and let stand for 5 minutes. Invert bread onto a serving platter while still hot.

NOTE: See tip 21 on page 7.

Classic White Bread

Makes 10–15 *servings*

1 (0.25-ounce) envelope
    or 2¼ teaspoons
    active dry yeast
1 teaspoon sugar
¼ cup warm water
1 egg
¼ cup vegetable oil
1 cup lukewarm water
1 teaspoon salt
¼ cup sugar
3½–4 cups flour,
    divided

In a bowl, combine the yeast,
1 teaspoon sugar, and ¼ cup warm
water. Allow the yeast to foam,
about 5 minutes. Add the egg,
oil, lukewarm water, salt, ¼ cup
sugar, and 2 cups flour. Beat with
an electric mixer on low speed for
2 minutes. With a wooden spoon,
stir in the remaining flour. Place the
dough in a greased 4- to 5-quart
slow cooker. Cover and cook on
high heat for 2–3 hours. Remove
the stoneware from the slow
cooker and let stand for 5 minutes.
Invert bread onto a serving platter
while still hot.

NOTE: See tip 21 on page 7.

Cranberry Orange Bread

2/3 **cup powdered milk**
2 cups warm water
3 cups flour, divided
1⅓ cups sugar
1 tablespoon baking
   powder
1/4 **teaspoon salt**
1/4 **teaspoon baking soda**
1 egg, beaten
1/4 **cup vegetable oil**
2 teaspoons finely
   grated orange peel
3/4 **cup dried cran-**
   berries, coarsely
   chopped

In a bowl, dissolve the powdered milk in the warm water. Stir in 2 cups flour, sugar, baking powder, salt, baking soda, egg, and oil. Beat with an electric mixer on low speed for 2 minutes. Add the remaining flour and beat on low until combined. With a wooden spoon, fold in the orange peel and cranberries. Place the dough in a greased 4- to 5-quart slow cooker. Cover and cook on high heat for 2–3 hours. Remove the stoneware from the slow cooker and let stand for 5 minutes. Invert bread onto a serving platter while still hot.

NOTE: See tip 21 on page 7.

Index

Metric Conversion Chart

Volume Measurements		Weight Measurements		Temperature Conversion	
U.S.	Metric	U.S.	Metric	Fahrenheit	Celsius
1 teaspoon	5 ml	1/2 ounce	15 g	250	120
1 tablespoon	15 ml	1 ounce	30 g	300	150
1/4 cup	60 ml	3 ounces	90 g	325	160
1/3 cup	75 ml	4 ounces	115 g	350	180
1/2 cup	125 ml	8 ounces	225 g	375	190
2/3 cup	150 ml	12 ounces	350 g	400	200
3/4 cup	175 ml	1 pound	450 g	425	220
1 cup	250 ml	2 1/4 pounds	1 kg	450	230